JUNIOR CERTIFIC

LESS STRESS MORE SUCCESS

Home Economics Revision

Mary Anne Halton

g GILL EDUCATION

Gill Education

Hume Avenue

Park West

Dublin 12

www.gilleducation.ie

Gill Education is an imprint of M.H. Gill & Co.

978 07171 4710 6

Design by Liz White Designs

Artwork by Oxford Designers & Illustrators

Print origination by Carole Lynch

The paper used in this book is made from the wood pulp of managed forests.
For every tree felled, at least one tree is planted, thereby renewing natural resources.

For permission to reproduce photographs, the author and publisher gratefully
acknowledge the following:

© 1996 FSC A.C.: 271B; © Alamy: 236, 237CR, 237BL, 279; © Corbis: 40T, 41, 57,
237BC; © Getty Images: 37, 38T, 38B, 39, 40B, 67T, 67B, 237CRB; Courtesy of
Australian Wool Innovation Limited: 289; Courtesy of BSI: 167T; Courtesy of
Excellence Ireland Quality Association: 166C; Courtesy of Guaranteed Irish: 166T;
Courtesy of National Standards Authority of Ireland: 166B, 167TB, 167C; Courtesy of
the Irish Organic Farmers and Growers Association: 95.

The authors and publisher have made every effort to trace all copyright holders, but if
any has been inadvertently overlooked we would be pleased to make the necessary
arrangement at the first opportunity.

CONTENTS

LESS STRESS MORE SUCCESS

Introduction

Course outline

Junior Certificate Home Economics is offered at two levels, **Higher level** and **Ordinary level**. The current syllabus is divided into two main sections:

- A **common core** of **five areas** of study.
- A **compulsory study/project** from a choice of three optional areas (you must choose **one** from these options).

The **Common Core** consists of the following **five** areas:

- Food Studies and Culinary Skills.
- Consumer Studies.
- Social and Health Studies.
- Resource Management and Home studies.
- Textile Studies.

The **three optional studies** are:

- Childcare.
- Design and Craftwork.
- Textile Skills.

 Note: Material that is to be studied only by those taking Higher level is indicated in the text.

How the course is examined and marked

The examination for **Higher level** and **Ordinary level** is through:

- A written examination.
- A practical examination in food and culinary skills.
- A study/project work.
- **The food and culinary skills examination** takes place either just before or after the Easter holidays in the presence of an external examiner.
- The **study/project work** must be completed by a specific date each year (your teacher will tell you the exact date and when it will be examined in your school).
- The **written examination** takes place in June.

key point

Be familiar with the content of the syllabus, the way the material is examined and the marking scheme. Know the marks given for the practical exam and each question on the written paper.

The marks for Junior Certificate Home Economics are allocated as follows.

	Higher Level	Ordinary Level
Written exam	50% (300 marks)	40% (240 marks)
Food and culinary skills	35% (210 marks)	45% (270 marks)
Study/project work	15% (90 marks)	15% (90 marks)
Total	**100% (600 marks)**	**100% (600 marks)**

Effective revision – Set smart goals!

Set your targets and aim high. To make the most of this revision guide, ask yourself how you learn best. Approach topics by:

- Carefully reading the material.
- Brainstorming.
- Making visual notes (less is always more!).
- Drawing spider or web diagrams or mind maps.
- Making tables of key information.
- Test yourself using past exam papers.
- Revise again and practise questions.
- Have a good filing system for your notes, etc.
- Reward yourself when you have completed a question, a topic or a section.

key point

Tick (✔) each aim when you are satisfied that you have read it, learned it and have tested yourself.

Format of the written paper

The written paper covers the five core areas of the syllabus.

The paper is divided into **Section A** and **Section B**.

Section	Types of questions	Higher Level	Ordinary Level
A	Short	Attempt 20 of 24	Attempt 16 of 20
B	Long with subsections	Attempt 4 of 6	Attempt 4 of 6
		300 marks	240 marks

Section A has short questions that students must answer in the spaces provided. Students must write on an **answer sheet** (Higher level) or in an **answer book** (Ordinary level).

Detailed knowledge of all the core areas is needed in order to achieve a good mark in Section A.

Section B carries the most marks and will take longer to complete. Students choose four out of six questions.

Students taking **Higher level** must use a separate answer book for Section B.

Students taking **Ordinary level** must use the same answer book for both Section A and Section B. The completed answer book is handed up to the examination supervisor at the end of the exam.

Types of questions in Section A

- Fill in the blanks.
- Label diagrams.
- Fill in a table or chart.
- Explain a symbol.
- True or false statements.

Other types of questions:

- Tick the correct answer (√).
- Choose or match the correct words/phrases.
- Fill in words from a list of words.

Types of questions in Section B

- This section is made up of six long questions, divided into four or five subsections and based on the five core areas.
- Answers must be sufficiently developed and focused in order to gain good marks. One- or two-word answers are not adequate.
- You must demonstrate a good knowledge and understanding of the topics and be able to analyse information given (charts, etc.) and apply the knowledge you have learned.
- Cross-linking is a feature of the questions in this section.

Questions and sample answers for Section B, both Higher and Ordinary Level, are included in this book.

Time

Higher level: 2 hours 30 minutes

Ordinary level: 2 hours

- Budget your time during the written exam.
- Allocate time to Section A and Section B.
- Answer the questions asked and do not spend time writing everything you know about a topic – **keep to the question asked.**

Level	Section	Timing (approx.)	Marks
Higher level	Read the questions	10 minutes	
	Section A	25 minutes	80
	Section B	1 hour 40 minutes	220
	Check your work	10–15 minutes	
Ordinary Level	Read the questions	10 minutes	
	Section A	20 minutes	80
	Section B	1 hour 20 minutes	160
	Check your work	10 minutes	

How long should the answers be?

- If you are asked for four points, give four points, not three or not five.
- Learn to use the marks as a guide.

LINKS
Check the questions and sample answers given in the different chapters. The key points are highlighted.

Preparing for the written exam

- Revise the complete course, taking note of what is needed for Higher and Ordinary Level papers.
- Leave nothing out in preparing for the written exam. Know the basics, e.g. how to label diagrams.
- The more information you have learned, the more likely it is that you will attain higher marks.
- Check how the questions are marked and use the marks allocated to determine the time you will spend on the answer.

exam focus

Refer back to questions continually to ensure that your answer is relevant to the question asked.

- Make notes in your own handwriting.
- Practise answering questions (Section A and Section B).
- Learn to label diagrams properly.
- Learn to use the information in questions to maximum advantage. You will learn this as you practise past questions.

GOLDEN RULES ON THE DAY

1. Write your exam number in the box provided.
2. Read the paper thoroughly.
3. Mark the questions you intend answering.
4. Mark all key words and phrases.
5. Allocate sufficient time to both sections.
6. Answer all subsections within each question in the spaces provided (Section A Higher Level; Sections A and B Ordinary Level).
7. Give focused answers.
8. Allocate time to go over the paper before the end of the exam. Ensure that you have answered the required number of questions and all the subsections. Check that you have put your exam number in the appropriate place.

Higher level – Section B

- **Leave space between each subsection** as you write so that when you read over the answer towards the end of the exam, you can add in information if needed.
- **Start each new question on a new page.**
- **Write in the number of each question** and the subsection e.g. Q.2 (a) (i).

> When answering questions, make sure you **understand** what is being asked and **how much information** is required to answer the question fully.

Key words

Watch out for **key words** when answering questions, such as the following.

advantages/disadvantages	benefits	checklist	classification/type
comment	compare	complete	cost
define	describe	discuss	effects
evaluate	examples	explain	factors
fill in	functions	give	guidelines
identify	indicate	label	list
match	name	outline	plan
precautions	properties	set out	sketch
sources	state	suggest	tick
uses	where		

Essential skills

Labelling diagrams

Know how to label the diagrams in this book and in your Home Economics textbook. **Always** give diagrams a title.

Check which diagrams you need to know for Higher and Ordinary level papers.

Body systems:

- Circulatory system
- Digestive system
- Reproductive systems
- Respiratory system
- Skin
- Teeth

Appliances:

- Cooker
- Fridge
- Microwave oven
- Plug
- Small appliances
- Work triangle

Food studies:

- Food pyramid (food groups)
- Structure of meat
- Where food is stored in the fridge

Symbols:

- Care labels
- Food labels
- Environmental symbols
- Fabric symbols (cotton, linen, silk, wool)
- Quality symbols
- Recycling symbols
- Safety symbol
- Smoking symbol

Textiles:

- Basic hand stitches
- Embroidery stitches
- Seam finishes
- Seams
- Sewing machine

Sketching

Be able to sketch:

- a household item made during the course
- a simple garment made during the course
- a kitchen layout
- a simple room layout (bedroom, living room, bathroom).

Understand and apply

Make sure you understand and can apply the following:

- decision-making process
- design process
- problem solving
- management principles
- work routines
- modifying a recipe
- rules or guidelines in all areas covered.

Analyse

Be able to analyse:

- case studies (in all areas)
- charts and information given
- food labels.

LINK

Terms are explained in each chapter or as part of a topic. Take note of them as you revise the course.

Twelve-week revision study plan

Check what you need to revise within each topic for Higher level and Ordinary level papers.

Week	Food studies and culinary skills	Consumer studies	Social and health studies	Resource management and home studies	Textile studies
1	Protein, fats, carbohydrates	Rights and responsibilities	The family	Resource management	Practice questions
2	Vitamins and minerals, the digestive system	Protection and legislation	Relationships and roles within the family, adolescence	Home studies	Textiles in the home
3	Healthy eating and balanced diets	Quality, packaging and labelling	Good health	Design principles in the home, design brief	Design and fashion
4	Special diets	Decision making	The skin	Design principles in the home	Fabric composition
5	Meal planning, preparing and serving	Practice questions	The teeth	Safety in the home	Fibres into fabrics
6	Food hygiene, safety, storage	Budgeting and money management	Respiratory system	First aid in the home	
7	Cereal and bread group	Shopping, consumer information	Practice questions	Technology – the fridge – the cooker	Fabric finishes
8	Fruit and vegetable group	Practice any questions	Circulatory system	The microwave oven; the small appliances	Caring for textiles
9	Milk and dairy group	Advertising and marketing	Practice questions	Services in the home	Sewing machine
10	Meat, fish and alternatives	Practice questions	Reproductive system (female)	The community	Needlework skills
11	Food processing and food preservation	Practice questions	Reproductive system (male)	Energy-friendly homes	Designing an item of clothing
12	Terms	Practice questions	Health hazards	Environmental issues	Designing a household item

Questions on past Junior Certificate examination papers

key point

Topics that have been asked on past Junior Certificate Home Economics papers are marked below. Areas that have been examined in the **short questions, Section A** are marked **SQ**. Areas that have been examined directly in **Section B** or have been included in a subsection of a question are marked **LQ**:

Remember that cross-linkage is a common feature of the Home Economics written examination. When revising, check out the links.

- SQ = Short Question (Section A)
- LQ = Long Question (Section B)

Check out past exam papers at www.examinations.ie.

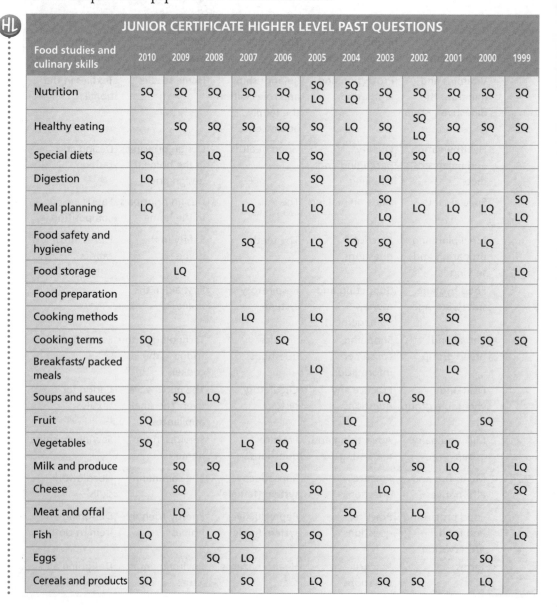

JUNIOR CERTIFICATE HIGHER LEVEL PAST QUESTIONS												
Food studies and culinary skills	2010	2009	2008	2007	2006	2005	2004	2003	2002	2001	2000	1999
Nutrition	SQ	SQ	SQ	SQ	SQ	SQ LQ	SQ LQ	SQ	SQ	SQ	SQ	SQ
Healthy eating		SQ	SQ	SQ	SQ	SQ	LQ	SQ	SQ LQ	SQ	SQ	SQ
Special diets	SQ		LQ		LQ	SQ		LQ	SQ	LQ		
Digestion	LQ					SQ		LQ				
Meal planning	LQ				LQ		LQ	SQ LQ	LQ	LQ	LQ	SQ LQ
Food safety and hygiene				SQ		LQ	SQ	SQ			LQ	
Food storage		LQ										LQ
Food preparation												
Cooking methods				LQ		LQ		SQ		SQ		
Cooking terms	SQ				SQ				LQ	SQ	SQ	
Breakfasts/ packed meals						LQ				LQ		
Soups and sauces		SQ	LQ					LQ	SQ			
Fruit	SQ						LQ				SQ	
Vegetables	SQ			LQ	SQ		SQ			LQ		
Milk and produce		SQ	SQ		LQ				SQ	LQ		LQ
Cheese		SQ				SQ		LQ				SQ
Meat and offal		LQ					SQ		LQ			
Fish	LQ		LQ	SQ		SQ				SQ		LQ
Eggs			SQ	LQ							SQ	
Cereals and products	SQ			SQ		LQ		SQ	SQ		LQ	

Food studies and culinary skills contd.	2010	2009	2008	2007	2006	2005	2004	2003	2002	2001	2000	1999
Baking	SQ				SQ		LQ			SQ	LQ	
Leftovers					SQ							
Food preservation		LQ				LQ				LQ		
Food processing		LQ	LQ	SQ	SQ LQ		LQ		LQ		SQ LQ	
Packaging, labelling, symbols	LQ		SQ	LQ					LQ		LQ	L

Consumer studies	2010	2009	2008	2007	2006	2005	2004	2003	2002	2001	2000	1999
Consumerism		LQ	SQ	SQ	SQ			SQ				
Rights and responsibilities	SQ	LQ	LQ	LQ					LQ		SQ LQ	
Protection		LQ		LQ	SQ		LQ		SQ	LQ		LQ
Consumer agencies			SQ	SQ		SQ	LQ			SQ	LQ	
Consumer action: Making complaints		LQ	SQ				LQ		SQ		LQ	
Money management and budgeting	SQ	SQ	LQ	SQ		SQ	SQ	SQ LQ	SQ		SQ	
Quality and symbols	SQ	SQ	SQ	SQ	SQ	SQ	SQ	SQ		SQ	SQ	SQ
Packaging and labelling										LQ		
Advertising			SQ			LQ		SQ	LQ		SQ	
Shopping	SQ	SQ	LQ		SQ LQ		SQ	LQ	LQ	SQ	SQ	SQ

Social and health studies	2010	2009	2008	2007	2006	2005	2004	2003	2002	2001	2000	1999
The family		SQ				LQ	SQ					
Rights, roles, relationships	SQ	SQ				LQ					SQ	
Adolescence	SQ			SQ				SQ	LQ	SQ	LQ	
Good health								SQ			LQ	
The skin and personal hygiene	SQ		LQ					SQ	LQ			LQ
The teeth		SQ	SQ		LQ		SQ			LQ	SQ	
Respiratory system (lungs)				SQ		SQ			SQ			SQ
Circulatory system (heart)		LQ		SQ	SQ		LQ	SQ		SQ		SQ
Reproductive system		SQ	SQ	LQ	SQ	SQ	SQ		SQ		SQ	
Human development			SQ	LQ	SQ							SQ
Health hazards	SQ	SQ	SQ	SQ		SQ	SQ			SQ	SQ	SQ

Resource management and home studies	2010	2009	2008	2007	2006	2005	2004	2003	2002	2001	2000	1999
Management	SQ											
The home					SQ							
Design in the home and room plans	LQ	SQ	LQ	SQ	SQ		LQ	SQ		SQ		SQ
Technology in the home	SQ							SQ				
Fridges/freezers		LQ							LQ			
Cookers		SQ						LQ				
Microwave ovens			LQ				SQ				LQ	
Small appliances		LQ										
Electricity					SQ	SQ	SQ		SQ		SQ	SQ
Gas				SQ								
Water			SQ						SQ			
Lighting	SQ	SQ	LQ				SQ			SQ		
Home heating					LQ			SQ				LQ
Ventilation									SQ			
Insulation				SQ						SQ		LQ
Community			SQ									
Environment		SQ	SQ	SQ	SQ	SQ		SQ		SQ		SQ
Home hygiene	SQ									LQ	SQ	
Safety and first aid	LQ		SQ			LQ			SQ		SQ	
State services											SQ	

Textile studies	2010	2009	2008	2007	2006	2005	2004	2003	2002	2001	2000	1999
Textiles		SQ						SQ LQ	LQ	SQ	SQ	
Household		LQ				SQ		LQ				LQ
Clothing and accessories	SQ	SQ	SQ	SQ LQ	SQ	SQ	SQ LQ		SQ	SQ	SQ LQ	SQ
Fibres and fabrics	LQ	LQ	SQ LQ	SQ LQ	SQ	LQ	SQ LQ	SQ	SQ LQ	SQ	SQ	SQ LQ
Fabric finishes		LQ						LQ	LQ			
Textile care	SQ LQ	SQ LQ	SQ LQ	SQ LQ	SQ	SQ LQ	SQ	SQ	SQ	SQ	SQ LQ	SQ
Sewing stitches and skills	SQ	SQ	SQ	SQ LQ	SQ LQ	SQ	LQ	SQ	SQ	SQ	SQ	LQ
Sewing machine	SQ	SQ			LQ	SQ	SQ	SQ		LQ		SQ

JUNIOR CERTIFICATE ORDINARY LEVEL PAST QUESTIONS

Food studies and culinary skills	2010	2009	2008	2007	2006	2005	2004	2003	2002	2001	2000	1999
Nutrition	SQ		SQ	SQ	SQ	SQ	SQ LQ	SQ LQ	SQ	SQ	SQ	SQ
Healthy eating	SQ	SQ	SQ	LQ	SQ	SQ	SQ	SQ LQ	LQ	SQ	SQ	SQ
Special diets	LQ		SQ LQ									SQ
Digestion												
Meal planning	LQ		SQ LQ	SQ			SQ LQ		LQ	SQ LQ	LQ	
Food safety and hygiene							LQ					
Food storage	LQ	LQ			LQ	LQ	SQ		LQ	SQ	LQ	
Food preparation							LQ		LQ			
Cooking methods					SQ	LQ	SQ			SQ	LQ	LQ
Cooking terms		SQ			SQ	LQ	LQ		SQ			
Breakfasts/ packed meals	SQ		LQ		LQ						SQ	
Soups and sauces		SQ		SQ	LQ					SQ	LQ	
Fruit		LQ		LQ					SQ	LQ		
Vegetables		LQ					LQ				LQ	SQ
Milk and produce	LQ								LQ			
Cheese					LQ			SQ				SQ
Meat and offal	LQ						LQ	SQ			LQ	
Fish	SQ			LQ					LQ		SQ	
Eggs	SQ	LQ				LQ				LQ	SQ	
Cereals and products			LQ					LQ				LQ
Baking							SQ	SQ			SQ	
Leftovers				SQ								
Food preservation												
Food processing					LQ		LQ		SQ			
Packaging, labelling, symbols		LQ		SQ		LQ						SQ

Consumer studies	2010	2009	2008	2007	2006	2005	2004	2003	2002	2001	2000	1999
Consumerism		SQ	SQ	LQ		LQ	SQ	SQ	SQ	LQ	LQ	
Rights and responsibilities			SQ			LQ					LQ	SQ
Protection											SQ	SQ
Consumer agencies						LQ						
Consumer action: Making complaints											LQ	
Money management and budgeting	SQ	SQ	LQ	SQ LQ	SQ	SQ	SQ		SQ LQ	SQ		SQ LQ
Quality and symbols	SQ	SQ LQ	SQ LQ	SQ	SQ LQ	LQ	SQ	SQ	SQ	SQ	SQ LQ	SQ
Packaging and labelling	LQ	LQ		LQ	LQ			LQ		LQ		SQ
Advertising	LQ		SQ			SQ	SQ		LQ		SQ	
Shopping		SQ	SQ LQ	SQ		SQ	SQ LQ	SQ	SQ LQ	SQ LQ	SQ LQ	

Social and health studies	2010	2009	2008	2007	2006	2005	2004	2003	2002	2001	2000	1999
The family	SQ			LQ			SQ	SQ			SQ	
Rights, roles, relationships				LQ		SQ	SQ				LQ	
Adolescence	SQ	LQ				SQ					LQ	SQ
Good health	SQ	SQ	SQ	SQ		SQ	SQ	SQ	SQ	SQ		SQ
The skin and personal hygiene	LQ	SQ			SQ	LQ	SQ			LQ	SQ	
The teeth			LQ				LQ		SQ			LQ
Respiratory system (lungs)				LQ					LQ			
Circulatory system (heart)												
Reproductive systems	SQ			SQ				LQ	SQ	SQ		
Human development		LQ	SQ	SQ			SQ		SQ			SQ
Health hazards		SQ			SQ	SQ	SQ	SQ	LQ		SQ	

Resource management and home studies	2010	2009	2008	2007	2006	2005	2004	2003	2002	2001	2000	1999
Management												SQ
The home												
Design in the home and room plans	SQ		SQ		LQ	SQ			SQ LQ		SQ	
Technology in the home												
Fridges/freezers	LQ					LQ						
Cookers		LQ								LQ		
Microwave ovens		SQ										
Small appliances				SQ			SQ				SQ	
Utensils												SQ
Electricity						SQ						
Gas											SQ	
Water				LQ		SQ				SQ		LQ
Lighting								SQ				
Home heating							SQ		SQ			
Ventilation										LQ		
Insulation	SQ	SQ	SQ		SQ			SQ			SQ	
Community												
Energy		SQ LQ								LQ		
Environment	SQ				SQ		SQ	SQ			LQ	SQ
Home hygiene			LQ				LQ					SQ
Safety in the home and first aid		SQ	SQ	SQ	SQ				LQ		SQ	LQ
State services												

Textile studies	2010	2009	2008	2007	2006	2005	2004	2003	2002	2001	2000	1999
Textiles	LQ								LQ			
Household textiles	LQ	SQ		LQ		SQ LQ			SQ	LQ	SQ	
Clothing and accessories	SQ	LQ	SQ		LQ	SQ	SQ	SQ	SQ LQ		SQ LQ	SQ
Fibres and fabrics	SQ	LQ			SQ	LQ		LQ	SQ LQ			
Fabric finishes						SQ			SQ			
Textile care and care labels	SQ	SQ		SQ	SQ		SQ	LQ	SQ	SQ LQ		SQ
Sewing stitches and skills	SQ	SQ	SQ		SQ	LQ	SQ	SQ	LQ	SQ	SQ	SQ
Sewing machine		SQ		SQ			LQ	SQ				LQ
Sewing equipment		LQ	LQ	SQ			LQ			LQ	SQ	

PART ONE

Food Studies and Culinary Skills

1 The Relationship between Food and Health

- To define the term 'food'.
- To list the functions of food.
- To identify factors affecting food choices and eating habits

What is food?

Food is any solid or liquid that provides nutrients to the body. Food is made up of protein, fats, carbohydrates, vitamins, minerals and water.

Functions of food

- To help the growth and repair of body cells.
- To provide the body with fuel (heat and energy).
- To protect the body against disease.
- To regulate body functions, e.g. temperature, breathing and digestion.

Good eating patterns are linked to good health.

We enjoy eating

We also eat because:

We like different foods, their flavour and their smell

We like eating with other people

We celebrate special events in our lives with special meals

Food advertising might make us feel hungry

Factors affecting food choices and eating habits

- Family budget (cost/income)
- Special dietary requirements or restrictions
- Nutritional value
- Lifestyle/eating patterns (parents, family and friends)
- Cultural or religious background
- Where we live (city, countryside, islands)
- Availability of different foods
- Knowledge of healthy eating
- Age (likes and dislikes at different ages)

- Our senses (sight, smell, taste, touch)
- Advertising.

 EXAM QUESTION AND SAMPLE ANSWER

Higher Level, Section A

Suggest **four** factors that influence a person's food choices. (4 marks)

- *Special dietary requirements or restrictions.*
- *Nutritional value.*
- *Family budget (cost/income).*
- *Parents, family and friends (lifestyle).*

Higher Level, Section A

Draw a diagram of the tongue and mark in the location of the taste buds and what flavour they taste. (4 marks)

Read the questions very carefully. Always take note of the **number of factors or examples** required and the **marks** allocated to the question.

Example 1:

List the **four** tastes that can be sensed by the taste buds on the tongue. (4 marks)

1. *Sweet,* 2. *Bitter,* 3. *Sour,* 4. *Salty*

Example 2:

Name the staple foods of the following countries: China, India, Italy, Ireland. (4 marks)

China: *Rice*

India: *Rice*

Italy: *Pasta*

Ireland: *Potatoes*

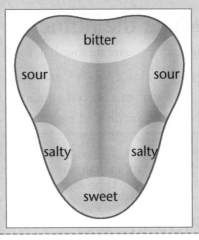

2 The Nutrients

aims
- To define a nutrient.
- To name/list the nutrients.
- To explain macronutrients and micronutrients.
- To list the nutrient sources, functions and deficiency diseases.
- To understand RDA. **HL**
- To list the effects of deficiency.

What is a nutrient?

A nutrient is a complex chemical substance found in food that is essential for the functioning of our bodies.

Name the nutrients

Six constituents are found in food, five of which are nutrients:

- Proteins ● Fats ● Carbohydrates ● Vitamins ● Minerals
- Water (this is a constituent, not a nutrient, but is essential for life).

Nutrients are divided into **two** groups: macronutrients and micronutrients.

Macronutrients	Micronutrients
Proteins, fats and carbohydrates – required by the body in large amounts	Minerals and vitamins – needed by the body in small amounts

Protein

Composition

- The basic protein unit is an amino acid.
- Amino acids join to form chains of larger protein units.
- The elements in amino acids are carbon, hydrogen, oxygen and nitrogen.

Protein Chain

PAST EXAM QUESTION
Higher Level 2004, Section A, Q.2: Macronutrients and micronutrients – put into a table.

key point

Protein is the only nutrient that contains nitrogen. It is needed for growth.

key point

During digestion, the amino acids are separated so that they can be used for growth and repair.

Classification and sources

High biological value (HBV)	Low biological value (LBV)
• Mainly animal sources. • Meat, fish, eggs, milk, cheese, yoghurt, soya beans.	• Mainly vegetable/plant sources. • Pulses (peas, beans, lentils), nuts, cereals (oats, wheat).

Functions

- Produces heat and energy.
- Growth of body cells (skin, blood, tissues).
- Repair of damaged cells (a cut).
- Production of enzymes and hormones.

key point

LBV protein (vegetable sources) contains fibre and is low in fat.

Effects of deficiency

- Stunted growth.
- Imbalance in hormones and enzymes.
- Cells slow to repair.
- Fewer antibodies produced.

exam Q   PAST EXAM QUESTIONS
Higher Level 2008, Section A, Q.1:
Sources of HBV protein.
Ordinary Level 2004, Section A, Q.1:
Sources of proteins.

LINKS

- Food pyramid (meat, fish and alternatives) (p. 35)
- Digestion (p. 53)

RDA for protein

- 1 gram protein per 1 kilo of body weight.
- Children and teenagers need more because they are growing.

Fats/Oils

Fats contain twice as much energy as proteins or carbohydrates. Fats are a concentrated energy food. At room temperature, fats are solid and oils are liquid. Fats can be visible or invisible.

Composition

- Fats are made up of a glycerol attached to three fatty acids.
- These are arranged in an E-shaped structure.
- The elements in fats are carbon, hydrogen and oxygen.

key point

During digestion, the links break in the E-shaped structure and the three fatty acids separate from glycerol.

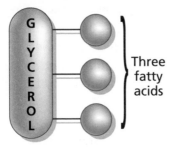

Glycerol and three fatty acids

Classification and sources of Fats/Oils (Lipids)

Classification	Sources
Saturated (mainly animal)	Unsaturated (mainly vegetable)
Milk, cream, cheese, butter, eggs, meat, lard, suet, meat products (sausages)	Nuts, whole cereals, oily fish, vegetable cooking oils, polyunsaturated margarine/spreads

Functions

- Produces heat and energy.
- Insulates the body with a layer of fat underneath the skin.
- Source of the fat-soluble vitamins A, D, E and K.
- Protects the kidneys, nerves and delicate organs.
- Gives a feeling of fullness and delays feeling hungry.

Effects of deficiency

Deficiency of fat is very rare.

- **Problems associated with high intake of fat**: Overweight, obesity.
- **Problems associated with high intake of saturated fat**: Heart disease and stroke.

- Excess fat is stored as adipose tissue.
- Saturated fats are high in cholesterol.

Current dietary guidelines

- Eat less saturated fats and more vegetable fats.
- Do not exclude fats from the diet, as they contain fat-soluble vitamins.
- Low-fat foods are unsuitable for babies.

HL RDA for fat

Deficiency in fat is unusual. It is recommended that daily fat intake be reduced to 30 per cent of the total energy in the diet (50 per cent saturated and 50 per cent unsaturated fats).

LINKS
- Coronary heart disease (p. 49)
- Obesity (p. 47)
- Special Diets (p. 49)
- Digestion (pp. 53-6)

PAST EXAM QUESTIONS
- **Higher Level 2006, Section A, Q.3:** Reducing intake of fat in diet.
- **Ordinary Level 2008, Section A, Q.3 (a):** Function of fat in diet.
- **Ordinary Level 2006, Section A, Q.1:** Sources of fat in the diet.

Carbohydrates

Carbohydrates are one of our energy foods, and are the cheapest and most plentiful nutrient.

Photosynthesis is the process that produces carbohydrates. The action of sunlight on chlorophyll in the leaves creates energy.

Composition

- The most basic unit of carbohydrate is glucose, a simple sugar.
- The elements in carbohydrates are carbon, hydrogen and oxygen.

key point

During digestion, glucose units are separated and used for energy (p.53).

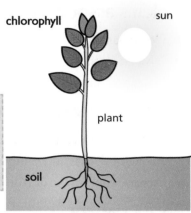

chlorophyll　　sun

plant

soil

Photosynthesis

Classification and sources

Classes	Sources
Dietary fibre	Fruits, vegetables, whole cereals (skins and husks), wholemeal brown bread, brown rice, oatmeal
Starch	Potatoes, root and pulse vegetables, rice, pasta, cereals, flour, bread
Sugar	Soft drinks, sweets, biscuits, cakes, sugar, milk, fresh and dried fruit, honey, jam

Functions of carbohydrate (Sugars, starches and dietary fibre)

key point

Sugar supplies energy in the form of 'empty kilocalories'. Sugar is not essential in the diet.

- Provides heat and energy (starchy foods and sugars).
- Excess carbohydrate is converted into fat (adipose tissue).
- Dietary fibre helps the movement of food through the body.
- Fibre gives a feeling of fullness.

Effects of deficiency

Deficiency is rare.

Fibre

LINKS
- Cereals (p. 82)
- Fruits (p. 90)
- Vegetables (p. 93)

Dietary fibre (Roughage/Cellulose)

- Fibre-rich foods are plentiful and reasonably cheap.
- Fibre is found in the outer skins of fruits, vegetables and the husks of cereals.
- Processed, convenience and refined foods are low in fibre.
- Fibre helps to prevent constipation and other bowel diseases.
- Fibre absorbs water and makes us feel full.
- Fibre picks up chemicals and toxins (eliminated in the faeces).
- Fibre-rich foods provide vitamin B (which helps the release of energy in the body).

Problems associated with low-fibre diets

- Constipation
- Diverticulosis
- Haemorrhoids

Current dietary guidelines

- Choose more dietary fibres and starches than sugars.
- Avoid foods that are mainly sugar.
- Increase your intake of fruit and vegetables.

RDA for dietary fibre

The RDA for dietary fibre is 30 grams per day. Irish people need to double their intake of fibre daily by increasing their intake of fruit, vegetables and whole cereals.

LINKS

- High-fibre diets (pp. 49–50)
- Cereals (p. 82)

QUESTIONS AND SAMPLE ANSWERS

Higher Level 2001, Section A, Q.1 (4 marks)

Name **two** foods which are good sources of dietary fibre.
(i) *Whole cereals* (ii) *Vegetables*

Higher Level 2006, Section A, Q.1 (4 marks)

Give **one** important source of each of the following.

Dietary fibre: *Brown wholemeal bread*

Vitamin C: *Blackcurrants*

PAST EXAM QUESTIONS

HIGHER LEVEL

- 2009, Section A, Q.1: Energy requirement.
- 2005, Section B, Q.1: Porridge, breakfast/menu.

ORDINARY LEVEL

- 2008, Section A, Q.1 (sources of fibre in the diet)
- 2003, Section B, Q.1 (pasta, spaghetti, carbohydrates)

Micronutrients

The two micronutrients are minerals and vitamins.

Minerals

The body needs minerals in smaller amounts than the macronutrients.

Examples: Calcium, iron, potassium, phosphorus, zinc, fluorine, magnesium, iodine, sodium, selenium.

Trace elements are minerals that the body needs in much smaller amounts, e.g. zinc and iodine.

Calcium

Food Sources	Functions	Effects of Deficiency
Dairy foods (milk, cheese, yoghurt), eggs, tinned fish (bones), green vegetables, white flour (fortified).	• Healthy teeth, bones, nerves and muscles. • Assists the clotting of blood. • Transmission of nerve pulses.	• Poor bones and teeth (dental decay). • Osteoporosis (adults and elderly people). • Rickets (children).

Calcium combines with phosphorus to make bones and teeth hard and strong. Calcium and phosphorus need vitamin D to be present in the diet so that they can be absorbed properly. By eating calcium-rich and vitamin D-rich foods, taking regular exercise and not smoking, you can reduce the risks of osteoporosis.

Iron

Food Sources	Functions	Effects of Deficiency
Lean red meat, offal (liver, kidneys), fortified breakfast cereals, wholegrain cereals, wholemeal bread, dark green vegetables (cabbage, broccoli), eggs.	• Needed to make red blood cells (haemoglobin), which carry oxygen around the body to give us energy.	• Poor concentration. • Anaemia is caused by a lack of haemoglobin. • Feeling tired, no energy, weakness.

key point

Eat vitamin C-rich foods to help the body absorb iron. A good intake of iron is necessary for toddlers, children, teenagers and women of childbearing ages. Increase iron intake during pregnancy to provide for the unborn baby. Women need a good supply of iron due to menstruation. Athletes and vegetarians are at risk of developing iron deficiency.

Iodine

Food Sources	Functions	Effects of Deficiency
Seaweed, sea fish, iodised salt, cereals, vegetables grown near the sea, eggs.	• Necessary for the functioning of the thyroid gland (regulates metabolism).	• Enlarged thyroid gland (goitre). • Slowdown of metabolism. • Weight gain and tiredness.

Iodine is added to salt to make up for the lack of iodine levels in soils in some areas. This is called iodised salt.

Phosphorus

Food Sources	Functions	Effects of Deficiency
Dairy foods (milk, cheese), meat, poultry, fish, eggs, whole cereals and pulse vegetables.	• Needed for healthy, strong bones and teeth.	• Rare, as it is in a variety of foods.

Phosphorus works with calcium to develop strong bones and teeth. Vitamin D is needed for its absorption.

Potassium

Food Sources	Functions	Effects of Deficiency
Most foods, dried fruits, wheat germ, milk (whole), fish, bananas, nuts, seeds, citrus fruits.	• Maintains the body's fluid balance. • Formation and functioning of cells.	• Rare, as it is found in a variety of foods.

Having a cup of dried fruit each day improves your daily supply of potassium.

Sodium

Food Sources	Functions	Effects of Deficiency
Snack foods, crisps, salted nuts, table salt, bacon rashers, stock cubes, some instant gravy, soya sauce, tomato ketchup.	• Helps to regulate the water balance in the body. • Important for the functioning of cells (muscles and tissues).	• Rare. • Cramps in muscles.

Too much salt in the diet raises blood pressure, which is a major risk factor for strokes, coronary heart disease and kidney damage. People suffering from high blood pressure need to reduce the amount of sodium in their diet. Irish people tend to have a high salt intake.

Fluoride

Food Sources	Functions	Effects of Deficiency
Drinking water, fish eaten with bones, tea.	• Prevents tooth decay.	• Tooth decay (dental caries).

Zinc

Food Sources	Functions	Effects of Deficiency
Oysters, meat and offal (liver, kidneys), poultry, dairy produce (cheddar cheese, milk).	● Aids general health, improves immunity. ● Assists healing of wounds (fights infection). ● Necessary for the metabolism of proteins and carbohydrates. ● Involved in the action of enzymes.	● Slow healing of wounds. ● Poor growth. ● Dry, flaky skin.

RDAs for minerals

HL

Mineral	RDA
Calcium	1,200 mg
Iodine	130 µg
Iron	10–14 mg
Phosphorous	none
Potassium	3.5 g (adults)
Sodium	1.6 g
Zinc	7–9 mg

Vitamins

key point

Deficiency diseases are caused by a lack of vitamins if a wide variety of foods are not eaten.

Classification

Fat-soluble vitamins	A, D, E and K
Water-soluble vitamins	B group and C

Fat-soluble vitamins

Vitamin A

Food Sources	Functions	Effects of Deficiency
Retinols (Foods of Animal Origin): Dairy foods (milk, butter), margarine, fish liver oils, oily fish, offal, eggs. **Carotene:** Red and yellow fruits (apricots, carrots, tomatoes, peppers), dark green vegetables.	● Healthy mucous membranes (lining of throat and nose). ● Growth and development. ● Healthy eyes, skin and hair.	● Retarded growth. ● Night blindness (poor vision in dim light). ● Dry mucous membranes. ● Dry, scaly skin.

Vitamin D

Food Sources	Functions	Effects of Deficiency
Oily fish, cod liver oil, liver, eggs, margarine, dairy products (cheese). Other sources: Action of sunshine on the skin.	• Helps the absorption of calcium in the body. • Formation of healthy bones and teeth. • Prevents rickets.	• Rickets (bone disease in children). • Osteoporosis. • Dental problems.

Vitamin E

Food Sources	Functions	Effects of Deficiency
Eggs, sunflower seeds and oil, margarine, cereals.	• Healthy red blood cells. • Natural antioxidant (prevents damage to cells). • Helps the healing of wounds.	• Rare. • Anaemia in newborn babies.

Vitamin K

Vitamin K is found in a limited range of foods.

Food Sources	Functions	Effects of Deficiency
Manufactured in the body by bacteria living in the digestive tract, green vegetables (spinach, cabbage), liver, peas.	• Essential for the clotting of the blood. • Works with calcium in the bones.	• Blood does not clot properly or takes longer to clot.

RDAs for fat-soluble vitamins

Vitamin A	Adolescents and adults	600-700µg per day
Vitamin D	Adolescents and Adults	15µg per day
Vitamin E		None

Water-soluble vitamins

Vitamin B group

There are many vitamins in this group. They share similar features but differ in their chemical structure. Examples of vitamins in this group are thiamine and folic acid.

Food Sources	Functions	Effects of Deficiency
Dairy foods (milk, cheese), meat, fish, eggs, wholegrain cereals, wholemeal bread, yeast, pulse vegetables and nuts.	• Helps the release of energy from foods. • Required for healthy nerves. • Needed for growth.	• Pellagra (disease of tongue and skin). • Beriberi (nerve disease). • Tiredness and irritability.

Vitamin C (Ascorbic acid)

Food sources	Functions	Effects of deficiency
Fresh fruit (citrus, blackcurrants, rosehip syrup, kiwi) and vegetables (dark green vegetables, salad vegetables, peppers, potatoes).	● Aids the absorption of iron. ● Necessary for general good health. ● Keeps the gums, skin, lining membranes and blood vessels healthy. ● Helps form connective tissue.	● Scurvy (gums and tongue swell and crack, skin bruises, teeth fall out). ● Slow healing of wounds. ● Iron is not absorbed properly.

RDA for water-soluble vitamins

Vitamin C	45–60 mg per day
Vitamin B group	Varies for each vitamin in the group

Summary of vitamins and minerals working together

Vitamin and mineral working together	What happens
Vitamin C + iron and calcium	Absorption of iron and calcium
Vitamin D + calcium and phosphorus	Absorption of both minerals
Vitamin K + calcium	Clotting of blood

Water

Composition

- The elements in water are hydrogen and oxygen (H_2O) in the ratio 2:1.

Properties

key point

The human body is about 70 per cent water. Daily water loss is on average 2–2.5 litres. Water lost must be replaced or dehydration will occur. Dehydration may also result from severe vomiting and diarrhoea.

- Boils at 100°C and freezes at 0°C.
- Changes to a vapour (steam) at 100°C.
- Is colourless, odourless and tasteless.
- Dissolves salt (brine) and sugar (syrup).

Sources

Drinks (tea, milk), water (tap, bottled), fruits, vegetables, most foods.

Functions

- Transports oxygen, nutrients and hormones around the body.
- Helps the digestion and absorption of food.

- Necessary for all body fluids, tissues and cells.
- Source of minerals, e.g. calcium and fluorine.
- Regulates body temperature (perspiration).
- Aids waste removal (kidney filters urine from the blood).
- Quenches thirst.

EXAM QUESTIONS AND SAMPLE ANSWERS

Higher Level 2007, Section A, Q.2 (4 marks)

Identify a **different** deficiency caused by a low intake of **each** of the following nutrients.

	Nutrient	Deficiency
(i)	Calcium	Poor bones and teeth, rickets
(ii)	Vitamin C	Scurvy, wounds take longer to heal
(iii)	Iron	Anaemia, tiredness, no energy
(iv)	Vitamin K	Blood does not clot properly

Ordinary Level 2009, Section A, Q.2 (4 marks)

Name **one** water-soluble vitamin and **one** fat-soluble vitamin.

(i)   *Vitamin C*   (ii) *Vitamin A*

Energy

What is energy?

Energy is defined as the ability to do work. We need energy for each body function, as well as sleeping, resting and any other activity.

What Is Oxidation?

The food we eat supplies energy. Energy is released from food during the process of oxidation when oxygen burns up food in the cells. The basic metabolic rate (BMR) is the minimum amount of energy needed to keep the body's organs working.

energy

oxygen

food

Oxidation

Functions of energy

- Growth (toddlers, children, adolescents, pregnant women).
- Physical activity and muscle movement (running, walking, dressing).
- To maintain the correct body temperature (37°C).
- To keep vital organs working (heart and lungs).

Body size (height and weight)

Pregnancy (pregnant and nursing women need more energy foods)

Age (younger people usually need more energy foods)

Factors that Influence Energy Needs

Climate (people living in colder climates need more energy)

Gender (women generally need less energy foods than men)

Activity (active people need and use more energy)

Remember:

- If we eat **more energy foods** than we need, the energy produced is converted into and stored as fat.
- If we eat **too few energy foods**, we can suffer from some deficiency disorders.
- If we eat **a balanced diet**, energy intake will be equal to energy output.

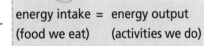

key point

energy intake = energy output
(food we eat)   (activities we do)

Measuring energy in food

Energy is measured in kilocalories (kcal) or kilojoules (kJ).

key point

1 kcal = 4.2 kJ

Energy values of nutrients

Nutrient	kcal/kJ
1 g protein	4 kcal/17 kJ
1 g fat	9 kcal/34 kJ
1 g carbohydrate	4 kcal/17 kJ

Estimated average daily energy needs (in kilocalories)

Age group	Daily requirements (kcal per day); sedentary to active
Children	1,400–1,500
Adolescents	2,300–2,800
Adult male	2,400–3,000
Adult female	2,100–2,400
Pregnant women	2,400
Breastfeeding women	2,800
Elderly male	1,800–2,200

3 A to Z – Some Definitions to Learn

aims
- To define terms clearly and give suitable examples.

exam focus

Definitions must be concise, clear and give relevant information. You must give sufficient information when explaining terms. Give a definition or explanation and an example where appropriate.

Anaemia results from a lack of iron in the diet.

A balanced diet contains a variety of foods that provide us with nutrients in their correct proportions.

Basal metabolic rate is the least amount of energy we need when our body is resting to keep it functioning.

Beriberi is a disease that affects nerve pulses. Lack of thiamine causes beriberi.

Cholesterol is a hard substance (sterol) that is produced in the body and is found in some foods of animal origin.

Coeliacs are people who are allergic to wheat and must follow a gluten-free diet (see also 'Gluten-free').

Deficiency symptoms result from a lack of or a reduced intake or poor absorption of nutrients.

Dietary fibre is the roughage found in whole cereals, fruit and vegetables. It prevents constipation.

Elements are the basic building blocks of each nutrient. Examples of elements are carbon, hydrogen and oxygen.

Empty kilocalories are produced by foods high in sugar and lacking in all other nutrients, such as alcohol, biscuits, cakes and sweets.

Emulsions are formed when oil and water or vinegar are mixed vigorously together (French dressing, mayonnaise). Emulsions can be temporary or permanent.

Energy is described as the ability to do work. Energy is produced in the body from the foods we eat.

Energy balance occurs when energy intake (the food we eat) is equal to energy output (activities). An imbalance results in either weight loss or weight gain.

Enzymes are chemical substances that cause a chemical reaction without changing themselves, as in the saturation of fruit or digestion of food.

Fortified foods are foods to which extra nutrients have been added during processing. Examples are bread, breakfast cereals, Super Milk and white flour.

Functions are what the various nutrients found in food do for the body.

Goitre results from an insufficient amount of iodine in the diet, causing the thyroid gland to swell.

Gluten-free means the food does not contain gluten and a coeliac can eat it.

Haemoglobin is a protein found in blood. It picks up oxygen and carries it to the body's cells.

Hypervitaminosis is excess vitamin A or vitamin D in the diet, which is harmful to the body.

Macronutrients are protein, fat and carbohydrate. They have a large structure that must be broken down by chemical activity in the digestive system before they can be absorbed.

Malnutrition results from an imbalance of nutrients in the diet. This imbalance causes deficiency diseases. Some people in the world do not have enough to eat and suffer from deficiency diseases and starvation. Other people eat a lot of the wrong types of foods because they make poor food choices. Malnutrition can occur in both cases.

Metabolic rate is the rate at which our bodies use up energy.

Micronutrients are vitamins and minerals. They are smaller in structure than macronutrients.

Nutritionists are people who study food and apply the knowledge they have acquired to help people develop healthy eating habits, balanced diets and in some cases special diets.

Obesity is the term used when a person is greatly overweight (the weight is not in proportion to the height).

Organic food is food that is produced without using artificial chemicals.

Osteomalacia is a bone disease in adults, similar to rickets in children.

Oxidation is the process whereby energy is released from food by the body. In the cells, oxygen combines with food to produce energy.

Perishable foods are foods that must be stored in a fridge. They have a short shelf life.

Peristalsis is the contraction and relaxing of the muscles moving food along the digestive tract.

Recommended daily allowance (RDA) refers to the amount of a nutrient the body needs every day to stay healthy.

Refined foods are foods that have been processed commercially and have had the cellulose removed (such as flour, packet soups, white bread and white rice).

Rickets is a bone disease in children caused by a deficiency or lack of vitamin D or calcium.

Staple Foods are the foods that are readily available and used frequently in a country (such as potatoes in Ireland, pasta in Italy and rice in Thailand). They are the foods traditionally used in that country.

Trace means a very small or tiny amount of the nutrient is present in the food.

Whole Cereals are cereals that do not have the outer layer removed.

EXAM QUESTION AND SAMPLE ANSWER

Higher Level 2006, Section B, Q.1 (e)

Explain **one** of the following: **fortified** or **homogenised**. (5 marks)

Fortified foods are foods to which extra nutrients have been added during processing. *Examples* are bread, breakfast cereals, Super Milk, TVP and white flour.

key point

- The key word in this type of question is **explain**.
- Examples are given.
- Choose only one of the terms.

4   Healthy Eating and Balanced Diets

What is a balanced diet?

A healthy, balanced diet is one that contains all the nutrients in the correct proportions.

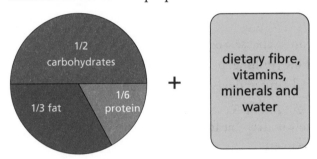

key point

Food should be selected from the different food groups (refer to the food pyramid). A healthy diet also takes special dietary needs of individuals or groups into consideration, e.g. diabetics, coeliacs, those suffering from coronary heart disease.

Healthy Eating Guidelines

Current dietary guidelines recommend that we:

- **Eat a variety of foods.** Choose foods from each of the food groups each day (eat the correct amount from each food group).
- **Increase intake of:**
  - Iron-rich foods (especially important for teenage girls and women).
  - Calcium-rich foods (especially important for teenage girls and women).
  - Fibre-rich foods.
- **Reduce intake of:**
  - Fats (especially animal or saturated fat). Do not eliminate fat from the diet completely, as it is a source of fat-soluble vitamins.
  - Salt, both when eating food and in the preparation and cooking of food.
  - Sugar in the diet.

How to increase iron

Choose from lean red meat, offal (liver, kidneys), dark green vegetables (cabbage), wholegrain cereals, wholemeal bread and sardines.

How to increase calcium

Choose from dairy foods (milk, cheese, yoghurt), eggs, tinned fish (bones), green vegetables and white flour (fortified).

How to increase dietary fibre

Choose from fruit, vegetables, whole cereals (with skins and husks – e.g. oatmeal), wholemeal brown bread, brown rice and commercially produced high-fibre breakfast cereals. Increase fibre when cooking by choosing fibre-rich ingredients and modifying recipes accordingly.

How to reduce fat

- Choose low-fat butter and margarine.
- Use spreads and butters sparingly on bread and potatoes.
- Choose lean meats and remove excess fat when preparing meat.
- Drain off excess fat when cooking food.
- Eat more pulse vegetables, fish and poultry.
- Choose low-fat dairy products (milk, cheese, yoghurt).
- Choose low-fat methods of cooking (grilling, poaching, boiling).
- Use vegetable oils rather than hard saturated fats.
- Avoid eating fried foods every day, e.g. chips.
- Do not use cooking oil indefinitely in deep-fat fryers – change the oil regularly.
- Drain all fried foods on kitchen paper.
- Reduce your intake of chocolate, high-fat sugary snacks, crisps, biscuits, cakes, sausages, peanuts, pastries, mayonnaise and cream.

SAMPLE EXAM QUESTIONS AND ANSWERS

- Suggest ways of **reducing the intake of sugar** in the diet of teenagers. (5 marks)
  (i)　Cut down on the intake of chocolate, sweets and honey.
  (ii)　Reduce intake of fizzy drinks and sugary drinks.
  (iii)　Limit intake of cakes, sugary snacks, bars and biscuits.
  (iv)　Choose unsweetened fruit juices, low-sugar breakfast cereals and porridge.
  (v)　Choose fresh fruit as snacks instead of sugary bars.
- Suggest ways of **reducing the intake of fat** in the diet. (6 marks)
  (i)　Bake, grill and steam instead of frying (low-fat methods).
  (ii)　Choose low-fat spreads instead of butters and spread butter thinly on bread.
  (iii)　Remove excess visible fat from meat.
  (iv)　Reduce intake of fat-laden foods, e.g. cakes, crisps, sausages.
  (v)　Choose low-fat cheese instead of full-fat products.
  (vi)　Reduce the amount of convenience/processed foods used.

- Suggest ways of **reducing the intake of salt** in the diet. (6 marks)
    - (i) *Reduce bacon, rashers, sausages, cheese and butter.*
    - (ii) *Choose porridge instead of other breakfast cereals.*
    - (iii) *Avoid stock cubes and tinned and packaged soups or sauces (convenience foods).*
    - (iv) *Reduce intake of salty snacks, e.g. crisps, nuts and snack foods.*
    - (v) *Avoid adding salt at the table and during cooking.*
    - (vi) *Choose low-salt products.*

How to reduce sugar

Choose from low-sugar or sugar-free foods, unsweetened fruit juices and low-sugar breakfast cereals. Reduce sugar at the table, in beverages and when cooking.

Reduce intake of sugary snacks, biscuits, cakes, fizzy drinks, high-sugar breakfast cereals, chocolates, sweets and tinned fruit in syrup.

Healthy food pyramid

key point

For younger children, begin with smaller and fewer servings and increase servings as they develop and grow older.

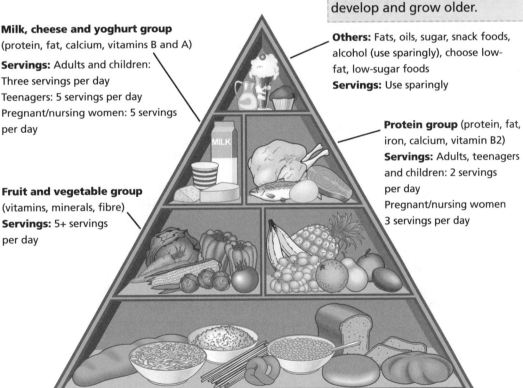

Milk, cheese and yoghurt group (protein, fat, calcium, vitamins B and A)
Servings: Adults and children: Three servings per day
Teenagers: 5 servings per day
Pregnant/nursing women: 5 servings per day

Others: Fats, oils, sugar, snack foods, alcohol (use sparingly), choose low-fat, low-sugar foods
Servings: Use sparingly

Protein group (protein, fat, iron, calcium, vitamin B2)
Servings: Adults, teenagers and children: 2 servings per day
Pregnant/nursing women 3 servings per day

Fruit and vegetable group (vitamins, minerals, fibre)
Servings: 5+ servings per day

Cereals, bread and potatoes group (main energy source)
Servings:
Children: 4+ servings per day
Teenagers: 6+ servings per day
Adults: 6+ servings per day

What are alternatives?

Alternatives include cheese, eggs, pulses and nuts. They are part of the protein group along with meat and fish.

What is a serving?

A serving is the recommended portion of a food that we should eat.

Examples of servings

Group	Serving examples
Protein group	2 eggs 90 g fish 60 g cooked poultry
Milk group	Glass of milk Carton of yoghurt Bowl of rice pudding
Fruit and vegetable group	Glass of fruit juice Bowl of vegetable soup 2 tablespoons cooked vegetables
Cereal, bread and potato group	Bowl of cereal (porridge) 1 slice of wholemeal bread 1 tablespoon of rice/pasta

Examples of modern dietary problems

- Cancer (e.g. cancer of the colon).
- Coronary heart disease.
- Digestive problems.
- High blood pressure.
- Obesity.
- Skin problems.

key point

The four main food groups provide a healthy, varied, balanced diet. All the essential nutrients are present. Avoid too many processed and refined foods.

Recommended daily servings from the food groups

Food Groups	Servings
Cereals, breads and potatoes	6+
Fruit and vegetables	5+
Milk, cheese and yoghurt	3+
Meat, fish and alternatives	2+
Others: fats, oils, sugars, snack foods, alcohol	Sparingly

Alternatives to high-sugar, high saturated fat, low-fibre foods

Replace	With
Biscuits	Crackers, unsalted nuts
Burgers	Fish, chicken burgers
Cheddar cheese	Low-fat cheddar cheese
Chocolate bars	Fresh fruit, yoghurt
Cream	Natural yoghurt
Crisps	Apple, yoghurt
Fizzy drinks	Fresh unsweetened fruit juice
Pasta	Wholewheat pasta
Pastry (shortcrust)	High-fibre pastry (wholemeal pastry)
Sugar	Sugar alternative
Sugary cereals	Porridge
White bread	Wholemeal brown bread
White flour	Wholemeal flour
White rice	Brown rice

Dietary guidelines

Babies

LINK
Healthy eating
guidelines (p. 33)

- Breastfeed a baby for the first six months of life. Breast milk has the correct balance of nutrients at the perfect temperature. It promotes mother–child bonding and the mother passes on immunity to the baby against specific illnesses.
- Infant formula milk is an alternative to breast milk (follow all instructions exactly as directed).
- Avoid skimmed milk – it is unsuitable for babies and children because it lacks fat and fat-soluble vitamins.
- Weaning takes place between four and six months. Introduce baby to solid foods slowly – one food at a time (puréed or mashed).
- Do not add salt, sugar or spices to the foods.
- Never give a baby tea or coffee.
- Babies are born with a six-month supply of iron. After that, introduce iron-rich and vitamin C-rich foods.

- By one year, a baby can eat most food, provided that it is cut into very small pieces.

Children

Growth is rapid but not as rapid as in the first year of life. Children are very active and need a good supply of energy-rich foods, protein, calcium and vitamins. Choose a wide variety of fresh foods to ensure a healthy, balanced diet:

- Proteins are needed to support growth and repair (meat, poultry, eggs and cheese).
- Starchy carbohydrate provides energy (avoid sugary foods).
- Fibre-rich foods prevent constipation (cereals, vegetables).
- Calcium-rich foods along with vitamin D give strong bones and teeth (milk, yoghurt, cheese).
- Iron and vitamin C protect against disease (vegetables).
- Other vitamins and minerals promote good health (fruits and vegetables).

Always:

- Give children frequent, regular meals and snacks (discourage faddy eating).
- Serve small portions to small children (not adult portions).
- Arrange the food attractively so that it looks tasty to eat.
- Provide healthy, well-balanced packed lunches (vary every day – always include fruit and yoghurt).
- Develop good eating habits and regular, relaxed family mealtimes.
- Restrict highly spiced, salty and fatty foods, sweets and biscuits.

Adolescents/Teenagers

This is a period of great change and rapid growth. Adolescents need protein, energy rich-foods, calcium, iron and vitamins to support this time of growth and development:

- Teenagers need proteins for growth (found in meat, poultry, fish and eggs).
- Calcium and vitamin D are needed for developing strong bones and teeth (milk, cheese).
- Iron-rich foods are important for teenage girls because menstruation results in iron loss and can sometimes lead to anaemia (red meat, offal (liver) and dark green vegetables).

- Vitamin C increases the absorption of iron (fresh fruit and vegetables).
- Energy-rich foods in the form of starchy carbohydrates are essential for this age group. Balance energy intake with energy output. Some teenagers are more active than others.
- Vegetables, salads, fresh fruit and lots of water promotes healthy skin.

What to avoid:

- Empty kilocalorie foods (crisps, fizzy drinks).
- Fast foods on a daily basis (chips, pizza, burgers).
- Too many sweets or chocolates.
- High-sugar, high-fat foods (bars, biscuits, cakes).
- Fatty or greasy foods (deep-fried foods).

Encourage:

- Regular meals (three a day) and healthy snacks.
- Yoghurt or fruit as a snack between meals.
- Breakfast before going to school.
- Healthy balanced mid-morning snacks and packed lunches for school.
- Fruit juices and water instead of tea or coffee.

Adults

Most people have finished growing by this stage. Nutritional requirements are changing and depend on gender and the amount of activity in one's life. Try to balance energy intake with energy output. Men tend to need more energy than women. Manual workers will need a higher intake of energy foods than sedentary workers, as they burn up energy faster.

- Proteins are needed for growth and repair of body cells and the manufacture of hormones, enzymes and antibodies (meat, poultry, fish, eggs).
- Eating polyunsaturated fats (such as oily fish) instead of saturated fats reduces the risk of heart disease.
- Carbohydrates provide energy (whole cereals, brown bread, vegetables).
- High-fibre foods (such as whole cereals, fruits and vegetables) prevent bowel problems.
- Vitamin B aids the release of energy.
- Vitamin C helps the absorption of iron.
- Calcium and vitamin D gives strong bones and teeth (milk, cheese).
- Iron (found in whole cereals, lean red meat, liver) prevents anaemia.

What to avoid or reduce:

- High-fat, high-sugar foods.
- Salt and salty foods.

- Low-fibre foods.
- Fried foods and too many saturated fat foods.

Pregnant or nursing mothers

- These women need proteins for the growth of the developing baby (meat, poultry, dairy products).
- Fats are necessary to help the baby develop a healthy nervous system (oily fish, liver, eggs).
- Carbohydrates provide the extra energy that is needed.
- Dietary fibre (wholemeal pasta and bread, fruits, vegetables) prevents constipation.
- Vitamin B (fortified foods, dark green vegetables) prevents neural tube defects.
- Iron-rich and vitamin C-rich foods prevent anaemia in baby and mother.
- Foods rich in calcium, phosphorous and vitamins A and D (milk and milk products) develop strong bones and teeth.
- Water preventing dehydration.
- Reducing salt intake prevents high blood pressure.

key point

Taking folic acid before and during pregnancy can prevent neural tube defects (spina bifida).

Foods to avoid:

- Cook-from-chilled foods, soft unpasteurised cheeses, raw and soft-cooked eggs (danger of *salmonella*).
- Spicy and fatty foods, fried foods.
- Coffee and strong tea.

key point

Do not smoke or drink when pregnant or breastfeeding.

The elderly

- Older people need proteins for the repair of cells (fish, chicken, eggs).
- Unsaturated fats give energy (oily fish, polyunsaturated foods).
- Carbohydrates also provide energy.
- Dietary fibre (whole cereals, fruits and vegetables) prevents constipation.
- Vitamin C (fruits, vegetables) fights infections and repairs cells.
- Vitamin A (eggs, liver, carrots) gives healthy skin and eyes.
- Calcium and vitamin D (milk, cheese, yoghurt) give strong bones and teeth.
- Iron and vitamin C can prevent anaemia (vitamin C aids the absorption of iron).
- Water prevents dehydration.

Choose:

- Fortified foods (with vitamins and minerals).
- Small portions of easy-to-digest foods .
- Low-energy foods (older people may need or use less energy).

Foods to reduce:

- Sugar (to prevent diabetes).
- Salt (to prevent high blood pressure).
- Fried, fatty and spicy foods (hard to digest).

Foods to avoid:

- Foods that are difficult to chew and difficult to prepare.

key point

A fortified food is one that has extra vitamins and minerals added to it during processing.

Invalids and convalescents

Follow the doctor's advice and guidelines.

- Easy-to-digest protein foods help in the repair of cells (chicken, white fish, milk dishes).
- Reduce the amount of fat in the diet (less energy is being used).
- Carbohydrates provide energy.
- Dietary fibre prevents constipation (drink lots of water).
- Vitamins aid healing and recovery.
- Calcium (milk and milk products) gives strong bones and teeth.
- Iron (offal, dark green vegetables) promotes healing and prevents anaemia.
- Water to prevent dehydration.

Other guidelines:

- Eat regular meals.
- Serve small portions of quality foods.
- Use light cooking methods, such as steaming, boiling or poaching.

Foods to avoid or reduce:

- Fried, reheated and spicy foods.
- Foods high in saturated fats.
- Processed and convenience food.

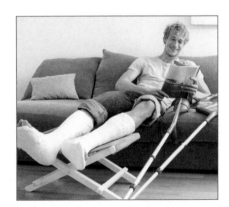

exam focus

Questions related to this chapter are found in:

- Section A (short questions).
- Section B (long questions).

They are also integrated with other related topics.

LINKS
The nutrients (p. 18)
Menu planning (p. 57)

SAMPLE SHORT EXAM QUESTIONS

- List four healthy eating guidelines.
- List four examples of modern dietary problems.
- Why is it better to breastfeed a baby?
- List three foods a pregnant woman should avoid.
- List four guidelines for a teenager's diet.
- List six guidelines for an elderly person's diet.
- Name two nutrients that are important in the diet of teenage girls.
- Make a list of the recommended servings for the different food groups.

5 Special Diets

Vegetarians

Definition – who are vegetarians?

Vegetarians are people who choose not to eat meat. The two main types of vegetarian are:

- Lacto-vegetarians.
- Vegans.

Types of vegetarians – what do they eat?

Lacto-vegetarians do not eat meat, poultry or fish.

Main sources of food for lacto-vegetarians are:

- Some foods of animal origin – milk, milk products (cheese, yoghurt, butter), eggs.
- Fruit, vegetables, nuts, cereals, textured vegetable protein (TVP), tofu, Quorn, seeds.

It is easy to plan a balanced diet for lacto-vegetarians, as they can eat a wide variety of foods.

Vegans are very strict about their diet. Vegans do not eat any foods or food products that come from animals.

Food sources for vegans:

- Vegetables, fruit, nuts, cereals, TVP, tofu, Quorn, fortified soya milk, seeds.

A balanced diet for a vegan requires careful planning, as the range of food they eat is limited.

Vegetarians, especially vegans, must read all food labels carefully to avoid foods of animal origin.

Why become a vegetarian?

People become vegetarians because of moral, religious or other personal reasons (health reasons, don't like the look of meat, hormones in meat, BSE, a desire to make better use of resources, etc.). They replace meat mainly with plant foods.

Dietary guidelines for Vegetarians

- A healthy balance of nutrients is needed. Vegetarians must keep an eye on their diet.
- For vegans, choose proteins from a wide variety of vegetable sources (pulses, nuts and meat substitutes such as Quorn, TVP and tofu).

- For lacto-vegetarians, choose proteins from vegetable sources and foods of animal origin (eggs, fish, milk, cheese, yoghurt).

> **key point**
>
> Meat substitutes include TVP (made from soy beans), tofu (from soya milk), pulse vegetables, nuts and mycoproteins (such as Quorn).

- For adequate fibre and vitamin B group, choose fibre-rich foods and fortified cereals (wholemeal bread, potatoes, nuts, pulse vegetables).
- Fortified foods will supply vitamin D (breakfast cereals, margarine).
- Calcium for lacto-vegetarians comes from milk and milk products.
- Calcium for vegans comes from fortified soya milk, leafy green vegetables and nuts.
- Iron to prevent anaemia comes from dark green leafy vegetables, dried fruits, nuts, whole cereals.
- Replace salt with herbs and spices.
- Cook with vegetable oils and fats when frying.

> **LINKS**
>
> Carbohydrates (pp. 20–1)
> Fruit and vegetables (p. 90)
> TVP (pp. 111–2)
> Eggs (p. 116)
> Fish (p. 114)

EXAM QUESTIONS AND SAMPLE ANSWERS

Higher Level 2006, Section B, Q.2 (55 marks)

'Vegetarian diets are becoming more popular in Ireland today.'

(a) Give **three** reasons why people may choose a vegetarian diet. (3 x 3 marks)
   - *Healthier option, lower in saturated fat.*
   - *Moral reason – do not wish to kill animals.*
   - *Religious reason – not allowed to eat meat.*

(b) Explain **each** of the following types of vegetarian diets: (i) vegan diet and (ii) lacto-vegetarian diet. (2 x 5 marks)
   (i) Vegan diet
      - *Does not eat meat, meat products, poultry, fish, dairy products or eggs.*
      - *Eats plant foods (pulses, fruits, vegetables, nuts and meat substitutes such as Quorn, TVP, tofu, fortified soya milk, nuts, dried fruits) and cereals.*
   (ii) Lacto-vegetarian diet
      - *Does not eat meat, meat products and poultry.*
      - *Eats dairy products, eggs, fruits and vegetables.*

(c) List the guidelines which should be followed when planning meals for a vegetarian. (3 x 4 marks)
   - *Balance the menu according to healthy eating guidelines.*
   - *Use meat substitutes, e.g. TVP, Quorn.*
   - *Use only vegetable fats and vegetable stocks.*
   - *Choose whole cereals, soya milk and yoghurts.*
   - *Include pulse vegetables and nuts.*

(d) Design a balanced **three-course** dinner menu suitable for a lacto-vegetarian.
(12 marks)

> *Three-bean salad*
>
> ***
>
> *Vegetarian curry*
> *Brown rice*
>
> ***
>
> *Fresh fruit salad*
> *Glass of freshly squeezed orange juice*

When answering:

- Use a menu format and the correct sequence.
- Make sure the menu is balanced.
- Include three courses in the menu: a starter or soup, main course and dessert.

(e) (i) What is TVP? (4 marks)

TVP (textured vegetable protein) is a meat substitute made from soya beans and is used in the diet of vegetarians.

(ii) Suggest two dishes in which TVP can be used. (2 x 4 marks)

1. Chilli con carne
2. Vegetarian lasagne

(Note: Other suitable dishes include Shepherd's pie and Spaghetti Bolognese.)

Coeliacs

What is coeliac disease?

Coeliac disease occurs in people who are unable to break down the protein gluten (found in wheat, barley, oats, rye and cereal products). The lining of the stomach becomes damaged. The gluten cannot be broken down for absorption into smaller units of amino acids.

Symptoms

- Anaemia, diarrhoea, stomach pain, extreme tiredness and weight loss. Stunted growth may also occur.

Dietary guidelines for coeliacs

- Eat a gluten-free diet. Choose gluten-free foods and food products.
- Read all food labels carefully. Watch out for hidden sources of gluten.
- Look for the gluten-free symbol.

Gluten-free symbol

- Gluten-free foods include poultry, fish, milk, milk products, fruit, vegetables, rice, cornflour, cornflakes, gluten-free flour, biscuits and breads.

Foods to avoid:

- Wheat, oats, rye, barley or products made from them (cakes, biscuits, sauces, soups, sausages, etc.).
- Convenience foods unless they display the gluten-free symbol.
- Stuffings, coated fish, pasta, spaghetti, batter, potato croquettes.

Diabetes

What Is diabetes?

Diabetes is a disease in which the body does not produce enough insulin (a hormone), or the body is unable to use the insulin it produces to control the level of glucose in the blood.

Types of diabetes

Type 1 (insulin-dependent) diabetes occurs when the body does not produce any insulin and not enough energy is produced. Glucose enters the bloodstream and is eliminated from the body in the urine. Too much or too little sugar will make the diabetic person feel ill. They might become unconscious.

Controlled by: Insulin injections and diet.

Type 2 (non-insulin-dependent) diabetes generally does not occur until adults are over 40 years of age. The insulin produced is not being used by the body for the conversion of glucose into energy. The glucose does not enter the cells but remains in the bloodstream. Sometimes this type of diabetes is associated with obesity.

Controlled by: Diet and weight loss.

Always consult your doctor and follow the guidelines given. Only eat the foods recommended in the diet plan given by the doctor.

Check labels on commercial diabetic products to make sure the product is suitable for your particular type of diabetes.

Dietary guidelines for diabetics

- Follow your doctor's recommended dietary and exercise programme.
- Maintain the recommended weight.
- Eat regular snacks and meals – *never* miss them.
- Eat starchy foods evenly and regularly throughout the day.
- Eat high-fibre carbohydrates for the slow release of energy.
- Reduce intake of salt and fat.
- Choose light methods of cooking (steaming, baking, grilling).
- Avoid foods high in sugar (pastries, cakes, biscuits, marmalades, jam, chocolate, sweets, fruits in syrup, sugary drinks).

LINKS
Low-sugar diet (p. 50)
High-fibre diet (p. 49)
Carbohydrates (p. 20)

Obesity

People are considered obese when they are 20 per cent over the recommended weight for their height.

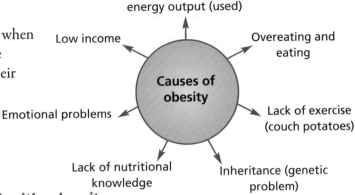

Energy intake is greater than energy output (used)

Low income

Overeating and eating

Causes of obesity

Emotional problems

Lack of exercise (couch potatoes)

Lack of nutritional knowledge

Inheritance (genetic problem)

Ten risks associated with obesity

1. Reduced life expectancy.
2. Coronary heart disease (CHD).
3. Increased risk of high blood pressure and strokes.
4. Varicose veins.
5. Gallstones.
6. Diabetes.
7. Difficulty during pregnancy and childbirth.
8. Chest infections.
9. Pains in joints, muscles and back.
10. Low self-esteem and maybe depression.

Dietary guidelines for dealing with obesity

- Consult your doctor and follow his or her guidelines.
- Eat a healthy, balanced, varied diet (do not diet without advice from a doctor).
- Choose foods that balance energy intake with energy output.
- Eat three regular meals each day – never skip meals.
- Always eat a healthy breakfast.
- Increase intake of high-fibre food.
- Increase intake of fruit and vegetables.
- Grill, bake, poach or microwave food (avoid frying).
- Increase intake of water.
- Modify recipes to increase dietary fibre and reduce fat, sugar and salt.
- Avoid convenience foods and take-aways.
- Exercise regularly (follow the doctor's guidelines).

Suitable foods

Fruits, green vegetables, lean meat, poultry, white fish, low-fat dairy products, low-sugar foods, salad vegetables (cucumber, peppers, lettuce, tomatoes), cottage cheese, whole cereals, root vegetables, citrus fruits, low-fat dairy products, fresh fruit juice.

EXAM QUESTIONS AND SAMPLE ANSWERS

Higher Level 2003, Section B, Q.2

(a) List the possible causes of obesity. (3 x 4 marks)
- *Imbalance between energy intake and energy output.*
- *Overeating due to emotional problems.*
- *Lack of exercise.*
- *Low income.*

(b) List **four** health problems associated with obesity. (4 x 3 marks)
- *Coronary heart disease (CHD).*
- *High blood pressure.*
- *Stroke.*
- *Diabetes.*

(c) Suggest **four** healthy eating guidelines which should be followed to reduce the risk of obesity. (4 x 3 marks)
- *Reduce intake of fatty foods.*
- *Reduce intake of high-salt foods.*
- *Increase intake of high-fibre foods (fruits, vegetables, whole cereals).*
- *Avoid convenience foods and take-aways.*

(d) Plan a **set of menus** for **one** day suitable for an adult who is obese. (15 marks)

> **Breakfast**
> *Glass of freshly squeezed orange juice*
> *Bowl of porridge with low-fat milk*
> *Wholemeal brown bread with low-fat spread*
> *Tea/coffee*
> ***
>
> **Lunch**
> *Fish bake*
> *Mixed green salad with low-fat dressing*
> *Fresh fruit (apple)*
> ***
>
> **Dinner**
> *Onion soup*
> ∞∞∞∞
>
> *Roast chicken*
> *Steamed mixed vegetables*
> *Baked potato*
> ∞∞∞∞
>
> *Apple and rhubarb crumble with low-fat yoghurt*

You are expected to:
- Provide three balanced meals (breakfast, lunch, dinner).
- Follow healthy eating guidelines.
- Use a Menu Format.

(e) Explain the term 'empty kilocalories'. (4 marks)
Empty kilocalories refers to foods that have high levels of sugar and lack other nutrients, e.g. table sugar.

Coronary heart disease (CHD)

What is CHD?

Coronary heart disease is caused by the build-up of cholesterol on the walls of the arteries, which results in blocked arteries and veins. Cholesterol sticks to the walls of the arteries.

Problems caused by CHD

- Heart attack • Stroke • Sudden death.

Causes of CHD

- Family history of CHD.
- Diet high in saturated fats, which raises cholesterol levels.
- Obesity.
- Lack of exercise.
- Stress.
- Smoking.
- Alcohol.

Dietary guidelines for CHD

- Reduce intake of saturated fats.
- Increase intake of oily fish (unsaturated fats).
- Replace high-fat products with low-fat varieties.
- Increase intake of dietary fibre.
- Omit salt from cooking and at the table.
- Avoid convenience foods and fast foods (take-aways).

Essential lifestyle changes

- Get active • Reduce stress • Stop smoking • Avoid alcohol.

High-fibre diet

Benefits of a high-fibre diet

- Prevents constipation.
- Prevents bowel problems.
- Gives a feeling of fullness.
- Prevents chemical build-up in the body.
- Low in fat.

Problems associated with low fibre intake

- Colon cancer.
- Constipation.
- Diverticulitis.
- Haemorrhoids (piles).
- Irritable bowel syndrome (IBS) .

Dietary guidelines for increasing fibre in the diet

- Eat wholegrain cereals and cereal products (brown bread, brown rice).
- Choose wholegrain breakfast cereals (porridge).
- Increase intake of fruit, vegetables, nuts and seeds.
- Eat the skins of fruit and vegetables.
- Increase intake of pulse vegetables.
- Avoid refined cereals, convenience foods and snacks.

> **key point**
> High fibre intake = 6 g or more of fibre per 100 g.

> **LINKS**
> Dietary fibre (p. 21)
> Cereals (p. 82)

Low-salt diet

Problems associated with high salt intake

- Coronary heart disease (CHD) • Fluid retention • Raised blood pressure • Stroke.

High-salt foods

Stock cubes, ketchup, convenience sauces and soups (tinned and packets), instant noodles, salty snacks (potato crisps, salted popcorn, salted nuts).

Dietary guidelines for reducing salt in the diet

- Avoid salt at the table and when preparing and cooking food.
- Replace salt with herbs and spices.
- Avoid convenience foods with a high salt content.
- Choose fresh meat, poultry, fish and vegetables.
- Read food labels.

> **LINKS**
> Minerals (p. 22)
> Coronary heart disease (CHD) (p. 49)

Low-sugar diet

Problems associated with high sugar intake

- Empty kilocalories.
- Obesity and being overweight.
- Tooth decay (dental caries).

High-sugar foods

Cakes, biscuits, bars, sweetened drinks, fizzy drinks, sugar-coated breakfast cereals, ketchup, sweets and sweet snacks/bars.

Dietary guidelines for reducing sugar in the diet

- Reduce the amount of sugar added when preparing and cooking foods.
- Avoid high-sugar foods (see list above).
- Choose fresh fruit, vegetables, seeds and nuts as healthy snacks.
- Use artificial sweeteners instead of sugar.
- Read food labels.

> **LINKS**
> Carbohydrates (p. 20)
> Healthy Eating Guidelines (p. 33)

Eating Disorders

There are **two** main types of eating disorders:

- Anorexia nervosa ● Bulimia nervosa.

Anorexia nervosa and bulimia nervosa require professional attention and counselling.

Anorexia nervosa

- Anorexia nervosa is a psychological condition where individuals suffer from anxiety and are obsessed with thinness and a fear of getting fat. They have a distorted body image and suffer low self-esteem.
- People suffering from aneroxia nervosa are convinced that they are overweight or fat when in fact they may be well below their recommended body weight.
- Symptoms may include severe dieting, excessive weight loss, starvation, self-induced vomiting, nutrient deficiencies, lack of menstruation and organ failure.
- Specialised treatment supervised by professionals is required.

Bulimia Nervosa

- Sufferers tend to turn to food in times of stress
- They engage in binge eating followed by self-induced vomiting
- People reduce their weight by taking laxatives with severe consequences
- Symptoms may include an inflamed oesophagus, irritation of the throat, tooth decay, nutrient deficiencies and dehydration.

 EXAM QUESTIONS AND SAMPLE ANSWERS

Higher Level 2009, Section B, Q.1 (b)
Outline the importance of including red meat in the diet of teenagers.
- *Red meat is a good source of iron, which is essential in the diet of teenage girls who, because of menstruation, lose iron. This sometimes leads to anaemia.*

HL

- *Iron is needed to make red blood cells (haemoglobin), which carry oxygen around the body to give us energy.*

Higher Level 2008, Section B, Q.1 (c) and (d)

(c) Explain the statement 'suitable for a gluten–free diet'. (4 marks)

The statement means:

- *The food product does not contain gluten.*
- *The food can be used by coeliacs who cannot break down gluten in their bodies.*

(d) (i) State the recommended daily salt intake of an adult. (2 marks)

The RDA of salt for an adult is 6 grams.

(ii) What effect can a high salt intake have on the body? (2 x 3 marks)

Effects of a high salt intake:

- *Coronary heart disease (CHD).*
- *High blood pressure.*
- *Stroke.*
- *Damage to kidneys – fluid retention.*

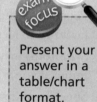

Present your answer in bullet points.

Higher Level 2006, Section B, Q.1 (b)

State which type of milk would be most suitable for (i) an energetic child and (ii) a pregnant woman. (10 marks)

	Type suitable and reasons for choice
(i) Energetic child	*Whole milk:* • *More fat present than in low-fat varieties.* • *Gives more energy.*
(ii) Pregnant woman	*Fortified milk:* • *High levels of folic acid to prevent neural tube defects.* • *High levels of calcium for developing bones.*

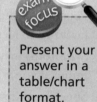

Present your answer in a table/chart format.

 SAMPLE EXAM QUESTIONS (4 MARKS)

1. What nutrients might be missing from a vegetarian diet?
2. Give four dietary guidelines to be followed by a coeliac.
3. List four foods coeliacs should not eat.
4. List four items high in salt and suggest an alternative.
5. Name four foods high in fat and suggest an alternative.
6. Give four ways salt can be reduced in the diet.
7. Name the two types of diabetes.

6 The Digestive System

aims
- To define key terms associated with the digestive system.
- To identify and label the digestive system.
- To outline the functions of the different parts of the digestive system.
- To explain how food is digested and absorbed.

Note: Chapter 6 is for Higher level students only.

Definitions

- **Absorption** is when soluble molecules/nutrients are passed into the bloodstream from the small intestine. The blood transports the nutrients around the body to where they are needed.
- **Digestion** is the breakdown of food into smaller molecules so that it can be used by the body.
- **An enzyme** is a chemical substance that causes a a reaction without changing itself.

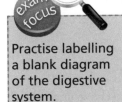

exam focus

Practise labelling a blank diagram of the digestive system.

key point

All nutrients present in the digestive system must be converted into their smallest molecules for absorption to take place.

Nutrients		Broken down into
Protein	→	Amino acid
Fat	→	Fatty acids and glycerol
Carbohydrate	→	Simple sugar, glucose
Cellulose	→	Cannot be broken down
Vitamins	→	Are already small units
Minerals	→	Are already small units

1.

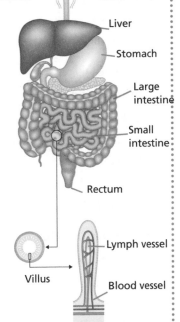

- Mouth
- Peristalsis (wave-like movement)
- Liver
- Stomach
- Large intestine
- Small intestine
- Rectum
- Lymph vessel
- Villus
- Blood vessel

The digestive system

1. Physically:

- Food is taken into the mouth, where it is broken up and chewed by the teeth.
- Food is churned in the stomach.

2. Chemically:

- Enzymes help break down protein, fats and carbohydrates. The enzyme causes a chemical reaction to take place without changing itself. Each enzyme works on breaking down **one** nutrient only.

The pathway of digestion

Mouth

Function: Physical and chemical.

Physical action:

- Teeth chop, grind and chew food into small molecules.
- Food is mixed with saliva.

Chemical action:

- Saliva contains an enzyme called salivary amylase.
- Salivary amylase changes cooked starch into maltose.

Oesophagus

Physical action:

- Mouth is linked to the stomach by the oesophagus.
- Rippling, wave-like muscular movements (peristalsis) push the food along into the stomach.
- No digestion takes place in the oesophagus.

Stomach

Physical action:

- Food is churned around the stomach until it forms chyme.
- Fats are melted by the heat of the stomach.

Chemical action:

- Hydrochloric acid destroys bacteria.
- Pepsin breaks down proteins into peptide chains.

Small intestine

Physical action:

- The small intestine joins the stomach and the large intestine.
- Peristalsis causes the food to move along the small intestine.
- Three digestive juices enter the small intestine:

   (a) Pancreatic juice from the pancreas.

   (b) Bile from the liver forms an emulsion with fats.

   (c) Intestinal juice from the lining of the intestine.

Chemical action:

- The digestive juices contain enzymes.
  - (a) Proteins and peptides are converted into amino acids.
  - (b) Sugars are converted into simple sugars, e.g. glucose.
  - (c) Fats are broken down into fatty acids and glycerol.
- Bile from the gall bladder:
  - (a) Emulsifies fat, breaking it into fatty acids and glycerol.
  - (b) Neutralises hydrochloric acid.

Absorption:

- Digested foods are absorbed into the villi of the small intestine.
- Each villus contains a lymph vessel and a blood vessel.
- Amino acids are absorbed into the bloodstream.
- Glucose is absorbed into the bloodstream.
- Fatty acids and glycerol go into the lymph system and then into the bloodstream.

Large intestine

Physical action/absorption:

- Digestion is completed as the remaining nutrients are absorbed.
- Bacteria break down dietary fibre, releasing gases and acids.
- Vitamins B and K are produced in the large intestine.
- Water is reabsorbed into the blood.
- Solid waste (faeces) is removed via the rectum.

Summary of absorption

What happens to the nutrients?

- Most absorption takes place in the small intestine.
- Amino acids, glucose, water-soluble vitamins and minerals are absorbed directly into the blood vessels and then transported to the rest of the body.
- Fatty acids, glycerol and fat-soluble vitamins pass into the lymph system, circulate around the body and eventually enter the bloodstream.

LINK
Nutrients (p. 18)

EXAM QUESTIONS AND SAMPLE ANSWERS

Higher Level 2003, Section B, Q.4

(a) State the functions of each of the following parts of the digestive system. (3 x 5 marks)

    (i) The mouth

- *Food is broken down and chewed by the teeth (physical action).*
- *Food is mixed with saliva, which contains the enzyme salivary amylase.*
- *Salivary amylase converts cooked starch into maltose (chemical action).*

    (ii) The stomach

- *Food is churned around the stomach until it forms chyme (physical action).*
- *Fats are melted by the heat of the stomach.*
- *Gastric juices containing hydrochloric acid and the enzyme pepsin are released from the walls of the stomach to work on proteins.*
- *Pepsin converts proteins into peptides (chemical action).*

    (iii) The small intestine

- *Bile breaks down fats into fatty acids and glycerol.*
- *Enzymes convert proteins and peptide into amino acids.*
- *Enzymes convert sugars into simpler sugars, e.g. glucose.*

(b) Describe **two** physical and **two** chemical changes which occur during digestion.

Physical changes (2 x 5 marks)

1. Food is churned around the stomach until it forms chyme.

2. Fats are melted by the heat of the stomach.

Chemical changes (2 x 5 marks)

1. Pepsin breaks down proteins into peptide chains.

2. Salivary amylase changes cooked starch into maltose.

(c) Explain what is meant by peristalsis. (5 marks)

Peristalsis is the rippling, wave-like movements of the muscles pushing the food along the oesophagus.

(d) What is the role of fibre in digestion?

Role of fibre in digestion:

- *Creates bulk by absorbing water.*
- *Helps the digestion of other nutrients.*
- *Prevents constipation.*
- *Prevents diverticulitis.*
- *Picks up and removes chemicals and toxins from the body.*

- To list the guidelines for planning meals.
- To explain/define table d'hôte and à la carte menus.
- To design sample menus for different meals using the menu format.
- To outline the guidelines for setting a table.
- To identify the guidelines for presenting and serving food.

Meal planning guidelines

Meal planning is influenced by:

- Food value (nutritious and balanced).
- Money/cost (family budget).
- Time available (must fit in with family commitments).
- Type of meal (occasion).
- Varying cooking methods, avoiding repetition.
- Availability and choice (variety and time of year).
- Equipment available (can speed up preparation and cooking).
- Special dietary needs/restrictions/preferences.
- Number of people.
- Skills of the cook.

Choice of individual dishes is influenced by:

- Variety of ingredients and dishes.
- Balance of colours, flavours.
- Presentation, garnishes and textures.

Menus

Definitions

key point

PLANNING AHEAD

- Make a shopping list based on the menus for one week.
- Serve hot dishes in winter and chilled dishes in summer.
- If time is limited, choose fast methods of cooking.
- Plan suitable accompaniments and garnishes/decorations.
- Plan to use all leftovers.

- **Menu:** A menu is an organised list of all the dishes to be served during a meal.
- **À la carte menu:** This menu lists every dish possible for all courses, with individual prices beside each dish. It offers more choice than the table d'hôte menu. A complete meal based on this type of menu is generally more expensive.

- **Table d'hôte menu:** This is a restaurant menu that has a fixed price for the complete meal. Three to five courses may be offered, with limited choices for each course. It is cheaper than the à la carte restaurant menu.

Writing menu cards

- Create an attractive design.
- Write courses in the order they will be eaten.
- Write names of dishes down the centre of the menu card.
- Be specific– for example name the type of meat and how it is cooked.
- List the accompaniments (vegetables, sauces).

Sample menus

Summer Breakfast

Grapefruit

∞∞∞∞

Homemade muesli and yoghurt

∞∞∞∞

Grilled sausage, bacon and tomatoes

∞∞∞∞

Wholemeal bread, jam
Milk/tea/coffee

Winter Breakfast

Fresh orange juice

∞∞∞∞

Porridge
Milk

∞∞∞∞

Poached eggs on toast

∞∞∞∞

Wholemeal bread, marmalade
Milk/tea/coffee

Summer Lunch

Lasagne
Mixed green salad
Carrot and raisin salad

∞∞∞∞

Natural yoghurt

∞∞∞∞

Tea/coffee

Summer Dinner

Grilled fillet of mackerel
Steamed vegetables
Boiled baby potatoes

∞∞∞∞

Fresh fruit salad

∞∞∞∞

Tea/coffee

Winter Lunch

French onion soup

∞∞∞∞

Grilled fillet of chicken
Rocket salad
Brown rice salad

∞∞∞∞

Apple crumble
Custard sauce

∞∞∞∞

Tea/coffee

Winter Dinner

Potato and leek soup

∞∞∞∞

Roast leg of lamb
Mint sauce
Creamed potatoes
Buttered carrots

∞∞∞∞

Baked apples
Custard sauce

∞∞∞∞

Tea/coffee

Summer Lunch

Carrot and coriander soup

∞∞∞∞

Quiche Lorraine
Mixed green salad

∞∞∞∞

Fruit flan

∞∞∞∞

Tea/coffee

Winter Supper Menu

Macaroni cheese
Mixed green salad
Wholemeal bread

∞∞∞∞

Light fruit cake

∞∞∞∞

Milk/tea/coffee

Summer Dinner

Chilled kiwi salad

∞∞∞∞

Baked stuffed fish
Boiled garden peas
Creamed potatoes

∞∞∞∞

Home-made chocolate ice cream

∞∞∞∞

Tea/coffee

Summer Supper Menu

Cold ham salad
Potato salad
Wholemeal bread rolls

∞∞∞∞

Apple tart

∞∞∞∞

Milk/tea/coffee

Food presentation

Guidelines for setting tables

- Table linen, crockery, glasses and cutlery should be clean.
- Arrange cutlery in the order in which it will be used.
- Allow sufficient space for each person.
- Fill all condiment sets and arrange in groups on the table.

Table setting suggestion

- Organise an attractive centrepiece (flowers, fruit or candles).

Guidelines for presenting and serving food

- Food should look attractive.
- Food should be arranged neatly on clean plates or dishes.
- Serve cold or chilled food on cold plates.
- Serve hot food piping hot on warmed plates.
- Use plain plates and dishes for serving savoury foods.
- Choose fancy plates and dishes for sweet foods.
- Serve meat towards the centre of the plate.
- Serve sauces in a sauce boat or on the plate around the meat.
- Garnish savoury dishes, decorate sweet dishes.

key point

Garnishes and decorations add colour and flavour to dishes.

Garnishes	Decorations
Chopped chives	Almond flakes
Cream or yoghurt	Cherries
Croûtons	Chocolate leaves
Finely chopped parsley	Grated chocolate
Juliennes of vegetables	Melted chocolate
Lemon twists or slices	Piped cream
Orange twists or slices	Sprigs of mint
Radishes	
Sprigs of parsley	
Twists of cucumber	

EXAM QUESTIONS AND SAMPLE ANSWERS

Higher Level 2003, Section A, Q.4 (4 marks)

Explain **each** of the following terms.

(i) Table d'hôte: *A menu with a limited selection of food for a fixed price.*

(ii) À la carte: *A menu where a large selection of dishes are priced individually.*

Higher Level 1999, Section A, Q.5 (4 marks)

Name a different food for which each of the following garnishes may be suitable.

Garnish	Food
(i) A wedge of lemon	*Baked fish pie*
(ii) Chopped parsley	*Omelettes*
(iii) Glace cherries	*Trifle*
(iv) A sprinkle of icing sugar	*Victoria sponge*

Ordinary Level 2008, Section A, Q.5 (5 marks)

Name a **different** garnish suitable for each of the following foods.

Food	Garnish
(i) Cheese omelette	*Finely chopped parsley/chives*
(ii) Fish cakes	*Lemon wedges*
(iii) Mushroom soup	*Swirl of cream*

Ordinary Level 2007, Section A, Q.6 (5 marks)

Explain the following.

(i) **Garnish:** *To decorate a savoury dish. Example: chopped parsley.*

Higher Level 2004, Section A, Q.5 (5 marks)

Name a different garnish suitable for each of the following foods.

Food	Garnish
(i) Soup	*Croûtons*
(ii) Fish cakes	*Lemon wedges*

Ordinary Level 2001, Section A, Q.3 (5 marks)

Name a different garnish suitable for **each** of the following foods.

Food	Garnish
(i) Grilled fish	*Tomato roses*
(ii) Shepherd's pie	*Tomato wedges and a sprig of parsley*

It is important to practise exam questions. In preparation for a question on menus, practise by designing menus for the following and outline reasons for your choice:

- A three-course dinner menu suitable for a family of four.
- A three-course dinner menu suitable for a lacto-vegetarian.
- A set of menus for one day suitable for an adult suffering from obesity.
- A menu, to include pizza in the main course, suitable for a group of teenagers.
- A balanced packed lunch suitable for a person on a low-cholesterol diet.

8 Designing Menus

aims
- To design menus for a variety of meals and individuals.
- To revise healthy eating guidelines, dietary needs and meal planning.
- To prepare for the practical cookery and written exams.

exam Q

Using the selection of dishes in this chapter, design the following menus:
- A two-course menu suitable for a family evening meal using a ready-to-cook fish pie.
- A balanced breakfast menu, to include porridge or muesli, suitable for a school-going teenager.
- A balanced breakfast menu for a school-going child, to include an egg dish.
- A three-course lunch for an adult that includes fresh fish.
- A three-course lunch for a teenager that includes homemade beef burgers.
- A packed lunch menu for a teenager that includes fish.
- A three-course dinner menu to include homemade vegetable soup.

key point

Menus for breakfast, lunch, dinner and a light evening meal can be created by selecting from the dishes below.

exam focus

To gain maximum marks when presenting menus, use the menu format and place menus in a box.

Breakfast

- **Fruit:** Grapefruit (segments or grilled half), melon, fresh fruit salad, stewed prunes, apples.
- **Cereals:** Breakfast cereals (porridge, muesli).
- **Breads:** Wholemeal brown bread, toast, croissants, scones, muffins, pancakes.
- **Cooked dishes:** Eggs (boiled, scrambled, poached), rashers, sausages, white and black pudding, liver, grilled tomato and mushroom, fish (trout, kippers), kedgeree (a fish and rice dish).
- **Others:** Yoghurt, cheese, marmalade, jam.
- **Beverages:** Juice (orange, grapefruit, apple, pineapple), tea, coffee, milk, smoothies, fresh fruit and vegetable juices.

Light lunch

Starters:

- **Soup:** Potato and leek, carrot, mixed vegetable, gazpacho, French onion.
- **Breads:** Wholemeal brown bread, bread rolls, garlic bread.
- **Sandwiches:** Salad, meat (beef, turkey, ham), cheese, mixed.
- **New trends:** Wraps, baguettes, paninis, bagels.

Main course:

- Baked potato with filling (chicken, ham, mushroom), green salad, coleslaw.
- Pizza, green salad, coleslaw.
- Lasagne, mixed green salad.
- Savoury pancakes, mixed salad, carrot and raisin salad.
- Vegetable stir-fry, noodles.

Desserts:

- Fresh whole fruit (apple, pear, orange).
- Yoghurt (natural, fruit flavoured, whole fruit).

Beverages: Tea, coffee, orange juice, milk.

Substantial lunch

Starters:

- **Soup:** Tomato, mushroom, minestrone, chicken broth.
- **Breads:** Wholemeal brown rolls and bread, dinner buns, melba toast.

Main course:

- Fish chowder, brown rolls/garlic bread.
- Grilled trout, green salad, brown rice salad.
- Kebabs, green salad.
- Omelette with salad and baked potato.
- Pasta dishes (lasagne, spaghetti Bolognese, salad).
- Quiche with salad.
- Salads (ham, beef, chicken, turkey, tuna).
- Savoury stuffed pancakes, mixed salad.
- Stir-fry (beef, chicken, vegetable).
- Stuffed peppers, mixed salads.

Desserts:

- Fresh fruit salad.
- Fruit flan.
- Piece of fresh fruit (orange, pear).
- Yoghurt with stewed fruit.

Beverages: Tea, coffee, orange juice, milk.

Dinner (Main meal of the day)

Starters:

- Melon balls.
- Mixed fruit salad.
- Salad niçoise.
- Seafood cocktail.
- Smoked fish pâté, brown bread.

Soups: Any soup (broths, clear, purée, thickened) or chowder served with garlic bread, brown bread, dinner rolls or buns.

Main course dishes and accompaniments:

- Baked stuffed fish, garden peas, creamed potatoes.
- Beef casserole, baked potato, French beans.
- Beef goulash, piped potatoes, green salad.
- Boiled bacon and cabbage, boiled potatoes, onion sauce.
- Chicken marengo, baked potato, green salad.
- Chicken risotto, mixed salad.
- Chilli con carne, boiled rice, green salad.
- Curry (beef or chicken), boiled brown rice, green salad.
- Goujons of fish, chipped potatoes, garden peas.
- Grilled mackerel, chipped potatoes, French beans.
- Grilled steak, baked potato, mixed green salad.
- Irish stew, root vegetables.
- Lasagne, mixed green salad, coleslaw.
- Roast chicken, roast potatoes, glazed carrots.
- Smoked haddock au gratin, creamed potatoes, broccoli.
- Steak and kidney pie, baked potato, green salad.
- Stir-fry (poultry, vegetables), Chinese noodles, salad.
- Stuffed pork steak, baked potato, mixed green salad.
- Vegetable stir-fry, boiled brown rice, green salad.
- Vegetarian casserole, stir-fried peppers and nuts.
- Vegetarian curry, brown rice, cooked green vegetables.
- Vegetarian lasagne, mixed green salad, nut salad.

Desserts:

- Apple or rhubarb crumble, custard sauce.
- Baked apples, custard sauce.
- Cheesecake (lemon, raspberry).
- Chocolate mousse.
- Fresh fruit salad.

- Natural yoghurt.
- Queen of puddings.
- Stewed fruit, yoghurt.
- Strawberries and cream.
- Stuffed pancakes, cinnamon cream.

Beverages: Tea, coffee, orange juice, milk.

Light evening meal (teatime)

Savoury dishes:

- Cold meat or poultry salad.
- Eggs (omelette, boiled, poached, scrambled).
- Potato and cheese pie.
- Selection of sandwiches.
- Shepherd's pie, green salad, tomato salad.
- Stuffed eggs, tomato salad.
- Stuffed savoury pancakes.
- Stuffed tomatoes, wholemeal bread.

Bread and cakes:

- Apple tart.
- Brown fruit scones, tea scones, rock buns.
- Fruit flan.
- Gingerbread.
- Light fruitcake.
- Swiss roll.
- Victoria sandwich.
- Wholemeal brown bread.

Beverages: Tea, coffee, milk.

LINKS

Revise
- Preparing for the practical cookery exam (p. 146)
- Healthy Eating Guidelines (p. 33)
- Individual dietary requirements (pp. 37–52)
- Meal Planning Guidelines (p. 57)

9 Food Hygiene and Food Safety

- To list the causes of foods spoiling.
- To list the sources of food poisoning. **HL**
- To list the rules for preventing food poisoning. **HL**
- Name four bacteria and explain how they contaminate food. **HL**
- Explain what is meant by 'acceptable levels of contamination'.

Causes of foods spoiling

- **Micro-organisms** (moulds, yeasts, bacteria).
- **Enzymes** (involved in the ripening of fruit and vegetables).
- **Oxygen** (causes fats to go rancid and food to discolour).

key point

To avoid the growth of micro-organisms in the kitchen, food contamination and cross-contamination, it is important to keep everything clean.

Food poisoning

Food poisoning can result if there are high levels of bacteria present in food.

Symptoms: Stomach pains, nausea, vomiting and diarrhoea.

HL Five food-poisoning bacteria

Bacteria	Sources
Salmonella	Intestines of humans and animals, raw meat, poultry, eggs, shellfish
Listeria	Soft cheese, cook–chill products, pâté, poultry, mayonnaise, prepared salads
Staphylococcus	Spread by humans (present in the nose, throat and skin)
Clostridium Botulinum	Incorrectly processed canned foods
E. Coli	Intestines of animals, spread by humans, minced meats (e.g. burgers), unpasteurised milk and cheese

Factors affecting food safety

- Personal hygiene.
- Kitchen hygiene.
- Food hygiene (food handling, preparation, cooking and serving).
- Food storage.

How bacteria spreads in the kitchen

- Cross-contamination between raw and cooked foods.
- Cuts and open wounds.
- Dirty equipment, surfaces, kitchen cloths, towels and bins.
- Flies and vermin (rats and mice).
- Incorrect handling of food.
- Incorrect storage of food.
- Pets in the kitchen.
- Poor personal and food handling hygiene.

How bacteria grow and multiply

Micro-organisms need:

- Food (moist, high-protein foods).
- Time (bacteria double every 20 minutes).
- Warmth (around 37°C). Boiling kills them; cold slows their growth.
- Moisture (damp conditions and moist food).
- Some need air (oxygen).
- Correct pH levels.

Food preparation: Rules for preventing food contamination

Personal hygiene

- Tie back and cover hair. Keep fingernails short.
- Wash hands after using the toilet and before handling food.
- Wash hands before and after handling food.
- Cover all cuts and sores.
- Handle food as little as possible and use food tongs.
- Do not cough or sneeze over food and dishes. If ill, do not prepare, cook or serve food.
- Use a clean spoon to taste food – never lick your fingers.

Kitchen hygiene

- Wash and disinfect kitchen utensils, equipment and surfaces.
- Keep the cooker, fridge and microwave oven clean.
- Wash and disinfect the kitchen sink daily.
- Wash and disinfect kitchen cloths and change daily. Use separate cloths for different tasks, e.g. kitchen, bathroom.
- Wipe up spills as they occur, use kitchen paper.
- Sweep and wash kitchen floor daily. Disinfect regularly.
- Empty the kitchen bin daily. Keep it covered. Disinfect weekly.
- Keep cats and dogs out of the kitchen.
- Do not smoke in the kitchen.

Food hygiene

- Store food at the correct temperature and in the correct location, e.g. perishables in the fridge. Check the fridge daily and use food within the expiry period.
- Keep foods clean, cool and covered until required.
- Keep raw foods and cooked foods separate.
- Use separate dishes and chopping boards for raw and cooked food.
- Prepare foods on clean surfaces using clean utensils.
- Cook food thoroughly to kill bacteria, e.g. meat, chicken, fish.
- Put leftovers on a clean plate, covered, cooled and stored in the fridge until required. Reheat leftover food thoroughly.

key point

Stop the multiplication of bacteria by using:

- Antiseptics (reduce the level of bacteria).
- Disinfectants (kill all bacteria).

EXAM QUESTIONS AND SAMPLE ANSWERS

HIGHER LEVEL SHORT QUESTIONS

Higher Level 2007, Section A, Q.5 (4 marks)
Explain the term 'cross-contamination'.
Cross-contamination is the transfer of bacteria from one food to another or from one surface to another. This increases the risk of food contamination and food poisoning. Examples: (a) preparing raw and cooked meat, poultry, fish and foods on the same surface (b) storing raw and cooked meat on the same plate.

Higher Level 2003, Section A, Q.5 (4 marks)
Outline **two** possible causes of food spoilage.
(i) Enzymes
(ii) Moulds, yeast and bacteria

HL

HIGHER LEVEL LONG QUESTION

Higher Level 2005, Section B, Q.2 (a), (b) and (c) (55 marks)

(a) Outline the conditions that favour the growth of micro-organisms. (12 marks)

- *Food*
- *Warmth*
- *Moisture*
- *Oxygen*
- *Correct pH*

(b) (i) Name **one** food-poisoning bacteria. (3 marks)

   Salmonella

   (ii) Name **two** possible sources of this bacteria. (6 marks)

   1. Poultry

   2. Eggs

(c) List **three** symptoms of food poisoning. (9 marks)

   1. Nausea

   2. Stomach pain/cramps

   3. Vomiting

ORDINARY LEVEL LONG QUESTION

Ordinary Level 2003, Section B, Q.2 (a)

List **four** guidelines which could be followed to ensure safe food preparation. (12 marks)

(i) Wash hands before and after handling food.

(ii) Store food in the fridge until required.

(iii) Never prepare raw and cooked foods on the same surface.

(iv) Use clean utensils and equipment.

LINKS

Revise:

Hygiene in the home (pp. 67–8)

Cleaning fridges and cookers (pp. 251–52)

Kitchen ventilation (p. 240)

Waste disposal (p. 269)

10 Food Storage

aims
- To explain the term 'good storage'.
- To list the guidelines for storing foods according to type.
- To be able to explain the star rating on frozen foods and freezers.
- To identify food storage and packaging materials.

Good storage

- Protects the food from contamination (flies and dust).
- Ensures the rotation of food.
- Prolongs shelf-life with good storage conditions.
- Keeps the food storage areas organised and clean.

> **LINK**
> Revise Chapter 9 (p. 66) for the causes of food spoilage.

Classification of foods

Foods are classified so that they may be stored correctly in the kitchen.

> **key point**
> Perishables are foods that must be stored in the fridge and have a short shelf life.

1. **Perishables**

   Examples: Milk, cream, meat, poultry, fish, eggs.

   Storage area: Fridge.

2. **Semi-perishables**

   Examples: Vegetables, fruits, salad vegetables, biscuits, bread and cakes.

   Storage area: Vegetable rack or basket, lower compartment in fridge, bread bin and biscuit tins.

3. **Non-perishables**

   Examples: Dried (pasta), tinned (beans), bottled foods.

   Storage area: Kitchen cupboard in original packages (unopened) or once opened, in airtight containers.

4. **Frozen foods**

   Examples: Prepared meals, vegetables, pastries.

   Storage area: Freezer (−18°C or below).

Storage information on food labels

- A **date stamp** in the form of 'sell by' date, 'best before' date or '**use before**' date (check the dates on all foods that you buy).
- **Storage instructions**, e.g. store in a dark, dry place away from direct heat and sunlight.
- **Star markings** on frozen foods giving date and storage rules.

Star markings for frozen foods and freezers

*   Food will keep for one week

**   Food will keep for one month

***   Food will keep for three months

**** Food will keep for up to one year

Rules for storing foods

1. Store the food according to its class and use in rotation.

2. Note the expiry dates and use by the date recommended.

3. Check the fridge daily and use leftover foods quickly.

4. Never place hot or warm food in a fridge – allow it to cool first.

5. Clean out food presses and fridge regularly.

6. Store opened dry foods in airtight containers.

7. Store foods away from chemicals or cleaning agents.

> **key point**
>
> The shelf life of a food refers to the length of time the food remains fresh and is safe to eat. It depends on the type of food and how it is stored.

Disposable and reusable packaging for food

Disposable

Category	Types	Uses
	Aluminium foil	Covering food in oven/fridge, packed lunches
	Cling film	Covering food for storage in fridge, packed lunches
	Foil containers	Storing food in the freezer, cooking food in the oven
	Greaseproof paper	Packed lunches, lining baking tins, wrapping cheese
	Microwave cling film	Covering food before microwaving
	Parchment	Lining baking tin
	Polythene bags	Storing dried foods, packed lunches (sandwiches)
	Roasting bags	Roasting meat in the oven to keep in moisture

Reusable

Category	Types	Uses
	Margarine and ice cream containers	Storing and freezing foods (soups, sauces, fruits)
	Pyrex jars/dishes	Storing a variety of foods
	Tin boxes	Storing cakes and biscuits (store them separately)

LINKS
The fridge (p. 249)
Labelling (p. 132)
Symbols (p. 166)

EXAM QUESTIONS AND SAMPLE ANSWERS

Ordinary Level 2007, Section A, Q.5 (5 marks)
Name **two** different types of packaging in which foods can be frozen.
1. Waxed cartons
2. Aluminium foil containers

Ordinary Level 2001, Section A, Q.4 (5 marks)
List **four** rules which should be followed when storing foods.
1. Cover perishables and store in the fridge.
2. Store non-perishables in a cool, dry place.
3. Store opened dry foods in airtight containers.
4. Check the fridge daily and use leftovers quickly.

SAMPLE EXAM QUESTIONS

Practise these questions for your written exams and then check the answers.
1. List four perishable foods and explain how they should be stored.
2. Explain what the star rating on a food label means.
3. What is the normal temperature of a freezer?
4. Explain the term 'shelf-life'.
5. What packaging would you use to store the following?
   - Food for the freezer
   - Bread
   - Biscuits
   - Packed lunch (sandwich)
   - Opened packet of porridge

11 Preparing and Cooking Food

Students must learn:
- To adapt recipes to dietary goals.
- The principles of each of the cooking processes.

Guidelines for starting to cook

- Tie back hair, remove jewellery and wear an apron.
- Wash hands, cover cuts.
- Check that equipment and kitchen surfaces are clean.
- Check the recipe and collect equipment.
- Weigh ingredients accurately and place on plates.
- Preheat the oven if required.
- Prepare dishes or baking tins.

exam focus

Remember guidelines can be asked as shorter questions relating to:
- Preparation of self.
- Preparation of utensils, equipment and oven.
- Preparation of ingredients/dishes.

Guidelines when preparing and cooking food

1. Follow the recipe step by step.
2. Keep everything clean and tidy, wipe up spills.
3. Do not lick food with fingers – use a spoon to taste.
4. Store perishable foods in the fridge until needed.
5. Use oven gloves when lifting hot dishes.
6. Be careful when using sharp knives – use a chopping board.
7. Cut ingredients away from you.

exam focus

Be able to explain the safety points when handling hot dishes, using sharp knives and working with electric equipment. For the practical cookery exam, be able to demonstrate safety skills.

8. Do not handle electrical items with wet hands.
9. Take care with steam from saucepans and kettles.
10. Turn the handles of saucepans away from the edge of the cooker.
11. Place dirty dishes neatly beside the sink.

Guidelines for washing and tidying up

- Scrape, stack, wipe down table/cooker, wash, rinse, drain, dry and stack dishes.

LINKS

- Food hygiene and food safety (p. 66–8)
- Food preparation guidelines (p. 73)
- Kitchen equipment (pp. 249–55)

exam focus

Learn four or five key guidelines in order to be able to answer short questions (Section A) and at least six points for longer questions (Section B).

Modifying a recipe

Reasons for modifying recipes

- To cater for people on special diets (coeliacs, vegans).
- To reduce the amount of fat, salt and sugar or to increase fibre so that it follows the latest dietary guidelines.
- To vary the recipe or if an ingredient is not available, substitute another.
- To make use of leftovers.

key point

Modify any recipe by reducing salt, reducing fat, reducing sugar, increasing fibre or adding a new ingredient.

General guidelines for modifying a recipe

- Change one ingredient each time the recipe is used and note the difference in the flavour, texture and appearance of the dish.
- Avoid changing core ingredients.
- Watch the proportions of ingredients and weigh accurately.

LINK

Healthy eating and balanced diets (p. 33)

key point

For special diets (e.g. coeliac, diabetes) follow the specific guidelines given by the doctor.

Cooking methods

Dry heat

- Baking ● Grilling or barbecuing.

Moist heat

- Boiling ● Braising ● Poaching ● Simmering
- Steaming ● Stewing.

Using hot fat

- Frying (shallow or deep-fat) • Roasting.

Microwave

(see p. 252)

Reasons for Cooking Food

- Bacteria are killed by heat, so food becomes safe to eat.
- Food looks more appetising and colour develops (roast beef).
- Food tastes better, flavours develop (omelette).
- Cooking aromas stimulate the appetite.
- Food becomes more digestible (rice, potatoes).
- Cooking preserves some foods (chutney, jam).

Coating foods:

- Seals in flavour.
- Reduces the absorption of hot fat.
- Makes them crispier and tastier.
- Prevents food from breaking up.

key point

Some foods can be eaten raw (fruit, vegetables). These can look and taste appetising. Some foods must be cooked.

Three methods of heat transfer

Conduction

Heat passes from one solid molecule to the next solid molecule.

COOKER HOB → FRYING PAN OR WOK → FOOD

Examples of cooking methods: Frying, stir-frying.

Conduction

Convection

Heat travels in convection currents through air and liquids (oil, water).

COOKER HOB → SAUCEPAN WITH LIQUID → FOOD

OVEN → CONVECTION AIR CURRENTS → FOOD

Examples of cooking methods: Boiling, stewing, roasting.

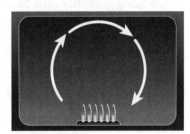
Convection

Radiation

Heat travels to food in straight lines in the form of rays.

GRILL → HEAT RAYS → FOOD

Examples of cooking method: Grilling, toasting, barbecuing.

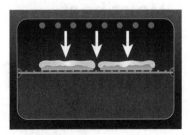
Radiation

Dry heat

Grilling

HL Cooking principles	Suitable foods
Grilling uses intense radiant heat at high temperatures to cook food in a short time under the cooker grill or on the barbecue. Heat is transferred by radiation	Rashers, sausages, burgers, steak, kidneys, chops, cutlets, fish, au gratin dishes, tomatoes, mushrooms, vegetables, toast, sandwiches.

Cooking guidelines for grilling:

1. Choose foods that can be cooked quickly.
2. Season food with pepper and avoid salt.
3. Always preheat the grill before cooking.
4. Brush the grill grid with oil to prevent food from sticking.
5. Brush food with oil to prevent burning or drying out.
6. Seal food quickly so that juices do not escape.
7. Turn food frequently using tongs (do not use a fork).

Baking

HL Cooking principles	Suitable foods
Baking uses dry radiant heat in an oven to cook food. Heat is transferred by convection.	Bread, cakes, biscuits, pastries (sweet and savoury pies), puddings, fish, fruit, vegetables, potatoes.

Cooking guidelines for baking:

1. Preheat the oven to the correct temperature.
2. Do not overfill the oven. Allow air currents to circulate.
3. Make maximum use of the oven. Do not use for one dish.
4. Avoid opening the oven door frequently.
5. To keep some foods moist, cover with foil.
6. Position food in the correct oven position.

LINK
Home baking (p. 86)

Moist heat

Poaching

HL Cooking principles	Suitable foods
Poaching is a method of cooking food in gently bubbling liquid between 85°C and 90°C in an open saucepan or poaching pan. Heat is transferred by conduction and convection.	Eggs, fish, fruit.

Cooking guidelines for poaching:

1. Never allow the water to boil.
2. Choose a suitable saucepan (shallow or deep).
3. Use a suitable poaching liquid: water, stock, milk, fruit juice, wine.
4. Barely cover the food with liquid.
5. Do not leave the saucepan unattended, as food can overcook.
6. Remove poached foods using a slotted spoon or a fish slice and drain on kitchen paper.

Boiling

HL	Cooking principles	Suitable foods
	Boiling is a method of cooking food in a fast-moving liquid at 100°C in a covered saucepan. Heat is transferred by convection.	Vegetables, fresh meat, salted meat, fish, eggs, cereals, rice, pasta.

Cooking guidelines for boiling:

1. Choose a saucepan with a well-fitted lid.
2. Place foods in boiling water, bring back to the boil, reduce to simmering and cover.
3. (a) Salted meat is put into cold water to draw out the salt.
   (b) Fresh meat is put in boiling water, then simmered.
   (c) Green leafy vegetables are put into fast boiling water.
4. Do not leave unattended, as food can fall apart.
5. Use leftover cooking liquid for sauces, stocks and soups.
6. Remove the food using a slotted spoon and drain.

key point

Boiling is also used when making sauce, jam, chutney, marmalade and syrups.

Stewing and casseroling

HL	Cooking principles	Suitable foods
	Stewing is a long, slow method of cooking even-sized pieces of food in a little liquid in a saucepan or casserole with a well-fitting lid. Heat is transferred by convection.	Tough, cheap cuts of meat (neck, shin or rib beef, mutton), poultry, fish, root/pulse vegetables, fruit.

Cooking guidelines for stewing:

1. Barely cover the food with liquid.
2. Bring liquid to boiling point, reduce the temperature and cook slowly – never boil.
3. Cover the saucepan or casserole with a tight-fitting lid.
4. Cook stew on the hob; cook casseroles in the oven.
5. Check from time to time.

key point

Stewing tenderises tough foods and is an economical method of cooking. The cooking liquid is generally served as part of the dish.

Steaming

HL Cooking principles	Suitable foods
Steaming is a slow method of cooking food over steam rising from a saucepan of boiling water. The food may or may not come into contact with the steam. The food does not come into contact with the boiling water. Heat is transferred by convection.	Thin pieces of meat, poultry and fish, puddings, egg custards, potatoes, root vegetables, rice.

Cooking guidelines for steaming:

1. Rapidly boiling water is essential.
2. Keep the water boiling.
3. Cover the saucepan with a tight-fitting lid.
4. Never allow the saucepan to boil dry. Add more water if necessary.
5. Never allow the water and the food to be in contact.
6. Steamed foods can lack flavour. Season or serve with a sauce.

key point

Steaming can be done using two plates over a saucepan, a steamer, bamboo baskets, a pressure cooker or in a pudding bowl.

Pressure cooking

HL Cooking principles	Suitable foods
Pressure cooking is cooking food under pressure in a steam-proof heavy saucepan with a specially designed lid. The lid may have different pressure combinations, which raises the temperature and forces steam through the food, cooking it more quickly than in a normal saucepan. Heat is transferred by convection.	Meat, fish, poultry, fruits, vegetables.

key point

Pay attention if using a pressure cooker for steaming. Follow the manufacturer's instructions. When steam is being released, be careful of the jet of steam. Always use the two handles to move the pressure cooker. Never leave the pressure cooker unattended.

Cooking guidelines for pressure cooking:

1. Follow the manufacturer's instructions.
2. Use the recommended amount of liquid.
3. Put on the lid and make sure it sits in place.
4. Arrange pressure regulator valves or weights (according to model of cooker).
5. Put on a high heat, and when steam begins to escape at a regular rate, reduce the heat.
6. Cook for the recommended time and then turn off the heat.
7. Allow the release of pressure (follow guidelines).
8. Open the pressure cooker and serve the dish.

Using hot fat

Roasting

HL Cooking principles	Suitable foods
Roasting is cooking food in hot fat at high temperatures in an oven or on a rotating spit. Food is placed on a roasting tin, rotisserie, casserole dish or in roasting bags. Heat is transferred by convection.	Tender joints of meat, poultry, game (pheasant, rabbit, venison), potatoes, root vegetables.

Cooking guidelines for roasting:

1. Preheat the oven to the recommended temperature.
2. Do not place food directly from the fridge into the oven. Allow food to reach room temperature first.
3. Prepare food and calculate the cooking time.
4. Meat may be roasted covered or uncovered.
5. Baste with hot fat during cooking to prevent food from drying out.
6. If the meat is tender, quick roast it. If tough, slow roast it.
7. Stand and drain for ten minutes before carving and serving.

Frying

HL Cooking principles	Suitable foods
Frying is a quick method of cooking food in hot fat or oil. Heat is transferred by conduction from the hob through the frying pan to the food.	Thin, tender pieces of meat, offal, poultry, fish, burgers, vegetables, rashers, sausages, potato chips, doughnuts, fritters, rissoles, coated foods (fish).

Methods of frying

- **Deep-fat frying:** Immersing food in hot oil or fat in a saucepan or a deep-fat fryer.
- **Dry frying:** Cooking food in a shallow pan without fat or oil.
- **Shallow frying:** Frying thin pieces of food in a small amount of fat or oil in a shallow pan.
- **Stir-frying:** Cooking small pieces of food very quickly in hot oil in a wok.

Cooking guidelines for frying:

1. Prepare the food before heating the oil or fat.
2. Dry food with kitchen paper to remove moisture.
3. Preheat the oil or fat before adding the food.
4. Do not put too much food in the pan.

key point

- Never leave frying pans, deep-fat fryers or woks unattended.
- Never allow water and hot oil to come into contact.
- Nutritionally, frying is not the best method of cooking and should be avoided where possible.

5. Remove cooked food carefully with a slotted spoon.

6. Drain fried food on kitchen paper to prevent greasiness.

When answering a question on the advantages and disadvantages of cooking methods, consider if the cooking method:

- is fast or slow.
- requires little or much preparation
- keeps the food moist or causes the food to dry out
- destroys the colour, flavour or texture of the food
- makes the food more digestible or indigestible
- is economical or expensive (give reasons why)
- keeps or loses nutrients.

Effects of heat/cooking on food

Type of food	Effect
Eggs	Protein coagulates and sets
Rice, pasta	Starches absorb liquid and swell
Fat in meat	Fat melts
Fish	Food shrinks due to loss of moisture
Bread (toast)	Colour changes
Vitamins B and C, minerals	Nutrients may be lost

Overcooking food has the following disadvantages:

- nutrients are lost.
- food becomes tough and indigestible.
- colour, flavour and texture may be lost.

LINK

Technology and cooking equipment (microwave ovens) (p. 252)

EXAM QUESTIONS AND SAMPLE ANSWERS

NOTE: Other acceptable suggestions are given in square brackets.

Higher Level 2003, Section A, Q.3 (4 marks)

Suggest a **different** food suitable for each of the cooking methods listed below.

Cooking method	Suitable food
(i) Pressure cooking	*Potatoes [puddings]*
(ii) Poaching	*Fish [eggs, fruit]*
(iii) Boiling	*Pasta [bacon, rice]*
(iv) Stir-frying	*Chicken [peppers, onions]*

Ordinary Level 2003, Section A, Q.6 (5 marks)

Suggest a method of cooking suitable for **each** of the following foods.

Foods	Cooking methods
(i) A pork chop	*Grilling [frying, baking]*
(ii) Pasta	*Baking [boiling]*
(iii) Whole chicken	*Roasting [casseroling, boiling]*
(iv) Brown bread	*Baking*
(v) Apples	*Baking [stewing, poaching]*

Ordinary Level 2001, Section A, Q.3 (5 marks)

Suggest **one** advantage and **one** disadvantage of grilling as a method of cooking.

Advantage: *Foods cook more quickly [little preparation needed, foods are healthier, less loss of nutrients, improved flavour – foods are crisper].*

Disadvantage: *Not suitable for tougher cuts of meat, only tender cuts can be used [foods can dry out, cannot be left unattended].*

12 The Cereals and Bread Food Group

- To list the average composition of cereals. **HL**
- To give the classification, nutritive value and structure of the wheat grain and the effects of heat/cooking and processing on cereals and cereal products.
- To identify raising agents and explain how they work.
- To outline the rules for home baking.
- To list the guidelines for making pastry.
- To classify and give the uses of pastry.

Composition of cereals

Nutrient	Composition of cereals
Protein	12%
Fat	2%
Carbohydrate	75%
Vitamins	B group (0.5%)
Minerals	Calcium, iron (1%)
Water	12%

key point

Cereals include wheat, oats, barley, rye, corn/maize and rice.

Nutritive value of cereals

Nutrient	Nutritive value
Protein	Low biological value (LBV) proteins in small amounts (gluten is a protein found in cereals)
Fat	Traces in the germ
Carbohydrate	Starch (75%) in the endosperm and fibre/cellulose in unprocessed cereals
Vitamins	B group vitamins in unprocessed cereals
Minerals	Calcium, iron and phosphorus
Water	Low water content

Value in the diet

- Cereals are important in everyone's diet.
- Cereals contain low biological value protein.
- Wholegrain cereals and their products provide dietary fibre and B group vitamins.

- When cereals are refined, they lose both fibre and vitamin B and a high percentage of starch remains. Because of the loss of nutrients during processing, some cereals are fortified.
- Cereals provide energy and fibre.
- Cereals are the staple food in some countries, e.g. China.

key point

Coeliacs do not eat wheat and wheat products because they contain a protein, gluten, that they cannot digest.

LINKS
Special diets (p. 43)
Menu planning (pp. 57–65)

key point

The bran and germ of the wheat grain are removed during the milling process.

Wheat grain

The wheat grain is made up of three sections: the outer bran layer, the inside layer (endosperm) and the germ.

- The bran provides dietary fibre, iron, some protein and vitamin B.
- The endosperm consists mainly of gluten and starch.
- The germ contains dietary fibre, protein, traces of fat and B group vitamins.

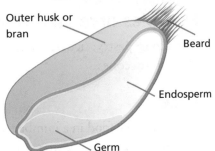

Outer husk or bran

Beard

Endosperm

Germ

Structure of wheat grain

Effects of cooking on cereals

- Starch grains absorb liquid or fat.
- Starch grains swell and burst.
- Starch grains become digestible.

Processing of cereals

Most cereal grains are processed to make them more digestible or to create different cereal products. The grains are crushed and parts are removed – and is called **milling**.

- **Wholegrain cereals** contain most of the cereal grain.
  Examples: Brown rice, rolled oats, wholemeal flour.
- **Refined cereals** contain mainly the endosperm.
  Examples: White rice, white flour, cornflour.
- **Fortified cereal products** have vitamins and minerals added because they were lost or removed during processing.
  Examples: Breakfast cereals, white flour.

Cereals and cereal products

Cereal	Cereal products
Barley	Pearl barley, beer, whiskey, barley water
Corn/maize	Corn on the cob, sweet corn, cornflour, corn oil, popcorn, tortillas, tacos, breakfast cereals (cornflakes)
Oats	Porridge, pinhead oatmeal, rolled oats, breakfast cereals (e.g. muesli, Ready Brek)
Rice	Brown and white rice, Rice Krispies, rice flour, rice cakes, rice paper, ground rice
Rye	Rye flour, bread, whiskey, crispbread (Ryvita)
Wheat	Wholemeal and white flour, wheat germ, noodles, couscous, semolina, pasta, breads, cakes, biscuits, bran, breakfast cereals

Examples of refined cereal products

Cornflour; pastry; rice flakes; rice flour; wheat germ; white bread; white flour; white rice; white scones

Rice

Rice is a staple food in a number of countries (China, India).

- **Brown rice:** The husk has been removed.
- **White rice:** The bran and germ have been removed.

Main types and uses of rice

Types	Uses
Basmati rice	Curries, stir-fried chicken
Brown rice	Brown rice salad, casseroles, curries
Easy-cook rice	Rice has been steamed already to make it easier to cook. Used in a variety of savoury dishes.
Ground rice	Milk puddings, biscuits and cakes
Instant rice (processed)	A 'boil-in-the-bag' product for faster cooking. Used in savoury dishes.
Long grain rice (patna)	Kedgeree, savoury dishes, sweet and sour pork, curries
Medium grain rice (risotto)	Risotto, rice and red pepper salad
Short grain rice	Milky rice puddings, paella

Rice can be:

- Boiled.
- Braised or baked.
- Fried.

Quantities per person: approx. 50 g.

LINK
Cooking Methods
(pp. 74–80)

Rice products

Rice products available include rice cakes, rice flour, breakfast cereals, tinned rice pudding and ground rice.

Effects of cooking on rice

- Rice grains soften and swell.
- Starch absorbs moisture and gelatinises.

Pasta

Pasta is made from durum wheat flour, mixed with water, shaped and cut. Pasta can be bought fresh, dried or tinned. It is available in a variety of shapes (spaghetti, macaroni, noodles, spirals) and colours (eggs, tomatoes, spinach). Pasta should be cooked until it is *al dente* – an Italian phrase meaning 'to the tooth', i.e. not too soft.

Uses of pasta

- Pasta salads (tuna and pasta shell salad).
- As part of a main course (cannelloni).
- As a main course, with a sauce (macaroni cheese, spaghetti Bolognese).
- As an alternative to potatoes or rice.
- As an accompaniment (buffet meal, Italian menu).

Effects of cooking on pasta

- Pasta softens, absorbs water and swells.

> **LINK**
> Cooking methods
> (pp. 74–80)

Flour

Types of flour

White flour is fortified or enriched with calcium, iron and B group vitamins.

Wholemeal flour	100% whole grain (nothing removed) *Uses:* Brown bread, scones, pastry
Brown flour	80–90% grain (some bran is removed) *Uses:* Brown soda bread, scones
White flour	Approx 70% grain (all the bran and most of the germ are removed, only the endosperm and some gluten remain) *Uses:* White soda bread, scones, pastry, cakes, sauces
Strong flour	Flour with a high gluten content *Uses:* Yeast bread, dinner buns
Self-raising flour	White flour with added raising agent *Uses:* Scones, cakes
Gluten-free flour	Gluten has been removed *Uses:* Bread, cakes, biscuits

Breads and cakes

Breads and cakes are made using flour, fat, sugar, a raising agent and liquid (water, eggs or milk). Bread is available in a variety of forms across the world, such as baguettes (France), soda bread (Ireland), naan bread (India) or tortillas (Mexico, Spain). Commercial bread and cake mixes are quick and easy to use but are expensive and may contain additives.

Raising agents

Raising agents are substances used to produce a gas in bread, cakes and batters. The gas expands when heated and raises the bread or cake. A crust forms to prevent the mixture from rising further.

Types of raising agents

- **Natural:** Air (added when sieving flour, rubbing in fat, creaming fat and sugar, whisking eggs).
- **Chemical:**
  - Baking powder + liquid (water/milk/eggs).
  - Bread soda and sour milk.

$$\text{ACID} + \text{ALKALI} + \text{LIQUID} \rightarrow \text{CARBON DIOXIDE (CO}_2\text{)}$$

- **Biological:** Yeast.

Yeast, a micro-organism, produces carbon dioxide in bread, dinner buns and some pastries.

Sequence

Gas produced in dough → dough put in oven → heat causes gas to expand and raise dough → heat forms a crust on dough and prevents dough rising further.

Raising agents in action

Bread/cake	Raising agent
Wholemeal bread	Bread soda + sour milk
Madeira cake/buns	Baking powder, air
Tea scones	Baking powder, air
Egg sponge	Air
Victoria sandwich	Baking powder, air
Barm brack	Yeast
Croissants	Yeast

Basic methods for making cakes

- **All-in-one:** All ingredients are mixed together at once, using soft margarine (madeira cake, pastry).

- **Creaming:** Fat and sugar are creamed together (fruitcake, Madeira buns/cakes).
- **Melted fat:** Melt fat and add to the dry ingredients (gingerbread).
- **Rubbing-in:** Fat is rubbed into flour (scones, pastry, cakes).
- **Whisking:** Sugar and eggs are whisked together (Swiss roll, egg sponge).

LINK
Cooking Methods
(pp. 74–80)

General guidelines for home baking

1. Prepare tins, baking tray or dish.
2. Arrange shelves and preheat the oven.
3. Follow the recipe exactly.
4. Weigh ingredients accurately.
5. Time the bread/cake in the oven; avoid opening the door too often.
6. Test, remove from the tin and cool on a wire tray. Turn off the oven.

Pastry

Pastry is made from a mixture of fat and flour which is usually held together with a small amount of water. Pastry is suitable for sweet and savoury dishes. The raising agent used is air.

General guidelines for pastry making

1. Weigh and measure ingredients accurately.
2. Keep utensils and ingredients cold.
3. Preheat the oven.
4. Handle the ingredients lightly. Lift your fingers above the ingredients to introduce as much air as possible.
5. Add the water gradually; avoid adding it all at once.
6. Use a knife to mix in the water.
7. Sprinkle flour on a clean surface.
8. Knead pastry lightly with the tips of your fingers.
9. Roll out the pastry evenly without stretching it.
10. Put it on a clean plate, cover and rest in the fridge for 15 minutes.
11. Make up dish and decorate.
12. Cook pastry in a preheated hot oven.

key point

To bake blind means baking a sweet or savoury pastry case without a filling.

Types and Uses of Pastry

Types	Uses
Shortcrust	Apple tarts, chicken pie, flans
Rich shortcrust	Tarts, pies
Wholemeal pastry	Rhubarb tart, pies, quiche
Cheese pastry	Quiche, cheese biscuit
Flaky and rough puff	Sausage rolls, fish pies, sweet pies, tarts and flans
Puff pastry	Mince pies, vol-au-vents
Choux pastry	Éclairs, profiteroles
Filo pastry	Fish pie, fruit parcels
Suet pastry	Steamed or baked puddings

EXAM QUESTIONS AND SAMPLE ANSWERS

Higher Level 2007, Section A, Q.3 (4 marks)

Name the parts of the cereal grain labelled A, B and C.

A. Bran

B. Endosperm

C. Germ

Higher Level 2006, Section A, Q.4 (4 marks)

List **four** raising agents used in home baking.

(i)   Air

(ii) Baking powder + liquid

(iii) Bread soda + sour milk

(iv) Yeast

Higher Level 2005, Section A, Q.5 (4 marks)

Name **one** different type of flour that matches each of the following descriptions

Description	Type of flour
(i) Contains outer husk and bran	*Wholegrain*
(ii) Contains extra gluten	*Strong flour*
(iii) Suitable for coeliacs	*Gluten-free*
(iv) Raising agent has been added	*Self-raising flour*

Higher Level 2003, Section A, Q.6 (4 marks)

Give **two** effects of cooking on cereals.

(i)   Starch grains absorb liquid, swell and burst.

(ii) Cellulose/fibre softens.

Higher Level 2001, Section A, Q.5 (4 marks)

Name **two** raising agents used in baking and suggest a different use for **each**.

Raising agent	Use
(i) Air	*Sponge*
(ii) Bread soda	*Brown soda bread*

Ordinary Level 2007, Section A, Q.3 (5 marks)

Name **two** different sweet dishes and two different savoury dishes that can be made using pastry.

Sweet dishes	Savoury dishes
(i) *Apple tart*	(i) *Cheese and bacon quiche*
(ii) *Lemon meringue pie*	(ii) *Chicken pie*

Higher Level 2004, Section B, Q.2 (55 marks) (long question)

(a) What guidelines should be followed when home baking? (5 x 3 marks)

1. Arrange shelves and preheat the oven.

2. Prepare tins, baking tray or dish.

3. Weigh all ingredients accurately.

4. Time the bread/cake in the oven; avoid opening the door too often.

5. Test, remove from the tin and cool on a wire tray.

(b) List **three** raising agents used in home baking and explain how one of them works. (3 x 4 marks)

(i) Natural raising agent → Air

(ii) Chemical raising agent → Bread soda + sour milk

(iii) Biological raising agent → yeast

How a chemical raising agent works

The chemical raising agent produces a gas in the bread or cake mixture. The gas expands in the oven and the bread/cake rises. The heat of the oven causes a crust to form on the surface of the mixture.

(c) (i) Explain the function of gluten in bread making. (5 marks)

When moistened, gluten becomes elastic. During baking, gases (CO_2) expand and the elastic dough rises. Heat in the oven causes a crust to form on the bread or cake. The dough does not expand any further.

(ii) Sketch the symbol found on gluten-free flour and products. (5 marks)

> **LINK**
> Revise the gluten-free symbol on p. 45.

(c) Give **two** advantages and **two** disadvantages of using commercial cake mixes. (12 marks)

Advantages (2 x 3 marks)

1. Useful in emergencies.

2. Saves time.

Disadvantages (2 x 3 marks)

1. Tends to be expensive.

2. High in salt, sugar and fat and low in fibre.

13 The Fruit and Vegetable Food Group

aims

- To list the average composition of fruit/vegetables. **HL**
- To classify fruit and vegetables and give examples.
- To outline the nutritive value of fruit/vegetables.
- To list the uses of fruit and vegetables.
- To outline the effects of cooking.
- To outline the guidelines for buying, preparing, cooking and storage fruit and vegetables.

Fruit

HL Average Composition of Fruit

Nutrient	Fresh	Dried	Tinned
Protein	Trace	Trace	Trace
Fats	0%*	0%	0%
Carbohydrates	5–20%	50–60%	20–30%
Vitamins	A, C	A	A, C
Minerals	Calcium, iron	Calcium, iron**	Calcium, iron***
Water	80–90%	15–25%	70–80%

*   Except avocados and olives
**   Increased iron content in dried fruit
***   Decreased iron content in tinned fruit

Nutritive value of fresh fruit

Protein	A trace of protein in a few fruits.
Fats	None except in avocados and olives.
Carbohydrates	Most fruits have sugars and starch; the outer skin contains dietary fibre.
Vitamins	<ul><li>Rich supply of vitamins A and C.</li><li>Vitamin C in fresh fruit (oranges and blackcurrants).</li><li>Vitamin A in green, red, yellow and orange fruits.</li></ul>
Minerals	Calcium and iron in dried fruit.
Water	High in fresh fruit, less in dried fruit.

Value of fruit in the diet

- Fruit is nutritious, versatile and economical. It can be eaten raw or cooked in a variety of dishes.
- Fruit is essential in the diet of children, teenagers, adults and those recovering from illness.
- Fruit is an excellent source of vitamins A and C and minerals. It is one of our main sources of vitamin C, which is needed for iron to be absorbed.
- Fruit provides a good supply of dietary fibre.
- Fruit is suitable for low-calorie diets, as it contains no fat.
- Fresh fruit has a high water content. In dried fruit, the water content is reduced and nutrients are concentrated.

LINKS

Nutrients (pp. 18–27)

Healthy eating guidelines (p. 33)

Healthy Food Pyramid (p. 35)

Classification of fruit

Class	Example
Citrus	Grapefruits, oranges, lemons, limes, tangerines, satsumas
Hard	Apples, pears
Soft fruit/berries	Strawberries, blackberries, gooseberries, raspberries, blackcurrants, redcurrants
Stone	Peaches, plums, cherries, apricots, damsons, avocados, olives
Dried	Raisins, prunes, sultanas, currants, figs, dates, apricots
Tropical	Mangoes, papayas
Others	Rhubarb, kiwis, pineapples, melons, bananas, grapes

Uses of fruit in cooking

Accompaniments	- Stewed apple with pork - Apricots with lamb - Sauces (orange, cranberry, gooseberry)
Baking	Bread, cakes, muffins, tarts, biscuits, pies
Beverages	- Milkshakes - Fresh juice (apple and carrot) - Smoothies (mixed berry) - High-energy drinks (oatmeal/raspberry)
Breakfast	On its own, fresh or stewed with yoghurt, on cereals
Cold sweets	Trifle, mousse, soufflé, yoghurt, fruit salads, cheesecakes
Hot puddings/ desserts	Baked, stewed, poached, flans, tarts, pies, puddings, crumbles
Packed lunch	Fresh, dried, mixed with yoghurt
Preserves	Jams, jellies, chutneys
Snack (fresh)	Apple, banana, kiwi
Starter	Grilled grapefruit, wedges of melon

Cooking fruits

Fruit can be:

- Baked ● Fried ● Grilled ● Poached ● Stewed.

LINK
Cooking Methods
(pp. 74–80)

Effects of processing and cooking on fruits

- The texture of fruit is changed, fruit softens.
- Fruits become more digestible, fibre breaks down.
- Cooking destroys micro-organisms and enzymes.
- Vitamins and minerals escape into canning and cooking liquids (use liquid for sauces).
- Up to 25 per cent of vitamin C is destroyed.
- Bacteria is destroyed.

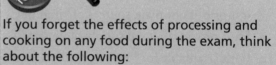

exam focus

If you forget the effects of processing and cooking on any food during the exam, think about the following:

1. What happens when you cook fruit at home, e.g. apples? What happens to the colour, flavour and texture?
2. What have you learned about the effects of heat on different nutrients, e.g. are nutrients lost or reduced during cooking? If so, which nutrients?

General guidelines for buying fresh fruit

1. Buy in season, when they are cheapest.
2. Check the grade of fruit.
3. Buy loose rather than prepacked whenever possible.
4. Buy fruit that is just ripe and brightly coloured.
5. Do not buy bruised or damaged fruits.
6. Use quickly; do not leave around for more than a few days.

LINKS
Vitamins (pp. 25–7)
Minerals (pp. 22–5)
Grading fruit and vegetables (p. 95)

key point

Choose a shop with a quick turnover to avoid buying stale fruit and vegetables.

Rules for preparing and using fruit

1. Eat raw and unpeeled when possible.
2. Prepare just before cooking or serving to avoid loss of vitamin C.
3. Wash thoroughly in cold water to remove dirt and chemicals.
4. Remove skin or peel only if necessary (rich in fibre).
5. Remove stones and cores, then cut into sections.
6. Cook or serve immediately.

key point

Toss pieces of bananas and apples in lemon juice to prevent oxidation (going brown when in contact with oxygen).

Vegetables

Average composition of vegetables

Nutrient	Greens	Roots	Pulses	Fruits
Protein	Trace	Trace	2–8%	Trace
Fats	0%	0%	Trace	0%
Carbohydrates	2–3%	5–20%	4–10%	2–5%
Vitamins	A, C	A, C	A, C	A, C
Minerals	Calcium, iron	Calcium, iron	Calcium, iron	Calcium, iron
Water	90–95%	75–95%	75–95%	90–95%

Nutritive value of vegetables

Protein	Good supplies of vegetable protein are found in pulse vegetables (peas, beans and lentils) – this is important for vegans.
Fat	Most are deficient in fat, although pulses contain a little.
Carbohydrate	• Starch: Good supply in potatoes, pulses and root vegetables. • Cellulose is found in all vegetables. • Sugar is found in beetroot, carrots, parsnips and onions.
Vitamins	Vegetables are important for their vitamin A (carotene) and C content; pulse vegetables contain vitamin B
Minerals	• Calcium in green leafy, root and pulse vegetables. • Iron in greens e.g. spinach and roots. • Trace elements in pulses.
Water	A large amount in fresh vegetables – 75–95% (especially greens and salad vegetables).

Value in the diet

- Vegetables are nutritious, versatile and economical.
- Vegetables are essential in the diets of all groups.
- Vegetables are an important source of dietary fibre, vitamins, minerals and water. Fibre adds bulk to the diet.
- Vegetables provide vitamins A and C.
- Green vegetables are an excellent source of calcium and iron.
- Pulse vegetables are a good source of vegetable protein, making them ideal for vegetarian diets.
- Vegetables are suitable for low-fat diets because of their low fat content.

Classification of vegetables

Greens	Roots and tubers	Pulses	Fruits	Others
Broccoli	Beetroot	Beans	Avocado	Artichoke
Brussels sprouts	Carrot	Lentils	Courgette	Aubergine
Cabbage	Onion	Peas	Cucumber	Chicory
Cauliflower	Parsnip		Pepper	Endive
Kale	Potato		Tomato	Fennel
Spinach	Turnip			Okra
				Squash
				Sweet potato

Processing fruits and vegetables

Fruits and vegetables can be bottled, canned, dried and frozen.

key point

Processing vegetables reduces or destroys some nutrients.

Uses of vegetables in cooking

As a starter of a meal	salmon salad
In soup	mixed vegetable soup
As a snack between meals	carrot or celery sticks
In savoury bread, tarts, pies	onion bread, quiche
As accompaniments to a main dish	buttered carrots
As a main dish	curry, casseroles, pizza
In chutney	tomato and onion chutney
Juices	carrot juice, tomato juice
Smoothies	carrot and avocado, cucumber and mint
Fresh juicing	carrot, orange and apple; celery, apple and red pepper
Packed lunches	sandwiches, snacks and dips

key point

Juices lack fibre, whereas smoothies contain most of the fibre. Some fibre may be lost if vegetables are peeled.

General guidelines for buying fresh vegetables

1. Buy vegetables when in season.
2. Buy loose rather than in plastic bags or prepacked.
3. Buy in small quantities and check the grade or class.
4. Choose fresh, clean, brightly coloured vegetables.
5. Avoid vegetables that are wilted, soft or with blemishes and broken skin.
6. Check the 'best before' date.

exam focus

Learn six to eight examples of uses of vegetables in cooking.

Rules for using vegetables

1. Eat raw where possible.
2. Use vegetables in rotation, prepare close to the cooking/serving time, trim sparingly.
3. Wash under running water, avoid steeping and soaking, scrub roots and tubers well, remove wilted outer leaves.
4. Do not mix washed and unwashed vegetables.
5. Use a sharp knife to prevent loss of vitamin C.
6. Cook frozen vegetables directly from the freezer.
7. Do not reheat cooked vegetables.

Cooking vegetables

Vegetables can be:

- Baked ● Boiled ● Braised ● Fried ● Grilled
- Microwaved ● Roasted ● Steamed ● Stir-fried.

> **LINK**
> Cooking Methods (pp. 74–80)

Effects of cooking on vegetables

- Starch cells burst, vegetables become more digestible.
- Cooking destroys micro-organisms and enzymes.
- Vitamins and minerals are lost into the cooking liquid.
- Most vitamin C is destroyed.
- Dietary fibre is softened.
- Cooking changes the flavour, colour and texture.
- Overcooking causes vegetables to break up.

Organic fruit and vegetables

These are fruits and vegetables that are grown without using harmful chemicals (e.g. artificial fertilizers, herbicides, pesticides). Organic products carry a special label.

Organic standard label

Methods of processing fruits and vegetables

- Bottling ● Canning ● Crystallising (fruit) ● Drying ● Freezing.

Grading fruit and vegetables

Under EU regulations, fruit and vegetables must be:

- Sound, clean and free from chemicals.
- Graded with produce of similar size.
- Marked with country of origin, variety, quality and class.

Grade	Quality
Class Extra	Best quality and most expensive
Class I	Good quality
Class II	Marketable: variation in shape or colour
Class III	Inferior but marketable and cheaper

Rules for storing fresh fruit and vegetables

1. Always remove from plastic bags and packaging and wash fresh produce before storing in the fridge.
2. Pulses are best stored in an airtight jar.
3. Salad vegetables and greens are best put into the vegetable drawer in the lower part of the fridge.
4. Store roots and tubers in a cool, well-ventilated vegetable rack in a dark, dry place.
5. Store frozen vegetables in the freezer (follow instructions on the packaging).
6. Never mix washed and unwashed fruit/vegetables.

exam focus

Six key points must be learned.

Retaining maximum vitamin and mineral content of fruit and vegetables

- Choose best-quality fresh fruit and vegetables.
- Buy in small quantities and use up quickly.
- Eat raw and unpeeled if possible, but wash or scrub before eating.
- Avoid steeping in water; wash under cold running water.
- Use a sharp knife to avoid damaging the cells.
- Prepare just before cooking.
- When cooking greens, do not use bread soda.
- Use the cooking liquid in sauces, stocks and soups.

key point

Cook vegetables with skins on or peel thinly, cook in a small amount of liquid for a short time and serve at once in order not to lose too many nutrients.

exam Q

EXAM QUESTIONS AND SAMPLE ANSWERS

Higher Level 2006, Section A, Q.5 (4 marks)

Give an example of a different vegetable under each of the following classifications.

Greens	Roots	Fruit	Pulses
Cabbage	Turnips (swedes)	Tomatoes	Beans

Higher Level 2004, Section A, Q.5 (4 marks)

Give **two** effects of cooking on vegetables.

(i) Starch softens and becomes digestible.

(ii) Minerals and vitamins dissolve into the cooking liquid.

exam focus

Check that you have included a vegetable under each class. Do not leave a blank space.

HL

Ordinary Level 2002, Section A, Q.3 (5 marks)

Place each of the fruits listed below under the correct headings.

oranges, plums, raspberries, grapefruit, blackberries

Citrus	Berries	Stone
Oranges	Raspberries	Plums
Grapefruit	Blackberries	

Ordinary Level 2007, Section B, Q.1 (40 marks) (long question)

> ### FRESH FRUIT SALAD
>
> | | | |
> |---|---|---|
> | 1 apple | 6 strawberries | 100ml apple juice |
> | 1 pear | 2 plums | juice of 1/2 lemon |
> | 1 orange | 1 peach | |

exam focus

Check that you have included each of the fruits listed in the question. **Do not leave any out.**

(a) Place **each** of the fruits listed above under the correct headings. (6 marks)

Citrus	Berries	Stone	Hard
Orange	Strawberries	Plum	Pear
Lemon		Peach	Apple

(b) Describe how you would prepare each of the following fruits for the fresh fruit salad. (9 marks)

  (i) Pear: (3 marks)
  - *Wash fruit and dry with kitchen paper.*
  - *Peel only if necessary.*
  - *Remove the core and slice with a sharp knife.*
  - *Toss in lemon juice or put in cold water to prevent oxidation (going brown).*

  (ii) Strawberries: (3 marks)
  - *Check for dirt and mould.*
  - *Discard damaged fruit.*
  - *Wash gently and dry gently in kitchen paper.*
  - *Remove stalk, leave whole or slice.*

  (iii) Peach: (3 marks)
  - *Wash and dry in kitchen paper.*
  - *Peel if necessary.*
  - *Cut around the peach with a sharp knife.*
  - *Twist and separate to reveal the stone.*
  - *Carefully remove the stone so as not to damage the fruit.*
  - *Slice for the fruit salad.*

(c) Why is lemon juice used in the fresh fruit salad? (7 marks)
  - To prevent the fruit from going brown.
  - To stop the action of oxygen in the air.

(d) Give **two** advantages of buying fresh fruit in season. (2 x 4 marks)
  1. *Fruit is cheaper and more plentiful.*
  2. *Fruit has a better flavour.*

14 The Milk, Cheese and Yoghurt Food Group

aims
- To give the average composition of milk and cheese. **HL**
- To classify milk and milk products.
- To outline the nutritive value of milk and dairy products.
- To list the value in the diet of milk and dairy products.
- To list the uses of milk, cheese and milk products.
- To list the effects of cooking on milk and cheese.
- To outline the guidelines for buying, preparing, cooking and storing milk, cheese and dairy products.

Milk

Average composition of milk

Nutrients	Whole	Skimmed	Breast milk
Protein	3.5%	3.5%	2.25%
Fats	4%	0.2%	3.5%
Carbohydrates	4.5%	5%	6.5%
Vitamins	A, B, D (trace)	B	A, B, C, D
Minerals	Calcium, phosphorous	Calcium, phosphorous	Calcium, phosphorous
Water	87%	90%	87.4%

Nutritive value of milk in the diet

LINK
Nutrients (pp. 18–28)

Protein	Good source of high biological value protein (HBV).
Fats	Mainly saturated fat .
Carbohydrates	In the form of milk sugar.
Vitamins	Good source of vitamin B group and fat-soluble vitamins A and D (A and D are removed in skimmed milk).
Minerals	Good source of calcium and phosphorous.
Water	Varies with type of milk (87–90%).

Value in the diet

- Milk is an excellent source of nutrients and is easy to digest.
- It contains HBV protein and calcium, which are needed for growth and development. Milk is essential in the diet of babies, children, teenagers, pregnant and nursing women, invalids and convalescents.
- Calcium works with vitamin D to develop healthy bones and teeth. Vitamins A and B are also present in whole milk.
- Skimmed milk is not suitable for children, as it lacks the fat-soluble vitamins A and D. Skimmed milk is suitable for low-calorie diets.
- Some low-fat milk and whole milk is fortified with extra calcium and vitamins.
- Serve milk with foods rich in fibre, starch and iron.

Types of milk

Whole milk	Standard milk (nothing removed), 3.5% fat present.
Skimmed milk	Low fat (0.1–0.3% fat). Not to be given to babies and toddlers. Lacks vitamins A and D.
Low-fat milk (semi-skimmed or Light milk)	Semi-skimmed with half the fat of whole milk (1.5–1.8% fat).
Fortified milk (e.g. Super Milk)	Extra vitamins (A, B, D, E), folic acid and calcium added to low-fat or skimmed milks.
Buttermilk	Liquid remaining after making butter. Used in baking, e.g. bread.
Pasteurised milk	Milk is heated to 72°C for 15 seconds, then cooled quickly. Heat process kills bacteria but the taste remains the same.
Homogenised milk	Fat globules are distributed evenly in the milk.
Dried or powdered milk	All water removed. Ideal for emergencies.
Condensed milk	Canned milk with 40–60% of the water removed and sugar added. Used in desserts.
Evaporated milk	Canned milk with 60% of the water removed. Used in desserts.
Long-life milk	Ultra heat-treated milk (UHT). Lasts for months. Milk is heated to 132°C for one second.

Plant-based milks used as milk substitutes:

- Soya milk (soya beans).
- Almond milk.
- Rice milk.

Uses of milk in cookery

- To enrich other foods (soups, sauces, breads, cakes).
- On its own or as part of a beverage (milkshakes).

key point

Soya, almond and rice milks are suitable for vegetarians and for those who are lactose intolerant.

- Over breakfast cereals (hot and cold).
- As part of a dish (macaroni cheese, chicken and broccoli bake, batters, quiches).
- In sauces (cheese sauce, parsley sauce).
- In puddings (rice pudding, bread and butter pudding).
- In desserts and puddings (pancakes).

Effects of heat on milk

- Protein coagulates, a skin forms on the surface.
- Changes the flavour.
- Loss of vitamins B and C .
- Bacteria are killed and milk lasts longer.

General guidelines for buying and storing dairy products

1. Check the 'use by' and 'best before' dates on the label.
2. If milk is delivered to the house, remove it from direct sunlight immediately.
3. Store all dairy products in the fridge.
4. Keep away from strong-smelling foods.
5. Cover the container when not in use.
6. Use milk in rotation; do not mix fresh and stale milk; pour into a clean jug when required.

> **LINKS**
> Food storage (p. 70)
> Food hygiene (pp. 66–8)

Milk products

- Cream ● Butter ● Yoghurt ● Cheese

Cream

Cream is made from milk fat. It contains fat and the fat-soluble vitamins A and D.

Types of cream

- Double cream (48 per cent fat).
- Single cream (40 per cent fat).
- Crème fraîche (30 per cent fat).
- Low-fat cream (30 per cent fat).
- Soured cream (18 per cent fat).
- UHT cream (long-life – 18 per cent fat).

Convenience creams

- Aerosol cream ● Tinned cream ● Whipped cream.

Uses of cream in cooking

- Decoration of sweet dishes (piped on flans).
- Filling for sponges (jam and cream sponge).

- Garnish for soup (blob of cream just before serving).
- In desserts (mousse, soufflé, ice cream).
- Decoration for fresh fruit salads (piped).
- Added to sauces, stews and casseroles.
- In salad dressings.

Butter

Butter is made from cream. Buttermilk is the liquid left behind.

Types of butter

- Cream butter (80–82 per cent fat).
- Low-fat spreadable butter (40 per cent fat).
- Spreadable butter (heat treated to make it soft).
- Unsalted butter (use for sweet dishes).
- Dairy spreads: 50 per cent butter + 50 per cent oil (olive or soya).

Uses of butter in cooking

- As a spread (sandwiches, garlic butter).
- In cake making (fruit cakes, butter filling).
- In sauces (cheese sauce).
- With potatoes (added to enrich mashed potatoes).
- For sautéing vegetables, meat, poultry.

Yoghurt

Yoghurt is a made from whole or skimmed milk that has been pasteurised and thickened by a culture of lactic acid bacteria. Full-fat and low-fat varieties are available. Yoghurt can be plain or flavoured.

Types of yoghurt

Bio yoghurts	New type with good bacteria added (acidophilus)
Fruit yoghurt	Fruit flavoured, fruit pieces, puréed fruit
Greek yoghurt	Unflavoured, creamy yoghurt
Low-fat yoghurt	Made from skimmed/low-fat milk
Natural yoghurt	Unflavoured from whole milk
Set yoghurt	Thicker yoghurts
Yoghurt drinks	Flavoured, sweetened and with added milk

Uses of yoghurt

- Alternative to cream.
- As a drink (milkshakes, smoothies).
- In cake making.
- In desserts.
- In stews, casseroles, sauces.
- As a marinade for meat and poultry.
- In packed lunches.
- In salad dressings.
- In savoury dips.
- As a snack.
- As a topping for breakfast cereals (muesli).

Cheese

Cheese may be made from the milk of cows, goats, sheep and some other animals.

Average composition of cheese

Nutrient	Hard (e.g. cheddar)	Soft (e.g. cottage)
Protein	26%	15%
Fat	33%	4%
Carbohydrates	0%	4%
Vitamins	A, B group	A, B group
Minerals	Calcium, sodium	Calcium, sodium
Water	34%	77%

Nutritive value of cheese

Protein	Rich in high biological value (HBV) protein.
Fats	High levels of saturated fats and cholesterol.
Carbohydrates	None present. Serve with carbohydrate-rich foods.
Vitamins	Rich source of vitamins A and B group.
Minerals	Excellent source of calcium.
Water	Varies depending on the type (hard or soft, 34–77%).

Value of cheese in the diet

- Cheese is a versatile and convenient food.
- Cheese is a high-energy food rich in HBV protein and calcium, which are needed for growth and development.
- Cheese is useful in the diet of children, teenagers, active people and pregnant and nursing women.
- Fats in cheese provide heat, energy and insulation.
- Cheese is high in saturated fat and should be used cautiously by those with high cholesterol problems or following low-cholesterol diets. Choose low-fat varieties.
- As it lacks carbohydrate, serve cheese with carbohydrate-rich foods.
- Cheese is a good alternative to meat, poultry and fish in the diet of vegetarians.

> **LINKS**
> Nutrients (pp. 18–28)
> Healthy Eating Guidelines (p. 33)
> Special diets (p. 43)

Making cheese

1. Milk is pasteurised and a culture of bacteria is added.
2. Rennet, an enzyme, is added to the milk.
3. The mixture separates into curds and whey.
4. The whey is removed.
5. After draining, chopping and salting, the curd is pressed into moulds and left to mature from three to 12 months.

Buying and storing cheese

> **LINKS**
> Food storage (p. 70)
> Food hygiene (pp. 66–8)

1. Check the 'best before' and 'use by' labels.
2. Buy in small quantities and use up quickly.
3. Remove plastic wrapping (except for Easy Singles).
4. Store in the fridge, loosely wrapped in greaseproof paper in the door compartment.
5. Remove from the fridge one hour before using to allow flavours to develop.

Uses of cheese in cooking

- In sauces (cheese sauce).
- As a snack on its own, in sandwiches and packed lunches.
- In salads (grated, sliced or diced).
- As a garnish (grated, diced or melted).
- As an accompaniment (sliced with cold meat salad).
- As part of a main course (quiche, macaroni, pizza).
- As part of a dessert (cheesecake).
- As a separate course (cheese board).

> **key point**
> Cheese is a versatile food, as it can be used in both sweet and savoury dishes.

> **exam focus**
> Be able to list sweet and savoury uses for cheese.

Improving the digestibility of cheese

This can be done by:

- Grating cheese.
- Using mustard.
- Combining cheese with starchy foods (bread, pasta, etc.).
- Using cheese raw rather than cooked.

Effects of cooking on cheese

- Fat in cheese melts.
- Cheese browns if grilled or baked.
- Protein coagulates.
- Cooking and overcooking makes cheese indigestible and stringy.
- Improves the colour of dishes, e.g. au gratin.

> **LINKS**
> Cooking Methods (pp. 74–80)
> Effects of cooking on nutrients (p. 80)

Types of cheese

Hard	Cheddar, Wexford, Emmental, Parmesan
Semi-soft	Blarney, Edam, farmhouse cheeses
Soft cheese	Brie, Camembert, Mozzarella
Blue-veined	Blue, Stilton, Gorgonzola
Processed	Spreads, slices, strings, singles
Farmhouse	Abbey Blue, Cooleeney, Derrynaflan, Durrus
Unripened	Cottage, feta, mascarpone, cream cheese

EXAM QUESTIONS AND SAMPLE ANSWERS

Higher Level 2009, Section A, Q.6 (4 marks)

Name **one** type of milk that matches each of the following descriptions.

Description	Type of milk
Contains 0.1–0.3% fat	*Skimmed milk*
Has all the water removed	*Dried or powdered milk*
Extra vitamins and minerals added	*Fortified milk*
A dairy milk substitute	*Soya milk*

Higher Level 2008, Section A, Q.5 (4 marks)

Give **two** effects of heat on milk.

1. *Bacteria is destroyed and milk keeps longer.*
2. *Protein coagulates, a skin forms on the surface.*

EXAM QUESTIONS AND SAMPLE ANSWERS

Higher Level 2005, Section A, Q.4 (4 marks)

Name **two** different classifications of cheese and give one examples of each class.

	Class	Example
(i)	Hard	Cheddar
(ii)	Soft	Cottage

Ordinary Level 2006, Section A, Q.3 (5 marks)

Name **three** types of milk available in supermarkets.

1. Skimmed milk.
2. Fortified milk.
3. Standard whole milk.

Ordinary Level 2003, Section A, Q.3 (5 marks)

Suggest **three** uses of cheese in cooking.

1. In sauces (cheese sauce).
2. As a snack on its own or in sandwiches.
3. As a garnish (grated, diced or melted).

Higher Level 2006, Section B, Q.1 (55 marks) (long question)

(a) Using the information given on the label, evaluate the nutritive value of fortified milk. (20 marks)

Fortified Milk

NUTRITIONAL INFORMATION	FORTIFIED MILK	WHOLE MILK
Typical Values per 100ml	205kJ/49kcal	269kJ/64kcal
Energy	3.4g	3.3g
Protein	1.5g	3.5g
Fat	5.2g	4.9g
Carbohydrate	166mg	118mg
Calcium	120µg	52µg
Vitamin A	0.24mg	0.17mg
Vitamin B	70µg	6µg
Folic Acid	1µg	0.03µg
Vitamin D	1.5mg	0.09mg
Vitamin E		

Pasteurised and Homogenised

exam focus

Read and analyse the information given before answering this type of question.

In your answer:

Refer to the nutrients (protein, fat, carbohydrates, vitamins and minerals) present and discuss each of them under the following headings in order to gain full marks:

- Quantity per 100ml and compare against the whole milk.
- Type(s) or classification.
- Functions in the body.

Be specific when commenting on vitamins and minerals – mention each one individually and its value in the diet.

Discuss the energy per 100ml.

(b) (i) State which type of milk would be most suitable for (i) an energetic child and (ii) a pregnant woman. (2 marks)

  (i) Energetic child: Whole milk.

  (ii) Pregnant woman: Fortified milk.

 (ii) Give **one** reason for your choice in each case. (6 marks)

  (i) Whole milk has more fat and provides more energy for active children.

  (ii) Fortified milk is higher in folic acid, which helps prevent neural tube defects.

(c) Explain why milk is pasteurised.

 Milk is pasteurised to kill bacteria and to increase its shelf life.

(d) (i) List **three** dairy products, other than milk, available in supermarkets. (6 marks)

  1. Cheese

  2. Yoghurt

  3. Butter

 (ii) Suggest **three** ways to include more dairy products in the diet. (9 marks)

  1. Have yoghurt as part of a packed lunch.

  2. Enrich mashed potatoes by adding milk and butter.

  3. Add grated cheese as a topping for baked potatoes.

(e) Explain **one** of the following: fortified or homogenised. (5 marks)

 Homogenised means that fat globules are distributed evenly throughout the milk.

Higher Level 2001, Section B, Q.1 (55 marks) (long question)

CHEESE	PROTEIN	FAT	CARBOHYDRATE	MINERALS	VITAMINS	WATER
CHEDDAR	27%	33%	0%	4% Calcium	A + B	34%
COTTAGE	15%	4%	4%	1% Calcium	A + B	77%

(a) (i) Using the nutritional information in the table, state which type of cheese would be most suitable for (i) an adult on a low-cholesterol diet and (ii) an energetic teenager. (2 x 2 marks)

  ● *For the **adult**, choose cottage cheese.*

  ● *For the **teenager**, choose cheddar cheese.*

 (ii) Give *two* reasons for your choice in each case. (12 marks)

  Cottage cheese:

  ● *Is low in cholesterol and saturated fats.*

  ● *Is low in kilocalories.*

Cheddar cheese:

- *Is a rich source of high biological value (HBV) protein, which is essential for growth and repair.*
- *Is a good source of calcium for healthy bones and teeth.*

(b) Using **one** of the cheeses named in the table, design a balanced snack suitable for a packed lunch. (6 marks)

> **Snack**
>
> Orange juice
>
> Wholemeal cheddar cheese and tomato sandwich
>
> Apple

(c) Classify cheese and give one example in each class. (12 marks)

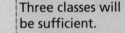

1. Hard: Cheddar.

2. Soft: Brie.

Three classes will be sufficient.

3. Blue-veined: Stilton.

(d) Outline the stages involved in the manufacture of cheese. (16 marks)

1. Milk is pasteurised and a culture of bacteria is added.

2. Rennet, an enzyme, is added to clot the milk.

3. The mixture separates into curds and whey.

4. The whey (liquid) is removed.

5. After draining, chopping and salting, the curd is pressed into moulds and left to mature from three to 12 months.

(e) Explain the term 'au gratin'. (5 marks)

Au gratin refers to food that has been covered in sauce, garnished with grated cheese and browned under a hot grill or in a preheated hot oven.

15 Meat, Fish and Alternatives

aims
- To list the composition, classification, nutritive value, value in the diet, structure, types, suitable cooking methods, effects of cooking and uses of meat, fish, poultry and eggs.
- To outline the guidelines/rules for buying and storing meat, fish, poultry and eggs.
- To list the uses, advantages and disadvantages of textured vegetable protein (TVP).
- To learn the composition of meat, fish and eggs. **HL**

Meat

Meat comes from:

- The flesh of birds and animals.
- Their internal organs, i.e. offal (kidney, liver).

Sources of meat

- **Cattle:** Beef, veal.
- **Game:** Rabbit, pheasant, duck, venison.
- **Pigs:** Pork, bacon, ham.
- **Poultry:** Turkey, chicken, duck.
- **Sheep:** Lamb, mutton.

Average composition of red meat

Nutrient	Composition
Protein	20–25%
Fat	10–30%
Carbohydrate	0%
Vitamins	B group
Minerals	Iron, calcium, phosphorus
Water	50–60%

Nutritive value of meat

Protein	Good source of HBV protein.
Fat	Contains saturated fat (visible and invisible fat). Varies with type of animal, e.g. beef and pork contain more fat than chicken.
Carbohydrate	None present in carcass.
Vitamins	B group vitamins. Offal (liver, kidney) is a good source of vitamin A.
Minerals	Red meat is an excellent source of iron and has some calcium, phosphorus and zinc (varies).
Water	Reasonably high water content (approx. 60%; more fat = less water).

Value in the diet

- Rich source of HBV protein, which is needed for growth and repair of cells. Important in the diet of children, teenagers (especially girls) and pregnant and nursing women.
- Because of its saturated fat content, it is recommended that people with high cholesterol or coronary heart disease should reduce their intake of red meat. Choose lean cuts of red meat or replace with low-fat alternatives, e.g. fish, poultry, meat alternatives (pulses, TVP).
- Lacks carbohydrates, so serve meat with potatoes, rice or pasta (carbohydrate-rich foods).
- An important source of B group vitamins, calcium and iron.

> **LINKS**
> Nutrients (p. 18–28)
> Healthy eating and balanced diets (pp. 33–42)

Structure of meat

Meat is made up of bundles of long meat fibres (filled with water, protein, minerals and extractives) and held together by connective tissue. Fat globules are found between meat fibres and on the surface of the meat.

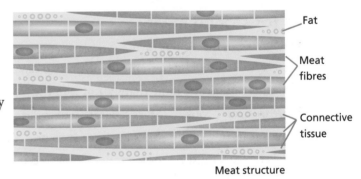

Fat

Meat fibres

Connective tissue

Meat structure

Causes of toughness of meat

Activity:

- Meat from active parts of the animal is tougher.
- Meat from less active parts of the animal is tender.

Age:

- Younger animals tend to have tender meat.
- Older animals have tougher meat.

> key point
>
> Extractives give meat its flavour and aid digestion.

Tenderising meat

- Mince or cut into small cubes.
- Marinate the pieces of meat.
- Pound with a steak hammer or a rolling pin.
- Use moist, slow cooking methods (stewing, braising).
- Use a chemical tenderiser.
- Correct hanging time allows enzymes to work.

General guidelines for choosing and buying meat

1. Buy from a clean, reputable butcher or supermarket.
2. Look for traceability information and symbols.
3. Cooked and raw meats should be stored, handled and wrapped separately to prevent cross-contamination.
4. Choose meat that has a good colour, moist flesh and fresh smell.
5. Avoid meat with too much bone, gristle and fat.
6. Choose cuts of meat depending on the dish/cooking method.
7. Cheaper cuts of meat are just as nutritious as more expensive cuts but need slower cooking methods (stewing, etc.). Offal is cheap and nutritious.

key point

Shop assistants should not handle both meat and money; gloves should be worn when handling meat. Money should be handled by someone else to avoid the danger of cross-contamination.

key point

When buying prepacked meat, check the 'best before' date.

Rules for storing meat

1. Unwrap fresh meats, put on a clean plate, cover and store low down in the fridge until ready to use. Use fresh meat within two days (check the 'best before' date).
2. If meat is not for use immediately, put it in the freezer.
3. Store fresh and cooked meats separately to avoid cross-contamination.
4. Leave meats in vacuum packs until ready to use/cook. Use before the expiry date.
5. Cooked meats must be cooled quickly, covered loosely, put in the fridge when cold and used within two days.
6. Never refreeze thawed meats and offal.

Rules for cooking meat

1. Remove meat from the fridge one hour before cooking.
2. If frozen, defrost thoroughly (can be done overnight in the fridge). **Never** refreeze thawed meat.
3. Avoid cross-contamination by never preparing fresh and cooked meats using the same board or knives.

4. Trim fat and gristle and remove bone if necessary.

5. Weigh meats to work out the cooking time. Choose a method of cooking that suits the cut of meat.

LINKS
Food hygiene (pp. 66–8)
Food storage (p. 70)

6. Unused cooked meats should be cooled, covered and stored in the fridge until required. Reheat thoroughly if serving hot.

Effects of cooking on meat

- Micro-organisms are killed, making meat safer to eat.
- Protein coagulates.
- Collagen changes to gelatine.
- Some amino acids and B group vitamins are destroyed.
- Meat becomes tender and digestible.
- Colour changes from red to brown.
- Fats melt and favour develops.
- Meat shrinks and water evaporates.

Methods of cooking meat

Tender cuts:

- Barbecuing ● Frying ● Grilling ● Roasting ● Stir-frying.

Tougher cuts:

- Baking ● Boiling ● Braising ● Casseroling ● Stewing.

LINK
Cooking methods
(pp. 74–80)

Processing meat

Meat can be processed by canning, curing, freezing and vacuum packing.

Meat products

Examples of meat products: Sausages, white and black puddings, burgers, pâté, samosas, pies and pasties, cook–chill products, canned meat.

Meat substitutes or alternatives

Meat can be replaced with the following foods from animal and plant sources.

Animal sources:

- Cheese ● Eggs ● Fish ● Poultry (chicken, turkey).

Plant sources:

LINKS
Meat (p. 108)
Fish (p. 114)
Poultry (p. 112)
Eggs (p. 116)

- Nuts.
- Pulse vegetables (peas, beans, lentils).
- Quorn, which is manufactured from a fungus (sliced, diced, shredded).
- Textured vegetable protein (TVP), from soya beans.
- Tofu (used in Chinese cookery).

Products and dishes made from TVP

- Burgers, chicken-based meals, sausages and sausage rolls, meat pies, meat sauces.

Advantages of TVP

- Less expensive than meat.
- Rich in protein, fibre and polyunsaturated fat.
- Intake of saturated fats is reduced.
- Easy to store, with a long shelf life.
- Saves waste and in some cases saves time.
- Can be used to extend meat dishes.
- Suitable for vegetarian diets.

Disadvantages of TVP

- Poor flavour compared to meat.
- Needs extra flavouring (herbs, spices).
- Unusual texture and aroma.

Uses of TVP

- As a meat extender, e.g. in stews and casseroles.
- As a meat substitute, e.g. in lasagne, curries.

Poultry

Poultry can be free-range, organic or factory reared. It can be bought fresh (whole or sections), prepacked or frozen.

Types of poultry

- **Domestic birds:** Turkey, chicken, duck, goose.
- **Game birds:** Pheasant, duck, grouse, etc.

Nutritive value of poultry

Protein	Good source of HBV protein.
Fats	Saturated fats vary – chicken and turkey have a low fat content, less than in meat.
Carbohydrate	None present.
Vitamins	Some B group vitamins, but less than beef or lamb.
Minerals	Traces of calcium and half the iron content of red meat.
Water	Amount varies (50–70%).

Value of poultry in the diet

- An excellent alternative for people who must reduce saturated fat in their diet. Remove skin, as most of the fat is located just under the skin.
- A versatile and easily digested food, chicken is suitable for invalids and convalescents.
- Serve with carbohydrate-rich foods, e.g. potatoes, rice, pasta, to make up for the lack of carbohydrates.
- Low in minerals and vitamins, so should be served with food combinations rich in minerals and vitamins.

> **LINK**
> Healthy eating and balanced diets (pp. 33–42)

Guidelines for choosing and buying poultry

Fresh:

1. Buy from a clean, reputable shop or supermarket.
2. Check the 'use by' label if prepacked.
3. Poultry should be fresh, with white skin and a pleasant smell.
4. Avoid poultry that looks discoloured.
5. The breast should be plump and the breastbone pliable.

Frozen:

1. Frozen poultry must be frozen solid.
2. Wrappers must not be damaged.
3. Do not buy if it has begun to thaw.

> **key point**
> *Salmonella* is the food-poisoning bacteria associated with poultry.

Rules for storing poultry

Follow the guidelines for storing meat (pp. 110) but add the following points.

- **Fresh:** Do not forget to remove the giblets.
- **Frozen:** If poultry has begun to thaw on the way home, do not refreeze (thaw fully, cook and use – do **not** refreeze).

> **LINKS**
> Personal hygiene (p. 67)
> Food hygiene (pp. 66–8)
> Food storage (pp. 70–2)

Rules for using/cooking poultry

1. Remove fresh poultry from the fridge and wipe dry.
2. Remove frozen poultry from the freezer and allow to thaw fully in the fridge before preparing for cooking.
3. Season with salt, pepper, herbs or garlic.
4. Do not stuff the central cavity (cook stuffing separately to avoid problems, e.g. *salmonella*).

Cooking methods

Poultry can be:

LINK
Cooking Methods (pp. 74–80)

- Boiled • Casseroled • Fried • Grilled • Roasted • Steamed • Stir-fried.

Fish

Fish is classified into three groups according to its nutritional value.

Classification of fish

White	Oily	Shellfish
Cod	Herring	Crab
Haddock	Mackerel	Mussels
Plaice	Salmon	Oysters
Whiting	Trout	Prawns

HL Average composition of fish

Nutrient	White	Oily	Shellfish
Protein	17–20%	17–20%	17–20%
Fat	0%	13%	2.5%
Carbohydrate	0%	0%	0%
Vitamins	B group	A, D, B group	B group
Minerals	Iodine	Iodine	Iodine, calcium
Water	70–80%	65%	72%

Nutritive value of fish

Protein	Rich source of HBV protein in an easy-to-digest form.
Fat	Oily fish is a good source of polyunsaturated fat. White fish has fat in the liver but none in the flesh.
Carbohydrate	None.
Vitamins	B group vitamins are in all fish. Because of its fat content, oily fish is a source of vitamins A and D.
Minerals	Good source of iodine and potassium. Calcium is found in the bones of tinned fish, e.g. salmon, sardines.
Water	Higher water content in white fish than in oily or shellfish.

Value of fish in the diet

- Good source of HBV protein in an easily digestible form, so is ideal for all groups – children, teenagers, adults, the elderly and invalids.
- High in polyunsaturated fats, so it is important in the diets of those suffering from CHD and those following low saturated fat diets.
- Lacking in carbohydrates, so serve fish with carbohydrate-rich foods.
- Good alternative to meat, as it is high in polyunsaturated fats, rich in HBV and contains a supply of vitamins and minerals.

LINKS

Healthy eating and balanced diets (pp. 33–42)

Healthy Food Pyramid (p. 35)

Guidelines for choosing and buying fish

Fresh:

1. Buy from a clean, reputable shop or supermarket.
2. Choose fish that is in season, when it is cheapest.
3. Fish should be fresh, with bulging eyes, firm flesh, bright red gills, a fresh smell and moist, unbroken skin.
4. Check the 'sell by' date (if prepacked).
5. If wrapped, check that it is not damaged.
6. Do not buy fish if it looks discoloured and smells stale.

Frozen:

1. Fish must be frozen solid.
2. Wrappers must be sealed and undamaged.
3. Put in the freezer as quickly as possible.

Rules for storing fish

Fresh:

1. Remove from the wrapping, rinse, put on ice if possible, cover and put in the fridge.
2. Do not mix with other foods, as fish has a strong smell.
3. Use within 24 hours (preferably the same day).

Frozen:

1. Put into the freezer as soon as possible.
2. Never refreeze thawed fish.
3. Use by the expiry date and follow the instructions given.

LINK

Food storage (p. 70)

Rules for preparing fish

1. Prepare according to its shape (round, flat).
2. Remove scales by scraping and cut off the head. Cut off the fins and tail with scissors. Remove the gut.
3. Rinse and wipe dry with kitchen paper.
4. Use whole or filleted or cut into steaks.

Effects of cooking on fish

- Fish changes colour (from transparent to opaque).
- Protein coagulates and fish becomes firm.
- Cooking dissolves connective tissue and the fish flakes.
- Vitamin B and minerals dissolve into the cooking liquid.
- Bacteria and parasites are destroyed.

Cooking fish

Fish can be:

- Baked • Fried • Grilled • Poached • Steamed • Stewed.

LINKS
Methods of cooking (pp. 74–80)
Effects of heat on nutrients (p. 80)

Processing and preserving fish

Method	Examples
Brine	Prawns, mussels
Drying	Anchovies
Canning	Tuna, salmon
Freezing	Cod, plaice
Pickling	Roll mops (herrings)
Smoking	Kippers, haddock

Eggs

HL Average composition of eggs

Protein	13%
Fat	12%
Carbohydrate	0%
Vitamins	A, D, B group
Minerals	1%
Water	74%

Nutritive value of eggs

Protein	High biological value (HBV) protein.
Fat	Yolk contains cholesterol and saturated fat.
Carbohydrate	None.
Vitamins	Fat-soluble vitamins A and D in the yolk, B group in the white.
Minerals	Calcium, iron, sulphur, phosphorus.
Water	Most found in the egg white.

Value of eggs in the diet

- A useful, cheap and easily digested source of HBV protein, eggs are useful in the diets of children, the elderly and invalids.
- The fat present is in a form that babies and children find easy to digest.
- As eggs contain saturated fat, they should be restricted in the diet of those with coronary heart disease.
- Serve eggs with foods rich in vitamin C, as it is needed for the absorption of iron, which is found in eggs.
- Serve with foods rich in carbohydrates, e.g. chips, toast.
- Suitable for lacto-vegetarians and a good substitute for meat.

Grading and labelling eggs

Under EU legislation, eggs are graded and the egg box has all the information (labelling) you need to choose the freshest and best-quality eggs.

Grading

- Graded according to quality and weight.
- Weight/size (large, medium and small).
- Quality/class (Extra, Class A, B, C).

Labelling

Information on the box:

- Country of origin, e.g. IE = Ireland.
- Name and address of the producer.
- Registration number of the producer.
- Quantity of eggs.
- Quality/class.
- Week number (1–52).
- Use-by date.
- Storage guidelines.
- Quality assurance marks.

Information on the egg:

- Farming method, numbered 0 to 3: organic (0), free-range (1), barn (2), cage (3).
- Country of origin, e.g. IE = Ireland.
- Farm and county (indicating the farm on which the eggs were produced and in which county the farm is located).
- Best before date, e.g. 07/FEB or 7 Feb.

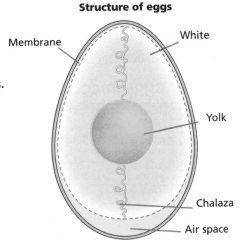

Structure of eggs

Membrane

White

Yolk

Chalaza

Air space

BEST BEFORE: 22 JULY   WEEK NO: 26
HAPPY HENS LTD
6
FREE-RANGE EGGS
SIZE: MEDIUM   COUNTRY OF ORIGIN: IRELAND   CLASS A

> **LINK**
> Consumer education (food labelling) (p. 170)

1IEA12
BB DAY/MONTH

Guidelines for buying eggs

1. Buy from a clean, busy shop or supermarket.
2. Check for the quality assurance symbol.
3. Check the labelling for the 'best before' date and week number.
4. Inspect eggs; do not buy cracked or broken eggs.
5. Eggs should be heavy for their size and have a rough shell.
6. Choose a size or class of eggs with a dish in mind.

Testing for freshness

- A fresh egg placed in salted water will sink to the bottom.
- A stale egg will float near or on the surface.
- A not-so-fresh egg will be suspended in the middle.

Uses of eggs in cooking

Uses	Examples
Binding ingredients	Burgers, rissoles
Coating foods	Fish dipped in egg and breadcrumbs
Eating on their own	Boiled, scrambled, poached, fried, salads
Emulsifying	Mayonnaise
Enriching	Increasing the nutritive value of dishes, e.g. mashed potatoes
Entrapping air	Sponges, meringues
Garnishing	Sieved, sliced on dishes, salads
Glazing	Tarts, scones, pastry, flans
Thickening	Quiches, custards

Rules for storing eggs

1. Store in the egg compartment of the fridge.
2. Store with the pointed end down to keep them fresh.
3. Do not wash the outer shell.
4. Avoid storing near strong-smelling foods.
5. Remove from the fridge one hour before using.

Rules for using eggs

1. Bring to room temperature to get better results.
2. Egg whites should be whisked in a bowl free from any trace of fat (including traces of egg yolk).

3. Add hot liquid slowly to eggs to prevent curdling.

4. Cook eggs thoroughly for babies, toddlers, children, pregnant women, invalids and elderly people (there is a danger of *salmonella* in undercooked eggs).

5. Check the 'best before' date and use eggs in rotation.

Effects of cooking on eggs

- Bacteria are destroyed.
- Protein coagulates and the egg white changes – it becomes opaque and hardens.
- Overcooking causes eggs to become indigestible.
- If high temperatures are used, eggs will curdle.

> **LINK**
> The nutrients (pp. 18–28)

Omelettes

Types of omelette:

- Plain ● Soufflé.

Examples of fillings for omelettes:

- *Savoury*: Cheese, ham, mushroom, tomato.
- *Sweet*: Jam, cream and puréed fruit.

Pancakes

Types of pancake:

- Sweet ● Savoury.

Examples of fillings for pancakes:

- *Sweet*: Crushed fruit, stewed fruit, whipped cream.
- *Savoury*: Cheese, mushroom, ham, cheese and ham.

 EXAM QUESTIONS AND SAMPLE ANSWERS

Higher Level 2007, Section A, Q.4
Name **two** classifications of fish and give one example of each class. (4 marks)

Classification	Example
White	Cod
Oily	Mackerel

Higher Level 2005, Section A, Q.3
Give **two** effects of cooking on fish. (4 marks)

(i) Protein coagulates and fish becomes firm.

(ii) Bacteria and parasites are destroyed.

Higher Level 2008, Section B, Q.2 (55 marks) (long question)

(a) State **three** classifications of fish and give **two** examples of each class. (12 marks: classification = 6, examples = 6)

HL

	Classification	Example 1	Example 2
(i)	White	Cod	Haddock
(ii)	Oily	Herring	Salmon
(iii)	Shellfish	Prawns	Oysters

(b) Give the nutritional composition of fish and outline its value in the diet. (24 marks)

Nutritional composition (6 x 3 marks)

Protein   17–20%. Rich source of HBV protein in an easy-to-digest form. Fish can be used as an alternative to meat.

Fat   Oily fish is a good source of polyunsaturated fat (13%). White fish has none in the flesh but a little fat in the liver.

Carbohydrate None.

Vitamins   B group vitamins are present in all fish. Oily fish is a source of vitamins A and D.

Minerals   Good source of iodine and potassium. Calcium is found in shellfish and the bones of tinned fish, e.g. salmon, sardines.

Water   Higher content in white fish than in oily or shellfish. Ranges from 65–80%.

Value of fish in the diet (3 x 2 marks)

- Good source of HBV protein in an easily digestible form and is ideal for all groups – children, teenagers, adults, the elderly and invalids.
- High in polyunsaturated fats, so it is important in the diets of those suffering from CHD and those following low saturated fat diets.
- Fish adds variety to the diet.

> **exam focus**
>
> You are expected to give two points related to nutrition and one other point.

(c) What guidelines should be followed when (i) buying and (ii) storing fresh fish? (8 marks)

(i) Buying fresh fish (2 x 2 marks)

1. Buy fish in season from a clean, reputable shop or supermarket.
2. Fish should be fresh, with bulging eyes, firm flesh, bright red gills, a fresh smell and moist, unbroken skin.

(ii) Storing fresh fish (2 x 2 marks)

1. Remove from the wrapping, rinse, put on ice if possible, cover and put in the fridge.
2. Do not mix with other foods, as fish has a strong smell.
3. Use within 24 hours (preferably the same day).

(d) (i) Suggest **three** methods of cooking fish. (3 marks)

     1. Poaching   2. Grilling   3. Baking

(ii) What are the effects of cooking on fish? (6 marks)

1. Protein coagulates and sets.
2. Bacteria and parasites are destroyed.
3. Connective tissue dissolves and the fish flakes.

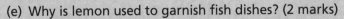

(e) Why is lemon used to garnish fish dishes? (2 marks)

1. *Adds colour.*

2. *Adds and improves flavour.*

Higher Level 2007, Section B, Q.2 (55 marks) (long question)

(a) (i) Outline the reasons why eggs should be included in the diet. (12 marks)

1. *High biological value protein is needed for growth and repair.*

2. *Calcium and vitamin D are present, for healthy bones and teeth.*

3. *Good substitute for meat, poultry or fish.*

4. *Eggs have a variety of uses in cooking.*

(ii) Name **two** important nutrients not found in eggs. (4 marks)

1. *Carbohydrate (starch, fibre).*

2. *Vitamin C.*

(b) What guidelines should be followed when (i) buying **and** (ii) storing eggs? (12 marks)

(i) **Guidelines for buying eggs** (2 x 3 marks)

1. *Check the labelling for the 'best before' date and quality assurance symbol.*

2. *Eggs should be fresh and heavy for their size. Do not buy cracked or broken eggs (danger of salmonella).*

(ii) **Guidelines for storing eggs** (2 x 3 marks)

1. *Store in the egg compartment in the fridge with the pointed end down.*

2. *Store away from strong-smelling foods.*

(c) List **five** culinary uses of eggs **and** name a different dish to illustrate each use. (Uses = 10 marks, 5 dishes = 5 marks)

Culinary uses	Dish
Binding ingredients	*Beef burgers*
Coating foods	*Fish dipped in egg and breadcrumbs*
Eating on their own	*Poached eggs*
Emulsifying	*Mayonnaise*
Enriching	*Increasing the nutritive value of dishes, e.g. mashed potatoes*

(d) Name **two** groups of people who should avoid eating raw eggs and **state why**. (2 groups = 6 marks, reasons = 2 marks)

1. *Pregnant women, because of listeria food poisoning.*

2. *The elderly, because of salmonella food poisoning.*

(e) What are 'free-range' eggs? (4 marks)

'Free-range' eggs are from hens that are free to run out of doors and are not kept inside in sheds in cages all day. The feed given to them is free of animal by-products and additives.

16 Stocks, Soups and Sauces

aims
- To list the advantages of using home-made stock.
- To outline the value of soups in the diet.
- To state the classification, thickening and garnishing of soups.
- To compare home-made and convenience soups.
- To list the characteristics of good soups and sauces.
- To identify the reasons for serving sauces.
- To classify sauces, roux sauce and variations.

Stocks

The quality of soups, sauces and gravies is influenced by the quality of the stock used. A stock is the basic liquid used when making soups, sauces and gravies. Bones, vegetables and/or meat are simmered in water to extract their favours during a long, slow cooking time. Stock has a low nutritive value because of the amount of water present.

key point

Home-made stocks and soups tend to be more nourishing than convenience varieties.

Advantages of home-made stock

- Lower in salt than commercial stock cubes.
- Excellent flavour.
- Does not have additives (you know what is in it).

Stock cubes and powders

These are a concentrated form of stock in beef, chicken, fish and vegetable flavours. They are:

- Convenient when time is not available to make stock.
- Useful in emergencies.
- High in salt compared to home-made stock.

key point

Check the label on convenience stock cubes, soups and sauces to determine how much salt is present.

LINK
Healthy eating (reducing salt in the diet) (p. 50)

Soups

Value in the diet

- As soups have a high water content, their nutritive value is determined by the other ingredients in the soup.
- Soups stimulate the appetite.
- Soups can be served at the start of a meal or used as a snack, for a light lunch or a packed lunch.

key point

Fresh vegetables, meat, poultry, fish, milk and cereals increase the nutritive value of soups.

Classification of home-made soups

Class	Types and examples
Thick soups	• **Puréed**: Ingredients are sieved or blended, e.g. mushroom soup. • **Thickened**: Contain a thickening agent such as roux, flour or cornflour, e.g. vegetable soup.
Thin soups	• **Clear soup**: Made from a rich stock, thin in consistency, e.g. beef consommé. • **Broth**: Thin liquid, finely chopped ingredients, thickened with whole cereals such as barley or rice, e.g. mutton broth.
Chilled soups	• **Vegetables**: Cold soup made from vegetables, e.g. gazpacho, iced cucumber, chilled guacamole. • **Fruit**: Cold soup made from fruit, e.g. Hungarian cherry soup.

Thickening soups

Soups can be thickened using:

- Roux – fat and flour in equal quantities.
- Starch – flour, cornflour, rice, potato.
- Egg yolk – egg yolk and cream (added to rich soups).
- Cereals – barley, rice.

LINKS
Menu planning (p. 57)
Designing menus (p. 62)

Characteristics of a good soup

- Good flavour, with the taste of the main ingredient
- Right consistency and colour
- Free from grease
- Well seasoned
- Served piping hot or chilled.

Garnishes for soup

- Croutons (fried cubes of bread)
- Cream or yoghurt
- Fresh herbs, e.g. parsley, chives
- Grated cheese, e.g. cheddar, parmesan.

Accompaniments to soup

- Brown bread/rolls/scones
- Dinner buns, breadsticks
- Garlic bread/tomato bread
- Herb bread/rolls/scones
- Melba toast.

LINK
Vegetables (p. 93)

Types of convenience soups

- Canned • Cook-chill • Dried.

Comparing home-made and convenience soups

	Advantages	Disadvantages
Home-made soup	<ul><li>Fresh ingredients</li><li>Good flavour</li><li>Good colour</li><li>No additives</li></ul>	<ul><li>Takes time to prepare</li><li>Can be more expensive</li></ul>
Convenience soup	<ul><li>Easy to prepare, saves time</li><li>Useful in emergencies</li><li>Adds variety to menu</li><li>Can be cheaper</li></ul>	<ul><li>Poor in flavour when compared to fresh varieties</li><li>May contain additives, e.g. flavour enhancers</li><li>High in salt</li></ul>

Sauces

Sauces can be very simple or elaborate, depending on the dish or type of meal. The ingredients used will determine the nutritive value of a sauce. Those made with water are less nourishing than those containing milk, cream and eggs.

Reasons for serving sauces

Sauces are served with food to:

- Stimulate digestion
- Improve the flavour of bland foods
- Provide variety in colour, flavour and texture
- Counteract the richness of foods
- Improve the nutritive value of food.

Classification of sauces

Class	Examples
Roux-based sauces	Cheese sauce, mushroom sauce
Cold sauce/dressings	Mint sauce, vinaigrette
Egg sauces	Hollandaise sauce, custard, mayonnaise
Fruit sauces	Apple purée, cranberry sauce
Other	Chocolate sauce

Roux

A roux is made from equal quantities of fat and flour.

The basic roux sauces are pouring, stewing, coating and panard.

Quantities of fat, flour and liquid in roux sauces

	Pouring	Stewing	Coating	Panard
Fat	25g	25g	25g	25g
Flour	25g	25g	25g	25g
Liquid	500ml	375ml	250ml	175ml

Variations of the basic roux sauce:

- Béchamel sauce
- Cheese sauce
- Egg
- Mushroom
- Mustard
- Onion sauce
- Parsley sauce
- Velouté.

Characteristics of a Good Sauce

- Well seasoned
- Correct consistency
- Free from grease
- Flour cooked thoroughly
- Nice flavour.

Convenience sauces

- Bottled ● Canned ● Cook-chill ● Dried.

Advantages:

- Useful in emergencies.
- Good variety available.

Disadvantages:

- May be high in salt/sugar.
- May contain additives.
- Expensive.

LINKS
Meal planning (pp. 57–60)
Designing menus (pp. 62–5)
Food processing (p. 129)
Food preservation (p. 137)

EXAM QUESTIONS AND SAMPLE ANSWERS

Higher Level 2002, Section A, Q.6 (4 marks)
Give **two** benefits of using stock when making soup.
1. Increases the nutritive value of the soup.
2. Improves the flavour of home-made soup.

Ordinary Level 2009, Section A, Q.5 (5 marks)

Match the sauce usually served with **each** of the following roast meats.

orange, parsley, apple, mint, cranberry

Ham	Turkey	Pork	Duck	Lamb
Parsley	Cranberry	Apple	Orange	Mint

Higher Level 2003, Section B, Q.1 (55 marks) (long question)

The following is a recipe for home-made cheese sauce.

> *HOMEMADE CHEESE SAUCE*
>
> Ingredients
>
> *25g margarine*   *50g grated cheddar cheese*   *25g flour*
>
> *1/4 tsp mustard*   *500ml milk*   *salt, pepper*

(a) Based on the ingredients listed above:

  (i) Evaluate the nutritive value of the home-made cheese sauce. (5 x 3 marks)

   • *HBV protein is provided by the cheese and milk.*

   • *Margarine provides fat.*

   • *Milk and cheese provide vitamins A, B group and D.*

   • *Milk and cheese are rich sources of calcium.*

   • *A little carbohydrate is provided by the flour.*

  (ii) Identify the ingredients which are combined to form a roux. (4 marks)

   • *Margarine and flour.*

(b) Name **three** dishes in which cheese sauce forms part of the main ingredients. (6 marks)

  1. Macaroni cheese

  2. Cauliflower au gratin

  3. Lasagne

(c) Give **four** reasons why sauces may be used to accompany food. (12 marks)

  1. Stimulate digestion.

  2. Improve colour, flavour and texture.

  3. Counteract the richness of foods.

  4. Enrich the nutritive value of food.

(d) Suggest a **different** sauce which is traditionally served with **each** of the following roast meats. (6 marks)

  1. Turkey: Cranberry sauce.

  2. Lamb: Mint sauce.

  3. Pork: Apple sauce.

(e) Give **two** advantages and two disadvantages of using convenience sauces.

  Advantages:

  1. Saves time and energy.

  2. Easy to make.

  Disadvantages:

  1. May contain additives.

  2. Low in fibre.

17 Leftovers

 aims

- To identify the value of leftovers in the diet.
- To outline the rules for using leftovers.
- To give examples of uses for leftovers.

Planning meals carefully will reduce the amount of leftovers. All leftover foods should be used. Leftovers can be used in hot or cold dishes.

Value in the diet

Reheated leftovers have a lower nutritive value than food just cooked. Improve the food value by serving with fresh ingredients.

Examples: Rissoles with steamed vegetables, stewed apple with yoghurt.

Rules for using leftovers

1. Reheat food thoroughly to avoid food poisoning.
2. Improve the nutritive value, colour, flavour and texture by serving with fresh salads and vegetables.
3. Handle the food as little as possible.
4. Use herbs and sauces to improve the flavour.
5. Do not reheat leftovers for a second time.
6. Use leftovers within 48 hours – do not store for long.

key point

Reheated leftovers could cause food poisoning if not stored correctly, reheated thoroughly or used quickly.

LINKS
Food storage (p. 70)
Food hygiene (p. 66)
Home management (wise use of resources) (p. 226)

 key point

Cover leftovers and store in the fridge until needed. Never leave them in a warm place.

Using leftovers

Food	Examples of use
Bread	Breadcrumbs, bread sauce, puddings, stuffing
Cakes	Trifle, puddings
Cheese	Grated for toppings, sauces
Egg	Cakes, garnish, glaze, mayonnaise, meringue
Fish	Fish cakes, fish pie, salads, sandwiches
Fruit	Crumble, flans, pies, tarts, trifle
Meat	Curry, shepherd's pie, sandwiches, salads
Potatoes	Toppings for pies, croquettes, potato cakes
Vegetables	Croquettes, savoury pies

LINKS
Balanced diets (p. 33)
Menu planning (pp. 57–65)

EXAM QUESTION AND SAMPLE ANSWER

Ordinary Level 2006, Section A, Q.4 (5 marks)

Suggest a different dish in which you would use each of the following leftover foods.

Leftover food	Dish
(i) Boiled potatoes	*Potato salad*
(ii) Roast turkey	*Turkey curry*
(iii) Half tin of tomatoes	*Shepherd's pie*

18 Food Processing

aims
- To identify the reasons for processing food.
- To give examples of processed foods.
- To evaluate convenience foods.
- To state the advantages and disadvantages of processed foods (convenience foods).
- To explain food labelling.
- To give the advantages and disadvantages of food additives.
- To classify and identify uses for processed foods.
- To outline legislations regarding standards and labelling. **HL**
- To list additives and why they are used. **HL**
- To list positive/negative effects of additives. **HL**

Reasons for Processing Food

- To make seasonal foods available throughout the year.
- To make some foods more digestible.
- To create new foods.
- To stop the action of micro-organisms and enzymes and extend shelf life.
- To add nutritional value (fortified).
- To respond to consumer needs for food that is easy to prepare/cook.
- To make storage and transportation of food easier.

Examples of processed foods

- Bottled foods • Butter • Canned foods • Cheese • Dried fruit • Frozen meals
- Fruit juice • Milk • White flour • Yoghurt • All types of convenience foods.

Examples of new food products

- Breakfast cereals • Cook-chill meals • Crisps
- Vegetable burgers • Yoghurt drinks.

> **LINK**
> Effects of processing on nutrients (pp. 130–31)

Convenience foods

What are convenience foods?

Foods that undergo commercial preparation, precooking and cooking which save cooking time and energy in the home are called convenience foods.

Advantages of convenience foods

- Save time and energy.
- Little cooking skill is needed.
- Foods can be used out of season.
- Easy to prepare and use.
- Provide variety and interest to meals.
- Useful in emergencies.

Disadvantages of convenience foods

- Expensive to use regularly.
- Portion size tends to be small.
- Easy to overuse.
- Tend to be high in salt, sugar and fat and low in dietary fibre.
- Incorrectly stored/cooked cook-chill products can cause food poisoning.

Types of convenience/processed foods

Bottled	Jam, chutney, carrots, sauces, dressings, oils
Canned	Peas, soups, pineapple, salmon, tuna
Cook-chill	Curries, lasagne
Dried	Soups, sauces, bread mixes, herbs, tea
Frozen	Pizza, fish, meat, vegetables, pastry, precooked meals such as lasagne and garlic bread
Ready-to-cook	Lasagne, fish pie, soups
Take-away	Chinese meals, pizza, fish and chips

Evaluating processed foods

Food value of canned, dried and frozen foods

Food	Food value
Canned	Vitamins C and B group are destroyed by processing.
Dried	Vitamins C and B group are destroyed by processing.
Frozen	Retain vitamins and minerals. Vegetables and fruits are processed very quickly after picking.

Colour of canned, dried and frozen foods

Food	Colour
Canned	Some loss of colour.
Dried	Some loss of colour.
Frozen	Most foods retain colour. Vegetables must be blanched before freezing to maintain colour.

Texture of canned, dried and frozen foods

Food	Texture
Canned	Loss of texture in fruits and vegetables.
Dried	Some loss of texture. Foods soften.
Frozen	Most foods retain texture. Changes in soft fruit on thawing, e.g. strawberries.

exam focus

If you get stuck during your exam for an example of convenience foods, just think of what you see on the supermarket shelves and in the freezer sections when shopping.

LINKS
Soups and sauces (pp. 122–26)
Food preservation (p. 137)

Guidelines for using convenience foods

1. Follow the instructions on the label.

2. Use convenience foods in emergencies only.

3. Include fresh foods to improve nutritive value.

4. Use no more than one or two convenience foods in a meal.

5. Heat cook-chill products thoroughly to destroy bacteria.

6. Use convenience foods in rotation.

Guidelines for storing convenience foods

- Follow the instructions on the labels.
- Store canned, bottled and dried foods in a dry, well-ventilated kitchen cupboard.
- Store cook-chill products below 4°C.
- Store perishables in the fridge.
- Use within the 'best before' or 'use by' date.

LINK
Food storage (p. 70)

Guidelines for buying convenience foods

- Choose quality convenience foods.
- Buy packets, cans, jars and containers that can be recycled.
- Check that packets are sealed correctly.
- Do not buy bulging or damaged tins.
- Choose low-salt, low-sugar and low-fat products.
- Check the 'sell by' date.

Food labelling

European Union law states that food labels should:

- Carry clear, specific and relevant information.
- Be in the language of the country.
- Be truthful.

The composition and hygiene of food is controlled by national and European legislation:

- General Food Regulations.
- Health Acts and European Community regulations.
- European Community foodstuffs Regulations.

Enforcement of regulations is through inspections.

Packet soup label

The information on food labels

- Name of the food product.
- List of ingredients in order of weight.
- Quantity (net weight).
- 'Sell by', 'best before' or 'use by' date.
- Instructions for storage, use and cooking.
- Name and address of the manufacturer.
- Country of origin.
- List of any GM or irradiated ingredients.
- List of any flavourings and sweeteners.
- Nutritional information.
- Quality.

Food additives

Food additives are ingredients or substances added to food by manufacturers. Under EU law, additives must be listed by name or E number. Amounts used are strictly controlled.

Why are additives used?

- To increase the shelf life of foods.
- To inhibit the action of micro-organisms and enzymes.
- To improve colour, flavour and texture.
- To add nutrients to foods (fortified).
- To prevent the food from reacting to the air.

Advantages of food additives	Disadvantages of food additives
• Improves flavour, colour and texture of food. • Reduces risks of food poisoning. • Increases shelf life and reduces waste. • Improves nutritive value. • Greater variety of foods.	• Allergic reactions, e.g. rashes, hyperactivity. • Colours may look unnatural and deceive consumers. • Foods do not follow a natural cycle until they decay.

key point

Special foods are provided for those suffering from diabetes and coeliac disease. Check the labels before you buy.

key point

Symptoms of allergic reaction include hyperactivity, rashes and headaches.

Classification, functions and uses of additives

Additives	Functions	Uses	Examples
Colourings (E100–199)	To maintain or improve the colour of the foods	Sauces, soups, sweets	Tartrazine (E102) (sunset yellow)
Preservatives (E200-E299)	To provide food out of season and prevent waste To prevent the growth of micro-organisms	Chutneys, pickles Bacon, ham, dried fruits	Salt, vinegar, spices Sulphur dioxide (E220)
Antioxidants (E300–399)	To prevent foods with fat from going rancid (rotten)	Vegetable oils, packaged foods	Vitamin C (E300) Vitamin E (E306)
Flavourings and sweeteners (no E numbers)	To improve or enhance the flavour of food	Cheese, stock cubes, sweets, breakfast cereals, soups, snack foods	Sugar, salt, spices, herbs, monosodium glutamate (E621)
Nutritive additives (no E numbers)	To replace nutrients lost during processing	Milk, breakfast cereals, flour	Vitamins A, D, B group (folic acid), calcium
Physical conditioning agents (no E numbers)	To form emulsions To stabilise foods To prevent lumps from forming in dried ingredients	Mayonnaise, ice cream, cakes, icing sugar, flour	Emulsifier: Lecithin (E422) Stabiliser: Guar gum (E412) Anti-caking agent

Genetically modified (GM) foods

These are foods whose chemical structure (DNA) has been altered to modify existing characteristics or to add new characteristics. Strict EU regulations control the use and labelling of GM foods.

What are the new characteristics/results of GM modification?

- Size and speed of ripening fruit and vegetables are altered.
- Fruits and vegetables are disease/pest resistant.
- Cereal crops are pest resistant.

Foods must be labelled as GM food if:

- Any ingredient has been genetically modified.
- It is produced from GM soya or maize.
- It has been contaminated by GM soya or maize.

Examples of GM crops from which ingredients have been derived include soya beans, maize, rapeseed oil and cotton seed oil. **You must read food labels carefully.**

EXAM QUESTIONS AND SAMPLE ANSWERS

HL

Higher Level 2007, Section A, Q.6 (4 marks)

Give **two** reasons why food is processed.

(i) To have seasonal foods available throughout the year (extend the shelf life of food).

(ii) To respond to consumer needs for foods that are easy to prepare/cook.

Higher Level 2006, Section A, Q.2 (4 marks)

Name **two** types of additives use in convenience foods.

(i) Colourings (E100–199).

(ii) Preservatives (E200–299).

Ordinary Level 2002, Section A, Q.5 (5 marks)

Give **two** reasons why convenience foods are becoming more popular.

(i) Easy to prepare and use, little skill required.

(ii) Useful in emergencies, saves time.

HL

Higher Level 2007, Section B, Q.1 (55 marks) (long question)

FARM-FRESH STEAM VEGETABLES
A delicious variety of fresh vegetables frozen. Gently steam to perfection...and enjoy!

NUTRITION INFORMATION	
Typical Values per Serving	
Energy	45 kcal
Protein	4.6 g
Carbohydrate	5.4 g
Fat	0.6 g
Fibre	3.4 g
Sodium	Trace
Vitamin C	34 mg
Folic Acid	99 µg

INGREDIENTS
Carrots, green beans, baby sweetcorn, peas.

A serving of 'Farm-Fresh Steam Vegetables' provides 1 of your recommended 5 daily portions of fruit and vegetables.

For best results STEAM for 5 minutes.

In this type of question, you must read and analyse the information given and use where relevant when answering the question.

(a) Using the nutritional information given on the product label on page 134, evaluate the nutritive value of Farm-fresh Steam Vegetables. (20 marks)

The latest nutritional guidelines recommend that we eat 5+ portions of fruit and vegetables each day. One serving of Farm-fresh Steam Vegetables provides one serving.

exam focus

When evaluating the nutritive value, you must name each nutrient, give the quantity per serving, state the class or type, list the functions of the nutrient in the diet and the latest nutritional information.

HL

1. Protein

A good supply of vegetable protein is found in this product.

Quantity: *4.6g per serving*

Class of protein present: *Low biological value (LBV) protein, found in carrots, green beans, baby sweet corn and peas.*

Functions of protein in the body:
- *Growth and repair of cells.*
- *Production of antibodies, enzymes and hormones.*
- *Produces heat and energy.*

2. Carbohydrates

Quantity of carbohydrates: *5.4g per serving.*

Quantity of fibre: *3.4g per serving.*

Classes of carbohydrates present:
- *Starches: Good supply in green beans, peas, sweet corn.*
- *Fibre is in all vegetables.*
- *Sugar: Good supply in carrots.*

Functions of carbohydrates in the body *(sugars, starches and dietary fibre):*
- *Provides heat and energy (starch and sugars).*
- *Excess carbohydrate is converted into fat, which insulates the body (stored as adipose tissue).*

Dietary fibre:
- *Helps the movement of food through the body.*
- *Helps to prevent constipation and other bowel diseases.*
- *Absorbs water and makes us feel full.*
- *Picks up chemicals and toxins.*
- *Fibre-rich foods provide vitamin B.*

exam focus

Discuss other nutrients using the same approach:
- Fat.
- Vitamins: C, folic acid (one of the B group).
- Minerals: Sodium.

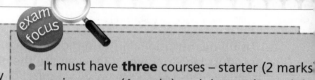

(b) Design a **three-course** dinner menu, to include this product, suitable for a family meal. (12 marks)

- It must have **three** courses – starter (2 marks) main course (4 marks) and dessert (2 marks).
- You must include the product in the main course.
- Follow a menu format (2 marks).
- Balance the menu (2 marks).

Crudités and yoghurt dip

***

Roast chicken

Baked potatoes

Farm-fresh Steam Vegetables

***

Rhubarb crumble

Custard sauce

(c) (i) Give **two** reasons why steaming is the recommended method of cooking for these vegetables. (6 marks)

1. *Healthier method of cooking, as no fat is added.*
2. *Vegetables are not immersed in water, so vitamins and minerals do not dissolve into cooking liquid.*

(ii) Name **two** other cooking methods suitable for vegetables. (4 marks)

1. *Stir-frying.*
2. *Microwave cooking.*

(d) How can teenagers include more vegetables in their daily diet? (9 marks)

1. *Drink vegetable juices, e.g. carrot juice.*
2. *Include vegetables and salads in packed lunches, starters for dinners and lunches.*
3. *Eat more vegetable salads, soups, vegetarian curries, stews and casseroles.*
4. *Add extra vegetables to meat/poultry/chicken curries, stews and casseroles.*

(e) What does this symbol mean? (4 marks)

This symbol means that the product 'Farm-fresh steam vegetables' is suitable for home freezing.

19 Food Preserving

- To identify the reasons for preserving food.
- To list the advantages and disadvantages of preserving food.
- To outline the methods of preservation.
- To state the effects of preservation on foods.

Reasons for preserving food

- To destroy micro-organisms.
- To inhibit the action of enzymes.
- To prevent micro-organisms from re-entering food.
- To maintain the nutritive value of the food.
- To keep the natural colour, flavour and texture.

Advantages of preserving food

- Prevents waste when foods are plentiful.
- Provides variety in the diet out of season.
- Saves time and energy.
- Saves money and waste.
- Flavour of home-made preserves is excellent.

Factors causing food to deteriorate include:

LINK
Food processing (p. 129)

- Action of enzymes.
- Bacteria, moulds and yeasts.

The conditions needed by micro-organisms to multiply are:

- Food.
- Warmth (around 37°C).
- Moisture (conditions and food).
- Time (bacteria double every 20 minutes).
- Some microbes need air (oxygen).

When one or more of these conditions is removed, micro-organisms will not grow/multiply and food will last longer. The main methods of preservation are freezing, drying, heat treatments, use of preservatives, pasteurisation and irradiation.

Methods of preservation

Drying	Removal of moisture
Freezing	Removal of warmth
Heat treatments	• Canning/bottling (removal of air) • Jam making (using sugar), chutneys (using vinegar)
Irradiation	Passing gamma rays through food to kill micro-organisms
Pasteurisation	Heat treatment of milk to kill bacteria
Using preservatives (includes heat treatments)	• Salt, e.g. salted fish • Vinegar, e.g. pickles, chutney • Smoke, e.g. ham, salmon, trout • Sugar, e.g. jams, jellies • Chemicals, e.g. commercial antioxidants
Vacuum packing	Air is removed, e.g. rashers

LINKS
Food processing (p. 129)
Milk and milk products (p. 98)
Food hygiene and food safety (p. 66)

key point

When preserving food, the colour, flavour and texture of many foods are changed. Some methods reduce the nutritive value of the food.

Freezing

Micro-organisms need moisture and heat to survive. All foods contain water. During freezing, heat is removed (−18°C to −35°C). Water turns into ice crystals. Micro-organisms cannot multiply or work when food is frozen. When the food thaws, they begin to act on the food once more.

key point

Food value of frozen food: Frozen food has a similar nutritive value to fresh food.

General rules for freezing

1. Choose top-quality foods.
2. Turn down the freezer to the lowest temperature in preparation for the food to be frozen (turn to 'fast freeze').
3. Pack and label foods correctly, follow guidelines.
4. Freeze food in small quantities in the 'fast freeze' compartment.
5. Do not pack the food tightly – allow the cold air to circulate.
6. Open freeze foods that stick together, e.g. berries, peas.

key point

Defrost the freezer at least twice a year.

LINK
Fridges (p. 249)

What is blanching?

Before freezing, some foods need to be blanched by placing them in boiling water and then plunging them into icy cold water for the same time, e.g. four minutes for carrots. Blanching kills micro-organisms and inactivates enzymes.

key point

Blanching helps vegetables retain their colour.

LINK
Vegetables (pp. 93–6)

To freeze or not to freeze?

Freeze:

- Bread and pastries • Cooked and uncooked pastry dishes • Desserts
- Fish • Meat • Most fruit and vegetables • Poultry • Sauces • Soups
- Stews and casseroles.

Do not freeze (foods with a high water content):

- Bananas • Cucumber • Cooked potatoes • Cream • Green leafy vegetables
- Lettuce • Melon • Milk • Whole eggs • Whole tomatoes.

Freezer packaging

Containers must be:

- Strong, durable and easily sealed (with ties/lids).
- Suitable for use at low temperatures.
- Moisture and vapour proof.

Freezer packaging includes:

- Freezer foil containers.
- Waxed cartons and tubs.
- Polythene bags and boxes.

Thawing frozen food

- Follow the guidelines on labels.
- Place food on a plate and thaw slowly overnight in the fridge. Use food quickly the next day.
- Thaw food using the auto-defrost on microwave ovens.
- Thaw frozen poultry completely before cooking.
- **Never** refreeze thawed foods.

key point

Some food can be cooked from frozen, e.g. sausage rolls, fish, vegetables.

LINK
Star marking rating for freezers (p. 71)

Jam making

In jam making:

- **High temperatures** destroy the micro-organisms, and by sealing the jar, they cannot re-enter the food.
- The **setting of jam** depends on the amount of pectin present and the use of acid to release the pectin during boiling.
- Jars are heated to a high temperature and are sterilised in the oven before the jam is added.
- Sugar acts as a preservative and jam contains a high percentage of sugar (65 per cent).

> **key point**
>
> Sure-set is a special sugar that contains pectin and helps jam set.

Canning and bottling

During the canning process:

- The food to be preserved is cooked and undergoes a sterilisation process at high temperatures in the can.
- Micro-organisms are destroyed by the high temperatures.
- Cans are made airtight to prevent contamination.
- Colour, flavour and texture change.

Food value of canned or bottled foods

During canning and bottling:

- Vitamins B and C are lost.
- Minerals dissolve into the canning liquid.
- The colour, flavour and texture change.

> **LINK**
> Food processing (evaluating colour, flavour and texture of canned foods) (pp. 130–31)

Buying and storing

- Do not purchase cans that are damaged (bulging, rusted or dented tins could cause food poisoning).
- Check the label and use before the expiry date.
- Store in a dry, well-ventilated place.

> **LINK**
> Food storage (p. 70)

Dehydration (Drying food)

During dehydration:

- Moisture is removed by heat.
- Micro-organisms are inactivated.
- Food is packed into air-proof and moisture-proof containers.

Rehydration

Water or other liquids are added to the dried foods in order to rehydrate the food for use. Micro-organisms may become active at this stage. Treat the food as a fresh food once it has been rehydrated.

Examples of dried foods

- Breakfast cereals.
- Casserole mixes and gravies.
- Dried milk powder.
- Fruit (raisins, sultanas).
- Herbs and spices.
- Packet soups, sauces, cake mixes.
- Vegetables (dried tomatoes).

Food value of dehydrated foods

- Some loss of vitamins A and B.
- One hundred per cent loss of vitamin C.
- Some dehydrated foods are fortified.

Buying and storing dehydrated foods

- Packaging must not be damaged.
- Check the expiry dates on labels.
- Store in an airtight container.
- Once opened, use as directed on the label.

EXAM QUESTIONS AND SAMPLE ANSWERS

Higher Level 2001, Section B, Q.2 (55 marks) (long question)

(a) Explain how freezing preserves food. (10 marks)

- *Micro-organisms need moisture and heat to survive. During freezing, heat is removed and micro-organisms are inactivated by temperatures between –18°C and –35°C.*
- *Upon freezing, water turns into ice crystals. Micro-organisms cannot multiply or work when food is frozen.*

(b) Give **three** advantages of using a freezer. (9 marks)

1. *Seasonal foods can be available throughout the year.*
2. *Suitable for storing a variety of foods.*
3. *Freezing is a simple and safe method of preservation.*

(c) Compare frozen vegetables with canned vegetables under each of the following headings. (16 marks)

	Frozen vegetables	Canned vegetables
(i) Food value (4 marks)	• Frozen food has a similar nutritive value to fresh food. • They are more nutritious than canned vegetables.	• Loss of vitamins B and C. • Minerals dissolve into the canning liquid.
(ii) Colour (4 marks)	Retain colour better than canned vegetables.	Loss in colour, may be replaced with additives
(iii) Flavour (4 marks)	No change in flavour.	Some loss during the canning process.
(iv) Texture (4 marks)	Texture of vegetables is retained.	Loss of texture, vegetables soften.

(d) What guidelines should be followed when (i) buying and (ii) thawing frozen food? (12 marks)

(i) Buying frozen food (3 x 2 marks)

1. Food should be frozen solid.
2. Packaging should be intact.
3. Check the expiry date.

(ii) Thawing frozen food (3 x 2 marks)

1. Follow the guidelines on the labels.
2. Place food on a plate and thaw slowly overnight in the fridge or thaw food using the auto-defrost on microwave ovens.
3. Thaw frozen poultry completely before cooking.

(e) Why should you not refreeze thawed food? (8 marks)

1. Conditions become favourable for bacteria to multiply.
2. There is a danger of food poisoning.

20 Cookery Terms

aims
- To define cookery terms.
- To provide examples where appropriate.

exam focus

Questions on cookery terms are asked in both Higher and Ordinary Level papers. It is important to be able to explain the term and know examples where appropriate. Be careful to note if you are asked to give an example as part of your answer.

Accompaniment: A food or dish that is traditionally served with a particular food or dish (e.g. roast beef and Yorkshire pudding).

Aerating: Introducing air into a bread or cake mixture to make it light (e.g. by sieving flour).

Á la carte menu: Each dish on the menu is priced separately.

Al dente: An Italian phrase describing cooked food that still has a bite.

Au gratin: Foods cooked in, or coated with, a sauce sprinkled with breadcrumbs or grated cheese and browned under the grill or in the oven.

Au naturel: Foods served raw and very simply presented.

Bain-marie: A large vessel with about 8cm of simmering water in which small saucepans or dishes containing food can be kept warm or cooked slowly.

Bake blind: Baking a pastry case without a filling (sweet or savoury).

Basting: To pour hot fat or cooking liquid over foods as they are cooking to keep them moist (e.g. hot fat over a roast).

Blanching: Plunging foods into boiling water to remove skins (from nuts and tomatoes) or to destroy enzymes when preparing vegetables for freezing, or done to whiten food.

Boquet garni: A bunch of fresh herbs tied together and used to flavour sauces, soups and stews.

Brine: A mixture of salt and water.

Buffet: A selection of dishes and courses set out on a table with appropriate accompaniments, condiments, plates and cutlery, from which people can help themselves.

Canapés: Appetisers of circles or fingers of bread, crackers, pastry, savoury biscuits or toast with savoury toppings.

Casserole: Cooking food slowly in a heatproof earthenware or Pyrex dish in the oven (e.g. chicken casserole).

Chowder: A thick seafood stew.

Condiments: Salt and pepper.

Consommé: A thin, clear soup.

Croquette: Potato or minced meat, fish or any savoury mixture coated with egg and breadcrumbs and deep fried.

Croûtons: Diced bread, fried or toasted, served as a garnish or an accompaniment to soup.

Crudités: Small, thin pieces of raw vegetables arranged on a plate and served as hors d'oeuvres.

Dicing: Cutting meat or vegetables into small cubes.

Dredging: Sprinkling flour, caster sugar, spices or herbs over a dish (flour sprinkled over the rolling pin, cinnamon over a rice pudding, caster sugar over apple tart).

Flan: An open pastry tart or sponge filled with sweet or savoury ingredients.

Garnish: A decoration for savoury dishes (sprig of parsley, lemon wedge) to improve the colour and appearance of the dish.

Gateau: A rich cake decorated and filled (cream and fresh fruit, butter icing and chocolate leaves).

Glazing: Brushing the tops of pastry and scones with beaten egg, milk or sugar and water to improve the appearance.

Grating: Foods are thinly cut using a grater or a food processor (grated cheese, carrot for coleslaw).

Hors d'oeuvres: Small pieces of savoury foods served before the soup to stimulate the appetite.

Infuse: Heating herbs, peppercorns, slices of vegetables or strips of lemon or orange rind in a liquid to flavour it.

Liaison: A thickening or binding substance used when making sauces, soups and stews.

Marinade: Oil, seasonings, wine and vinegar mixed together. It is used to flavour and tenderise meat by steeping the meat in the liquid before cooking.

Panard: A very thick sauce made from fat, flour and liquid. It is used to bind ingredients.

Parboil: Half-cooking food by boiling and then finishing cooking using another method.

Petits fours: Small fancy cakes.

Pulses: Pulse vegetables (peas, beans, lentils).

Purée: A smooth mixture of fish, fruit, meat or vegetables which has been sieved.

Roux: A mixture of equal quantities of fat and flour cooked together, used as a basis for sauces (pouring, stewing, coating, panard).

Sautéeing: Frying or tossing food quickly in a small amount of hot fat or oil (sautéed potatoes).

Seasoning: Adding salt, pepper, herbs or spices to improve the flavour of a dish.

Shortening: Fats used when making breads and cakes.

Sweat: To cook vegetables in a small amount of melted fat.

Syrup: Sugar added to water to make a concentrated solution.

Zest: The outer skin of oranges and lemons containing the essential oils which produce the flavour.

exam focus

Make sure you know what all the cookery terms mean.

Check out the following cookery terms before your exam:

appetiser	caramelise	menu	skimming
bagel	chilling	miso	stewing
baguette	chowder	organic	stir-frying
bap	consistency	fruit/vegetables	textured vegetable
bean curd	creaming	panini	protein
beating	crêpe	poaching	to modify a recipe
blending	feta	quiche	tofu
bouillon	free-range	raising agent	waffle
braising	herbs	rubbing-in	whisking
canapé	julienne	simmering	wrap

EXAM QUESTIONS AND SAMPLE ANSWERS

Higher Level 2006, Section A, Q.6 (4 marks)

Explain **each** of the following cookery terms.

(i) **Roux**: *A mixture of equal quantities of fat and flour cooked together is used to thicken soups and sauces.*

(ii) **Sauté**: *Frying or tossing food quickly in a small amount of hot fat or oil, e.g. sautéed onions.*

Higher Level 2000, Section A, Q.6 (4 marks)

Explain any **two** of the following cookery terms.

(i) **Sauté**: *To toss food very quickly in hot fat, e.g. onions.*

(ii) **Marinade**: *A mixture of oil, seasonings, wine and vinegar used to flavour and tenderise meat by steeping the meat in the liquid before cooking, e.g. grilling, baking.*

Ordinary Level 2007, Section A, Q.4 (5 marks)

Explain **each** of the following.

(i) **Garnish**: *To decorate a savoury dish to improve the colour and appearance, e.g. sprig of parsley, lemon wedge.*

(ii) **Raising agent**: *An ingredient added to bread and cake mixtures to make them rise, e.g. baking powder.*

21 The Practical Cookery Exam

Exam Time

The practical cookery exam is 1 hour 30 minutes long with 30 minutes' preparation time beforehand.

Drawing the Assignment

For the practical cookery exam, you will draw an assignment two weeks before the exam, so there will be plenty of time to prepare.

When You Draw the Assignment

Analyse the assignment selected.

	Steps involved	Questions to ask
1.	Read the task statement.	Is the task a design brief or a comparison/investigation?
2.	Analyse the task.	What am I asked to do?
3.	Identify the factors involved. Am I asked to modify a dish?	Which of the following factors might be relevant to the task: nutritive value, time, ingredients, cost, equipment, number of people, e.g. a dish for four, season, type of meal, preparation, cooking and serving of dish. ◀ Give three factors relevant to the task. Do I have to reduce salt, sugar or fat or increase fibre?
4.	Research possibilities.	Discuss the task with my teacher. Look up cookery books for solutions.
5.	List possible solutions.	Choose two solutions for each part of the task. ◀ Write up menus boxed in menu format. Solutions must meet the key requirements of the brief.
6.	List the chosen solution.	State **two** reasons for your choice. Remember what the assignment is asking you to do, healthy eating guidelines and balanced diets. ◀ Solutions must meet the brief.
7.	Name the dish(es) or menu. ● Ensure your list of ingredients and equipment is complete. ● Add up the costs of the dish.	Fill out assignment sheets with a list and cost of ingredients, equipment and method, including what you will do during the preparation time.

	Steps involved	Questions to ask	
8.	Timing.	Do not forget the time plan.	Refer to work sequences (method) and time for preparation, serving and tasting, washing up and evaluation.

Always remember to fill in the appropriate sections of the assignment sheet, following the guidelines given by the teacher.

Listen carefully to the advice given by your teacher.

Get organised

exam focus

Choose a wide variety of fresh ingredients. Keep convenience foods to a minimum. Test the recipe and try out a time plan before the examination day.

- Shop for the ingredients. Keep receipts so that you can work out the cost of the dish.
- Know what you have to do.
- Know what equipment is needed. Choose labour-saving appliances when possible to save time. Check you have the equipment needed for weighing and measuring, preparing, cooking and serving the dishes.
- List the items needed for the sink and cooking areas.
- Devise the time plan, then test and evaluate it. Make any changes that are needed **before** the exam (not on the exam day).

You are ready

Get up early and have breakfast. Do not arrive into school without having something to eat. You have nothing to worry about. You will show the examiner how well you have prepared and how hard you have worked to perfect the skills you need for the practical exam. Best of luck!

On the day – exam preparation (30 minutes)

Checking

- Make sure you have a hairnet, apron or coat, tea towel, oven gloves, dishcloth, your ingredients, equipment, cooking and serving dishes.
- Make sure you remember how to turn on/off the cooker and how to use equipment.

Getting ready

- Tie back hair, cover with a hairnet and wear a cookery apron or coat.
- Remove watch and jewellery.
- Cover cuts and wash hands before handling food and after using the toilet – you are now ready to start.

Preparation time (30 minutes)

- Display the examination number, task number and names of your selected dish/menu on your unit.
- Set the table. Organise the sink, cooking and serving areas. Organise bins/basins for rubbish.
- Organise the equipment and utensils.
- Place cutlery on a plate.
- Weigh ingredients accurately, put on plates, cover and place in the fridge if appropriate.
- Check with your teacher what preparation is to be done in advance (just in case in your enthusiasm you do too much!). **Remain calm** – you know exactly what to do; you have done this before in cookery class.
- Make sure you have your assignment sheets with you. Place the sheets in an appropriate place for the examiner to check.
- **Wear flat, comfortable shoes** during the examination.

> Do not over prepare. If you over prepare, you do not have an opportunity to show the examiner your skills during the examination, e.g. setting the oven temperature, peeling/slicing/dicing vegetables, grating cheese, lining baking tins.

The exam

- Listen carefully to the examiner's directions.
- Do not talk to or distract others during the exam.

Get started

- Wash your hands before beginning the assignment.
- Preheat the oven if necessary. Choose the correct cooking temperatures and cooking times. Line tins if necessary.
- Follow the time plan and recipe step by step. **Demonstrate good time management skills.**
- Follow the correct procedures for cutting, slicing, dicing, kneading, rolling, assembling and presenting dishes, etc. **Show your skills to the examiner.**
- Place any extra or leftover ingredients on a plate and cover as appropriate. **Show your economical approach** by wrapping and storing leftovers for future use.

> Dishes should be well presented, simply garnished and edible (not over- or undercooked).

- Observe all the kitchen hygiene and safety rules. **Show your hygienic work and safety practices.**
- **Show your environmental awareness skills** by separating waste and disposing of it correctly.
- Keep the table, cooker and sink tidy and clean.
- Place dirty cutlery and dishes neatly beside the sink. Wash up as you go along.

> Demonstrate safe and efficient use of appliances and equipment as you work.

- **Do not leave dishes unattended.** Check regularly. Watch that they are not undercooked or overcooked.
- Clean the edges of oven-to-table dishes before serving.
- Garnish or decorate the finished dish and serve.
- Fill out the Evaluation Sheet (check guidelines).
- Return all equipment to its correct place (once the examiner or teacher has checked it).

Avoid the following:

1. Over preparation.
2. Overuse of convenience foods.
3. Undercooking, e.g. poultry, fish, potatoes.
4. Overcooking, e.g. pasta, rice, vegetables.
5. Incorrect oven/hob temperatures.
6. Poor time management.
7. Inadequate seasoning.
8. Poor consistency of sauces and soups.

You need to comment on all problems on the evaluation sheets at the end of the exam.

What should you do if something goes wrong?

If something goes seriously wrong, e.g. glass breaks or you cut your fingers because a knife slips, let the examiner know immediately. Never be afraid to tell the examiner.

You will probably be able to deal with other problems yourself, e.g. heat was too high under the milk and it boiled over, the dish burnt in the oven.

Washing up guidelines

- Scrape, stack, wipe down table/cooker, wash, rinse, drain, dry and stack for examination by the teacher or examiner.

Presenting the finished dishes

- Serve dishes on clean plates (hot, chilled or cold, depending on the dish). Garnish or decorate.
- The serving area/table should be spotlessly clean.
- Put a spoon, knife and fork on another small plate. These can be used by the examiner when tasting the dish and checking its consistency. Leave a glass of water beside the plate for the examiner.
- Place the assignment and evaluation sheets neatly on the table for the examiner to read.

Tasting of dish by students

Taste the dish using clean cutlery and place used cutlery on a plate. Do not forget to taste food and adjust the seasoning.

Filling out the evaluation sheet

Comment on:

- Colour, appearance, presentation, taste and texture, consistency and doneness of the dish.
- Timing: How the time plan worked.
- Skills: Your preparation, cooking and serving skills.
- Problems: Any aspect of the assignment that went wrong at the exam (give the reason(s) why it happened and make suggestions as to how it could have been prevented).
- How well the dish fits the brief given and state why.
- Any changes that could be made to improve the dish.

Never complete the evaluation before the examination. Marks will not be given if this happens.

Watch your time. Allow sufficient time for filling out the evaluation sheet towards the end of the examination. One-word comments are not sufficient. You must give a proper comment that shows you have analysed what has happened.

Safety rules in exams or cookery classes

- Follow all safety guidelines given by the teacher.
- Always cut ingredients away from you.
- Know the safety rules if a fire breaks out.
- Know where the fire blanket and extinguisher are kept. Know the evacuation plan for the classroom.
- Walk in the kitchen, do not run.
- Know how to use all the equipment. Never use equipment without having a demonstration.
- Use oven gloves when removing hot dishes from the oven.
- Do not use any equipment that is faulty. Report faulty equipment to the teacher.
- Wipe up spills as they occur.
- Take care with steam from saucepans, kettles and casserole dishes.
- Do not leave the saucepan handles sticking out from the cooker.

After the exam

- Put food into suitable dishes to take home.
- Tidy up the kitchen, cooker and sink areas.
- Return dishes to their correct places.
- Leave everything spotlessly clean.

REMEMBER: There may well be other students using the kitchen in the afternoon or the following day for their practical cookery.

PART TWO

Consumer Studies

22 Consumer Education

- To define consumer education.
- To explain consumer terms and give examples.
- To categorise and give examples of consumer services.
- To explain needs, wants and luxuries.
- To list the factors that influence decision-making.
- To outline the steps involved in the decision-making process.

What is consumer education?

Consumer education provides consumers with the opportunity to:

- Develop decision-making skills in order to prioritise when choosing goods and services.
- Gain valuable information and skills to use in everyday situations.

What is a consumer?

A **consumer** is any person who buys and uses goods and services.

- Consumers pay for services and goods with money (cash, credit card, cheque and taxes).
- Consumers use the resources available to them (e.g. information, personal knowledge, money, time and skills) to achieve their goals.

What are services?

A **service** is work done for payment. Services are used, e.g. public transport.

What are goods?

Goods are consumed or worn, e.g. food, clothing.

What is an informed consumer?

An **informed consumer** is a person who knows their rights and responsibilities when they buy goods and services. An informed consumer should know about consumer laws, product labelling, quality, etc.

Consumer services

- **Local:** Doctor, dentist, dry cleaning.
- **State:** Education, health services, postal service.
- **Voluntary:** St Vincent de Paul, youth clubs, sports clubs.

- **Other services:** Gas, electricity, water, telephones, public library, public transport, roads, public lighting.
- **Direct services:** Local shops, cinemas, laundries, doctors.
- **Indirect services (paid for through taxes):** Roads, public lighting, libraries, public parks, schools, health services.

Characteristics of good service

- A friendly atmosphere.
- Clean, well-organised and efficient premises.
- Good facilities for people with disabilities.
- Helpful, friendly and efficient staff.
- Immediate attention.
- Short queues.

Goods used by consumers

- Books ● Central heating oil ● Food ● Furniture
- Houses ● Petrol ● Stereos ● Water for washing clothes.

> **LINK**
> Consumer protection (p. 159)

Needs, wants and luxuries

What is a need?

A **need** is something we must have to survive and live. **Examples:** Food, housing, warmth, clothing, water.

What is a want?

A **want** is something we desire but do not need to survive (e.g. holidays, CDs). Some wants might be considered to be needs by individuals, depending on their priorities (e.g. a car to get to work because there is no public transport). **Examples:** A holiday, an iPod, a laptop.

What is a luxury?

A **luxury** is not essential for survival. Luxuries are the extras in life that money can buy. Depending on the amount of money available, chocolate could be considered a luxury in some situations. **Examples:** Extra clothes, fillet steak, gold, expensive furniture and furnishings, two cars, new shrubs for the garden, magazines.

> **key point**
> Needs, wants and luxuries vary from family to family due to different circumstances, priorities and values.

Impulse buying

Impulse buying means buying an item on the spur of the moment without considering the consequences.

Factors influencing decision-making and consumer choices

We use our **decision-making skills** to make the best choice when selecting goods and services. Factors that influence us include:

- Priorities and values.
- Needs and wants.
- Resources available (money).
- Fashions, trends and environmental awareness.
- Family, peer pressure.
- Advertising, marketing, trends, sales techniques.

The decision-making process

1. Define the decision or the problem
2. Collect information (cost, size, etc.)
3. Consider the options or alternatives
4. Consider the consequence for each alternative
5. Make a decision/choice
6. Take action
7. Evaluate the outcome (positive or negative)

Be able to apply the decision-making process when answering questions to show that you have an awareness of consumer competence and management.

EXAM QUESTIONS AND SAMPLE ANSWERS

Higher Level 2007, Section A, Q.11 (4 marks)

Explain **each** of the following consumer terms.

(i) **Priority**: *A priority is something a person considers important to them.*

(ii) **Monopoly**: *This means that there is only one provider of a good or service. There are no other choices available.*

Ordinary Level 2008, Section A, Q.10 (5 marks)

List **two** basic human needs.

(i) Food. (ii) Shelter.

Higher Level 2007, Section B, Q.3 (a) and (b) (13 marks)

(a) What is a consumer? (5 marks)

> *A consumer is a person who buys and uses goods and services.*

(b) (i) Explain the difference between needs and wants. Give examples in your answer. (2 x 4 marks)

Note that questions in Section B incorporate information from different sections of the course. You must be able to apply information and knowledge.

> 1. *Needs are what we need to survive, e.g. food, water, clothing and shelter.*
> 2. *A want is something we desire but do not need to survive, e.g. holidays, CDs, an iPod, an iPhone.*

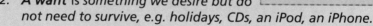

- To list consumer rights and responsibilities.
- To explain rights and responsibilities.
- To explain consumer terms.

What is a right?

A **right** is something to which you are entitled.

What is a responsibility?

A **responsibility** is something for which you are accountable.

Consumer rights and responsibilities

Consumer rights	Consumer responsibilities
Consumers have a right to:	**Consumers must:**
- Accurate information.	- Be informed, know consumer laws.
- Value for money.	- Examine goods and services.
- Choice.	- Read labels before using/buying.
- High standards of safety.	- Understand symbols and warnings on the labels.
- High standards of quality.	- Use the product according to the manufacturer's instructions and for the task intended.
- Redress (Replacement, repair or refund).	- Make a complaint when necessary.

Right to accurate information

Information provided must be accurate and clear. It must not be misleading or false. It is the consumer's responsibility to get the necessary information *before* buying a product/service.

Sources of consumer information and advice

When planning	When shopping	Agencies
- Newspapers, magazines	- Sales staff	- Consumer Association of Ireland
- Leaflets	- Examine the product brochure	- Office of Consumer Affairs
- Programmes on TV/radio	- Labels	- Citizens Information Centre
- Advertising	- Symbols on products	- Health Promotion Unit
- Friends (word of mouth)		- NSAI
- Exhibitions/showrooms		- European Consumer Centre

Right to value for money

The consumer pays the appropriate price for services and goods based on the true quality of the product. Sale items are only bargains when first-quality items are reduced in price and the consumer needs them.

Right to choice

Consumers are entitled to a variety of products and services provided by different manufacturers and providers who are in competition with each other.

If a company has a monopoly, they may not feel obliged to offer competitive prices.

> **key point**
>
> A monopoly is when there is only one provider of a good or service. There are no other options available.

Right to high standards of safety

Consumers are entitled to safe goods and services.

Right to high-quality goods/services

Consumers can make demands that raise quality and increase the range of goods and services.

> **LINK**
>
> Standards of safety (quality, safety and hazardous materials/substances) (pp. 166–68)

> **LINKS**
>
> Quality (pp. 166–67)
> Packaging and labelling (pp. 168–70)

Right of redress

A consumer may be entitled to a repair, replacement or a refund if an item or service bought is faulty or unsatisfactory, i.e. does not do the job for which it was intended.

It is the **consumer's responsibility** to know:

> **LINK**
>
> How to make a complaint (p. 160)

> **exam focus**
>
> Learn the terms associated with consumer studies and be able to give examples.

- Their rights and laws covering such rights.
- How to make a complaint.
- Where to go to make the complaint.

EXAM QUESTIONS AND SAMPLE ANSWERS

Higher Level 2007, Section A, Q.10 (4 marks)
List **four** state services paid for by taxation.
(i) Health services
(ii) Education
(iii) Roads
(iv) Gardaí

Higher Level 2006, Section A, Q.7 (4 marks)

List **four** sources of consumer information.

(i)   Billboards

(ii) Newspapers, magazines

(iii) Health Promotion Unit

(iv) Internet

Higher Level 2005, Section A, Q.9 (4 marks)

Give **two** features of a good-quality service.

(i)   Materials used should be of high quality and safe.

(ii) Providers should pay attention to care, diligence and safety.

Ordinary Level 2008, Section A, Q.7 (5 marks)

List **three** consumer rights.

(i)   Right to choice.

(ii) Right to honest information.

(iii) Right to value for money.

Ordinary Level 2008, Section A, Q.8 (5 marks)

What information does this symbol give to the consumer?

- *Doubly insulated symbol.*
- *It is a safety symbol.*
- *Found on small electrical appliances.*

Ordinary Level 2004, Section A, Q.6 (5 marks)

Choose the correct word from the following list to complete (i) and (ii) below.

Redress   Wants   Quality control

*(i)   Goods are tested during manufacturing. This is called **quality control**.*

*(ii) A consumer has the right to **redress** when an item is faulty.*

Higher Level 2007, Section B, Q.3 (c)(24 marks) (long question)

(a) Outline (i) **four** consumer rights and (ii) **four** consumer responsibilities. (24 marks)

  *(i) **Consumer rights** (4 x 3 marks)*

    *1. **Right to choice:** A variety of goods and services provides a selection and consumers can shop around for the best quality at the cheapest prices.*

    *2. **Right to accurate information:** Information given about goods and services must be true and honest.*

    *3. **Right to quality and value for money:** Items must be of merchantable quality.*

    *4. **Right to redress:** A consumer may be entitled to a repair, replacement or a refund if an item or service bought is faulty or unsatisfactory, i.e. does not do the job for which it was intended.*

(ii) **Consumer responsibilities** *(4 x 3 marks)*

1. *To be informed about prices, goods and services.*
2. *To follow the manufacturers' instructions.*
3. *To know consumer rights and consumer laws.*
4. *To make informed choices.*

Ordinary Level 2005, Section B, Q.3 (40 marks) (long question)

(a) What is a consumer? (8 marks)

A consumer is anyone who buys goods and services.

(b) List **three** rights and **three** responsibilities of a consumer. (18 marks)

Rights of a consumer (3 x 3 marks)

1. *Right to honest information.*
2. *Right to value for money.*
3. *Right to redress.*

Responsibilities of a consumer (3 x 3 marks)

1. *To know consumer laws.*
2. *Follow the manufacturer's instructions.*
3. *To read and understand labels.*

(c) (i) Name **one** agency that provides consumer information. (5 marks)

Consumer Association of Ireland.

(ii) Explain how the agency you have named protects consumers. (5 marks)

It carries out research and surveys and provides unbiased consumer information.

(d) Sketch a safety symbol a consumer would expect to find attached to an electric appliance.

Draw either the Double Insulation symbol or British Safety Standard symbol (see p. 167).

24 # Consumer Protection and Legislation

aims
- To list and describe the consumer laws.
- To define a guarantee, a quotation and an estimate.
- To outline the guidelines for making consumer complaints.
- To explain how to make a complaint in writing.
- To examine two consumer case studies.
- To list and explain statutory and non-statutory agencies.

Consumers are protected by:

- Legislation (laws and the courts).
- Statutory agencies (government agencies).
- Voluntary agencies.

Consumer laws/legislation

Consumer information act 1978

This Act states that it is an offence for providers of services or manufacturers of goods to:

- Advertise misleading or false claims about the price.
- Make misleading claims about price reductions.
- Create false claims about services or goods.
- Display an advert that might mislead consumers.

LINK
How to make a complaint (p. 160)

This Act is protected by the Office of the Director of Consumer Affairs.

Sale of goods and supply of services act 1980

This Act covers goods, services, guarantees and illegal signs. The Act states that **goods** should be:

- Of merchantable quality (in perfect condition).
- Fit or suitable for the task or purpose (can do the job).
- As described in the advert, on the label, etc.
- The same as samples displayed in the store.

Illegal signs

Shops may not put up notices that attempt to interfere with consumer rights.

Examples of unacceptable notices:

ONLY CREDIT NOTES GIVEN	NO REFUNDS GIVEN	NO LIABILITY FOR FAULTY GOODS

GOODS WILL NOT BE EXCHANGED

Provision of quality services

Consumers are entitled to have the service provided by suppliers using skilled or qualified staff and quality materials and paying attention to care, diligence and safety.

Guarantees, quotations and estimates

What is a guarantee?

A guarantee is a contract between the manufacturer and the buyer, but it can be extended to include a person who receives an item as a gift. Most guarantees have a time limit, e.g. one year from date of purchase.

What is meant by 'under a guarantee'?

Manufacturers state that all faults that develop during the period of the guarantee will be fixed or faulty goods will be replaced.

What is a quotation?

A quotation is a written, itemised, fixed price for a job.

What is an estimate?

An estimate is a general rough price for a job. It is not usually written down.

LINK
Consumer rights (p. 155)

Consumer action

LINK
Consumer responsibilities (p. 155)

Limiting consumer rights

Consumers can limit their own rights by not following the manufacturer's instructions or deciding that they do not like the colour, etc. when they get home.

Guidelines for making a complaint

1. Stop using the product, find the receipt.
2. Make the complaint as soon as possible.
3. Return the product and the receipt to the shop immediately.
4. Explain the complaint clearly and calmly.
5. If the assistant cannot help, ask to speak to the manager.
6. State what you want them to do.
7. Allow the seller/shop time to address your complaint.

key point

Know what you are entitled to when you return faulty goods to the shop. Solutions might involve a replacement, refund or repair. If the complaint is valid and is in breach of the consumer laws, a consumer is not obliged to accept a credit note.

General guidelines for complaining in writing

If the problem is not solved, put the complaint in writing to the manager or director, outlining clearly:

1. The item purchased (manufacturer's name, make and model).
2. The date of purchase.
3. A copy of the receipt of purchase.
4. The nature of the problem.
5. The return visit to the shop and the name of the person spoken to.
6. The action you expect the company to take.

key point

- Be polite at all times, whether complaining in person, by phone or in writing.
- Follow the guidelines and keep the original copy of the receipt and copies of letters written and received.
- Take note of the date of phone calls made to the company/shop, who you spoke with and the outcome.

Sample letter

> *Customer's address*
>
> *Date*
> *Name and address of shop*
>
> *Dear Sir/Madam,*
>
> *I wish to complain about a Hannon CD player that I bought in your shop on 12 January 2011. A copy of the receipt and guarantee are enclosed.*
>
> *While using it for the fourth time it made strange sounds and stopped working. Also, a favourite CD is stuck in the player. I followed the manufacturer's instructions in using it.*
>
> *I returned to the shop and the assistant refused to give me a refund, but offered to send it back to the manufacturer to be fixed.*
>
> *As there is a fault with the product, I am entitled to a refund of the cost of the CD player.*
>
> *Yours faithfully,*
>
> *Maria Jones*

Taking further action

If the visit to the shop and the letter do not produce a satisfactory solution, the consumer may have to consider contacting the relevant consumer organisation and taking legal action.

HL

Case study type of exam question

Kate bought a new iron and discovered when using the iron for the first time it was leaking.

(a) List the **steps** Kate should follow when returning the faulty iron to the electrical shop.

1. *Bring the iron in its packaging, the receipt as proof of purchase and the guarantee back to the shop.*

2. *Go to the customer services desk if there is one or to the shop assistant who sold the iron.*

3. *State your case, what happened and what you expect them to do about it.*

(b) Name **two** agencies/organisations Kate could contact if the store refuses to accept responsibility for the faulty iron.

1. *Consumers' Association of Ireland.*

2. *Small Claims Court.*

(c) Write a letter of complaint for Kate to send to one of the organisations you have named.

Kate's address

Date

Consumers' Association of Ireland

Address

Dear Sir/Madam,

I wish to complain about Murray's Electrical Shop, where I bought an Arrow iron that I discovered was leaking when using the iron for the first time. I followed the manufacturer's instructions when using it.

I bought the iron in Murray's Electrical Shop on 5 May 2011. I enclose a copy of the receipt and guarantee.

I returned to the shop and the assistant offered to send it back to the manufacturer to be fixed. As there is a fault with the product and it was not fit for its purpose, I am entitled to a full refund of the cost of the iron. Please advise me of the next step I should take.

Yours faithfully,

Kate Redmond

(d) What conditions are outlined in the Sale of Goods and Supply of Services Act 1980?

1. *Goods must be:*
   - *Of merchantable quality.*
   - *Fit for their purchase.*

- *As described.*
- *Exactly the same as the sample.*

2. *Redress must be available.*

3. *A service must be provided by suppliers using skilled or qualified staff and quality materials and paying attention to care, diligence and safety.*

Be prepared for similar types of questions about other types of products, e.g. CD player, a jumper or coat, shoes or runners, and just apply the knowledge you have gained in relation to making complaints.

Case study type of exam question

You are going on holiday and plan to buy a new camera.

(a) List **four** guidelines you should follow when buying the new camera.

   1. Consider the budget. How much can I afford to spend?

   2. Choose a reliable shop that specialises in cameras.

   3. Consider the quality of the camera.

   4. What are the terms of the guarantee?

(b) List **two** sources of information which would help in making the choice.

   1. Family and friends who are interested in photography.

   2. Brochures.

(c) Name **two** methods of paying for the camera.

   1. Cash. 2. Laser card.

(d) Why are receipts important?

   1. They are proof of purchase.

   2. A receipt is needed if you want to exchange items.

(e) List **four** points of information that you should find on the receipt for the camera.

   1. Date and time of purchase.

   2. Name of the camera shop.

   3. Cost of the camera.

   4. Name of the camera.

Statutory and non-statutory agencies

(HL) Statutory

Comhairle	Operates the Citizen Information Agencies.
European Consumer Centre	Walk-in advice centre that provides consumers with information about rights and protection in Ireland and the EU.
Office of the Director of Consumer Affairs	<ul><li>Informs the public of consumer rights.</li><li>Enforces consumer legislation.</li><li>Controls standards of advertising.</li><li>Monitors safety standards.</li></ul>
Small Claims Court	<ul><li>Deals with consumer complaints in relation to poor service, faulty goods, inadequate workmanship, etc.</li><li>Is inexpensive, only a small fee charged (€15).</li><li>Fast process.</li><li>No need to employ a solicitor; procedure is less formal.</li><li>Values of claims = up to €2,000.</li></ul>
The Ombudsman	<ul><li>Is appointed by the government.</li><li>Provides help for consumers who wish to make complaints against a government agency, e.g. An Post, Health Boards.</li><li>Makes recommendations.</li></ul>

Non-statutory (voluntary)

Advertising Standards Authority of Ireland	<ul><li>A voluntary body that makes sure all advertisements are truthful, legal and decent.</li><li>Investigates consumer complaints.</li></ul>
Consumers' Association of Ireland	<ul><li>Is a non-profit voluntary organisation.</li><li>Carries out research and surveys.</li><li>Provides unbiased consumer information.</li><li>Produces a magazine, *Consumer Choice*.</li><li>Aims to improve consumer legislation.</li></ul>
Trade associations	<ul><li>Encourage higher standards among their members.</li><li>Members must follow a code of practice.</li><li>Examples:<ul><li>Licensed Vintners Association.</li><li>RGDATA (grocers/shopkeepers).</li></ul></li></ul>

Citizen Information Centres

- A network of Citizen Information Centres provide face-to-face contact to the public.
- Centres are run by volunteers.
- Centres are supported and funded by the Citizens Information Board.

exam focus

When answering questions on statutory and non-statutory agencies, ensure you give the **correct name** and **list their functions clearly**. Do not waffle or produce essay-type answers.

EXAM QUESTIONS AND SAMPLE ANSWERS

Higher Level 2006, Section A, Q.10 (4 marks)

Give **two** advantages of the Small Claims Court procedure.

(i) Inexpensive; only a small fee is charged.

(ii) There is no need to employ a solicitor, as the procedure is less formal.

Higher Level 2005, Section A, Q.7 (4 marks)

What is the function of the Office of the Ombudsman?

The Ombudsman deals with complaints made by consumers about government agencies or public services, e.g. An Post.

Higher Level 2008, Section A, Q.7 (4 marks)

Outline the function of the National Consumer Agency.

1. Informs the consumer of rights.

2. Monitors advertising.

Higher Level 2008, Section A, Q.10 (4 marks)

List **four** items of information that should be included in a letter of complaint to a retailer.

(i)   Consumer's name, address and date.

(ii) Copy of receipt and guarantee.

(iii) Nature of complaint.

(iv) Action the consumer expects the retailer to take.

Higher Level 2007, Section A, Q.9 (4 marks)

Give **two** functions of the Consumers' Association of Ireland.

(i) Publishes the Consumer Choice magazine.

(ii) Provides the consumer with information, e.g. leaflets, websites.

Ordinary Level 2002, Section A, Q.8 (5 marks)

Choose the correct word from the following list to complete (i) and (ii).

budget, consumer, credit note, guarantee

(i) A consumer is a person who buys or uses a product or service.

(ii) A guarantee is a contract between the manufacturer and consumer.

Higher Level 2007, Section B, Q.3 (d) (14 marks) (long question)

(d) Name **two** consumer laws and explain how each protects the consumer. (2 x 7 marks)

1. **The Consumer Information Act** *1978 states that it is an offence for providers of services or manufacturers of goods to make false or misleading claims about good, services or prices. This Act is protected by the Office of the Director of Consumer Affairs.*

2. **The Sale of Goods and Supply of Services Act** *1980 covers goods, services, guarantees and illegal signs. This Act states that goods should be:*

   *   *Of merchantable quality (in perfect condition).*
   *   *Fit or suitable for the task or purpose (can do the job).*
   *   *As described in the advert, on the label, etc.*
   *   *The same as samples displayed in the store.*

   Services: *Consumers are entitled to have the service provided by suppliers using skilled or qualified staff and quality materials and paying attention to care, diligence and safety.*

25 Quality, Packaging and Labelling

Quality

Quality guarantees that services and goods are of a high standard.

Quality control

Quality control or testing is carried out by the manufacturers of goods and providers of services to assure the consumer of the quality.

Quality management

Quality management encourages manufacturers and providers of services to continually improve their products and services to meet consumer demands.

> **key point**
>
> Good-quality goods are suitable for their purpose, of good design and are long-lasting.

Quality marks

Name of symbol	Symbol	Where is it found?
Approved Quality System/Quality Irish		Awarded to Irish businesses and services
Guaranteed Irish		High-quality goods manufactured in Ireland
Irish Standards Mark	QUALITY I.S. EN ISO 9001:2008 NSAI Certified	Goods of high quality

Name of symbol	Symbol	Where is it found?
Kitemark (BSI)		Goods of high quality and safety standards
National Standards Authority of Ireland	NSAI	Granted under license to products that meet the NSAI regulations

LINK
Textiles (care labels) (p. 299)

Textiles (care labels) (p. 299)

key point

BSI is the British Standards Institute mark.

Safety symbols, marks and logos

Name of symbol	Symbol	Where is it found?
Communauté Européenne (CE)	C E	Toys, electrical goods
Double Insulated		Electrical appliances, e.g. hairdryers
Irish Mark of Electrical Conformity	Electrical Safety **NSAI Certified**	Electrical goods

Hazardous substances or materials

Name of substance	Symbol	Where is it found?
Corrosive		Some chemicals
Flammable		Furniture polish
Harmful and irritant		Bleach

Name of substance	Symbol	Where is it found?
Toxic	☠	Garden chemicals

Packaging

Purposes of packaging

- Helps to sell a product, advertises the product.
- Protects the products and prevents damage.
- Contains information, instructions and bar code.
- Preserves foods and keeps them fresh.

Types, advantages and disadvantages of packaging

Types	Advantages	Disadvantages
Cans	<ul><li>Can be recycled</li><li>Hygienic</li></ul>	<ul><li>Can rust</li><li>Danger of food contamination</li></ul>
Glass	<ul><li>Strong</li><li>Hygienic</li><li>Easy to clean</li><li>Can be recycled</li></ul>	<ul><li>Can break easily</li><li>Dangerous if it splinters</li></ul>
Paper	<ul><li>Variety of uses</li><li>Can be recycled</li><li>Biodegradable</li><li>Clean</li></ul>	<ul><li>Not strong</li></ul>
Plastic	<ul><li>Variety available</li><li>Can be recycled</li><li>Easy to clean</li><li>Strong</li></ul>	<ul><li>Can taint food</li><li>Non-biodegradable</li></ul>

key point

Aerosols are dangerous and add to the destruction of the ozone layer. If heated, they will explode and cause serious damage.

key point

Packaging should be environmentally friendly and reusable.

Uses of packaging

Foods	Packaging
Bread	Unwrapped, in plastic covers or wax paper
Cereals	Waxed paper
Cream	Plastic tubs
Eggs	Paper or plastic cartons
Jams	Glass jars
Juices	Lined wax paper cartons, glass, cans
Milk	Lined wax cartons, glass
Sauces	Waxed sachets, glass jars, cans

Problems of over-packaging

Problems include:

- Use of limited natural resources.
- Not environmentally friendly.
- Adds to waste and litter.
- Increased price of products.

> **LINK**
> Food storage (packaging for foods) (pp. 70–2)

Consumer response to over-packaging

- Refuse packaged goods and plastic bags/containers.
- Buy/choose loose items.
- Reuse containers.
- Recycle everything.

Labelling

Labels should be easy to read, clear, honest and in the language of the country the item is being sold in.

Examples of labels

- Instructions (appliances, cooking).
- Food labelling.
- Care labelling (caring for clothes).
- Date stamping (best before, use by, expiry date).
- Quality and safety labels.
- Government health warnings (smoking kills).

> **key point**
>
> The Food Safety Authority of Ireland (FSAI) is responsible for legislation related to food labelling.

Food labelling: information found on packaged foods

- Name of product.
- List of ingredients (in descending order).
- Net quantity.
- Country of origin.
- Name and address of the manufacturer, packer or seller.
- Instructions for storage.
- Instructions for cooking.
- Date stamp.

> **LINK**
>
> Eggs (packaging and labelling) – check out the label on foods in your kitchen at home (p. 117)

Food labelling: information found on non-packaged foods

- Name of the food (on food or shelf).
- Price per kilo.
- Country of origin, variety and class for fruit and vegetables.

> **LINKS**
>
> Revise the following:
>
> - Shopping (bar codes, price labelling) (p. 181)
> - Caring for textiles (care labelling) (pp. 299–301)
> - Technology (energy labels) (p. 249)
> - Quality and safety symbols (pp. 166–68)
> - Environmental issues (recycling symbols) (p. 271)

Reasons for labelling food

1. To inform consumers about the item.
2. To give nutritional information.
3. To give storage instructions.
4. To give cooking instructions.

SAMPLE EXAM QUESTION, HIGHER LEVEL, SECTION B (LONG QUESTION)

'Packaging adds to the consumer's weekly bill and is wasteful of natural resources.'

(a) List **four** reasons why food is packaged.
  1. Packaging protects food from contamination.
  2. Packaging on food carries nutritional information, storage and cooking instructions.
  3. Packaging makes it easier to transport and store food.
  4. Packaging helps to sell foods.

(b) List **three** characteristics of good packaging.
  Good packaging should be:
  1. Strong and durable.
  2. Waterproof.
  3. Biodegradable.

(c) Give **four** types of packaging and state a different use for each type.

Types	Use
(i) Waxed paper	Sliced bread
(ii) Glass jars	Jams
(iii) Aluminium foil trays	Freezing prepared meals
(iv) Plastic tubs	Cream

(d) List **five** items of information that are on the label of packaged foods.

1. Name of product.
2. List of ingredients (in descending order).
3. Country of origin.
4. Name and address of manufacturer, packer or seller.
5. Instructions for storage and cooking.

(e) List **four** disadvantages of over-packaging.

1. Wastes valuable natural resources.
2. Increases the cost of the item.
3. Can deceive the consumer.
4. Adds to waste and litter.

EXAM QUESTIONS AND SAMPLE ANSWERS

Higher Level 2007, Section A, Q.7 (4 marks)

(a) What information does this symbol give to the consumer?

- British Standards Institute Safety Mark (BSI Safety Mark).
- Found on items that have reached a specific safety standard.

(b) Name **one** item on which it is found.

Gas appliance [or electric appliance].

Higher Level 2004, Section A, Q.7 (4 marks)

What information does this symbol convey to the consumer?

- Doubly insulated.

Higher Level 2003, Section A, Q.8 (4 marks)

What information does this symbol convey to the consumer?

- This symbol indicates that the product can be recycled.

26 Budgeting and Money Management

aims

- To define budgeting and money management terms.
- To outline the principles/system for money management.
- To list the rules for planning a personal budget.
- To outline the rules for planning a household budget.
- To list the advantages of budgeting.
- To state the advantages and disadvantages of saving money.
- To identify the advantages and disadvantages of buying on credit.
- To list the benefits of a home filing system.
- To learn money management principles and be able to apply them.

Definitions

A budget is a personal plan for saving and spending money. It balances income and expenditure.

Deductions are PAYE (taxes), PRSI and voluntary deductions (pension, health or saving schemes, etc.).

Expenditure is money spent out of income. Examples are rent, mortgage, food, clothing, energy and entertainment.

Gross income is income earned before tax and other items are deducted.

Income is the money earned from work done and from investments.

Income tax, PAYE (Pay As You Earn), is taken out of gross income by employers and the tax is used by the government to pay for a variety of state services.

Net income is the money left after deductions.

PRSI (Pay Related Social Insurance) is deducted from your income and used to pay for benefits if you are unable to work due to injury or ill health or if you lose your job.

Tax credits is a system used by the Revenue Commissioners to calculate the amount of tax to be paid by workers.

Voluntary deductions include private pension schemes, health insurance, savings and salary protection insurance.

Money management system

A good money manager will:

1. Decide on the goal.
2. Look at the resources available (time, skills, money).
3. Plan and write up the budget.
4. Put the budget into action.

5. Evaluate the budget and make adjustments.

6. Make out a new budget.

Steps in planning a personal budget

1. Identify personal needs and priorities.

2. List all sources of income (weekly, monthly).

3. List expenditure, expenses and savings (weekly, monthly).

4. Add all the columns to see the totals.

5. Examine income and expenditure results.

6. Make out a budget.

7. Put the budget into action.

8. Evaluate the results.

Write the budget down using a table/chart that shows what is happening on a weekly and monthly basis.

When planning personal or household budgets, list:

- **What you know,** e.g. what you earn, what you spend.

- **What you must decide**, e.g. priorities based on needs, wants and luxuries, arrangements for saving each week/month, what you will spend your money on.

LINKS
Gross income (p. 172)
Net income (p. 172)
Voluntary deductions (p. 172)

Skills needed when budgeting

- Decision-making ● Financial
- Management ● Problem-solving ● Research.

Examining a budget

When examining a budget, ask the following questions:

- Do income and expenditure balance?
- Have you overspent?
- Did you borrow money or use an overdraft facility?
- Did you save money?
- Do you need to reorganise spending?

LINK
Consumer education (decision-making) (p. 154)

Planning a household budget

1. List all the family needs.

2. List all the sources of family income.

3. List all expenditure (fixed, irregular, variable).

4. Examine income and expenditure.

5. Make out the budget.

When planning any budget, write it down.

6. Put the budget into action.

7. Evaluate the results.

key point

Revise budgets regularly.

Examples of expenditure

Regular (monthly, annual)	Regular (daily/weekly)	Occasional
Rent/mortgage	Food	Clothing
Insurances	Transport	Gifts
Savings	Pocket money	Entertainment
Electricity		Household
TV licence		Holidays

Advantages of budgeting

- Security, reduces financial worries.
- Income and expenditure will be balanced.
- Prevents overspending on wants and luxuries.
- Arrangement for larger bills can be made (electricity).
- Encourages saving for seasonal spending (Christmas).
- Encourages saving for holidays, a 'rainy day', education.
- Budgeting is a good discipline for all the family.
- Budgeting controls the use of ATM cards.

exam focus

Learn six key advantages of budgeting for the exam from this list.

Savings

- Places to save include credit unions, banks and building societies.
- Check ease of withdrawal, interest rates, security and conditions.

LINK

Family budgets must be revised regularly and be flexible in order to cope with bills and changing family needs.

Advantages	Disadvantages
Interest is earned.	Must not touch 'rainy day' savings for wants and luxuries, e.g. holidays.
No debt to cause stress.	
Price may be cheaper than buying on credit.	

Buying on credit

- Means 'buy now, pay later'.
- Examples include credit cards, loans, hire purchase and overdrafts.

Advantages	Disadvantages
Use of item before it is paid for.	Cost more than cash.
Large items would take too long to save for, e.g. house.	Interest is paid.
	Consumers may buy more than they can afford.

Home filing system

A good home filing system is:

- Used for storing bills, receipts and guarantees.
- Useful when planning budgets, as documents are easy to find.

Examples

- Filing cabinets • Folders • Any medium-sized box.

EXAM QUESTIONS AND SAMPLE ANSWERS

Higher Level 2003, Section A, Q.10 (4 marks)

Give **two** advantages of using a household filing system. (4 marks)

1. Useful when planning a budget.

2. Makes it easier to monitor income and spending.

Higher Level 2003, Section A, Q.11 (4 marks)

List **four** essential expenses that should be considered when planning a household budget.

1. Mortgage/rent.

2. Food.

3. Electricity.

4. Savings.

Ordinary Level 2007, Section A, Q.10 (5 marks)

List **three** major expenses which should be included in a household budget.

(i)   Food.

(ii) Clothes/shoes.

(iii) Insurance.

Ordinary Level 2007, Section A, Q.8 (5 marks)

List **three** types of credit available when buying goods.

(i)   Credit card.

(ii) Interest-free credit.

(iii) Hire purchase.

Higher Level 2008, Section B, Q.3 (55 marks) (long question)

(a) In relation to income, explain the difference between statutory deductions and voluntary deductions. Give one example of each type of deduction. (8 marks)

Deductions	What they mean (4 marks)	Examples (2 x 2 marks)
Statutory	*Deductions taken from gross income by the government.*	*PAYE (PRSI, pension levy)*
Voluntary	*Deductions taken from gross income at the discretion of the employee.*	*Health insurance (savings schemes)*

HL

(b) Explain the term **'tax credit'**. (5 marks)

This is the part of a person's income that is not taxed by the government.

(c) State the advantages of budgeting. (3 x 3 marks)

1. Provides financial security.

2. Reduces stress and worries about money.

3. Helps balance income and expenditure.

(d) (i) Discuss **five** points that should be considered when planning a household budget. (5 x 3 marks)

1. List all sources of family income.

2. List all essential expenditure and allocate money to each expense.

3. Allocate money to savings and emergencies, e.g. household problems such as burst pipes.

4. Allocate money for seasonal spending, e.g. Christmas.

5. Balance income and expenditure and reduce expenses if necessary.

(ii) Plan a household budget based on an average weekly income. (5 x 2 marks)

Housing	25%
Food	25%
Household expenses	15%
Personal expenses	10%
Entertainment	10%
Education	5%
Emergencies	5%
Savings	5%

(e) Outline ways to ensure **'value for money'** when shopping. (4 x 2 marks)

1. Make a shopping list (and keep to it).

2. Shop around.

3. Check out special offers.

4. Compare products.

Ordinary Level 2008, Section B, Q.3 (40 marks) (long question)

(a) Tick (✔) the correct answer. (3 marks)

A budget is:

(i) The part of the income that is not taxed

(ii) *A money management plan* ✔

(iii) To buy now and pay later

(b) Give **two** reasons why it is important to save money. (2 x 2 marks)

(i) Reduces financial stress and worries.

(ii) Interest is earned on the money saved.

(c) (i) Name **two** different places where a consumer can save money.
(2 x 3 marks)

1. Credit Union

2. Bank

(ii) List the guidelines that should be followed when choosing a place to save. (3 x 3 marks)

1. Check the interest rate on offer.

2. Check the rules about the withdrawal of money.

3. Check the opening hours.

(d) State **two** disadvantages of borrowing money. (2 x 3 marks)

(i) Encourages consumers to overspend.

(ii) Inability to make repayments.

(e) Describe **three** methods used in the shops to encourage customers to spend more money. (3 x 4 marks)

(i)   Pleasant music and aromas.

(ii) Special offers, e.g. buy one, get one free.

(iii) Essentials are placed at the back of the supermarket.

exam focus

Note that different sections of consumer studies have been integrated in this question. Be ready to use the knowledge you gained in other chapters.

27 Shopping, Advertising and Marketing

aims

- To describe and evaluate different types of outlets.
- To identify differences between self-service and counter service shops.
- To list techniques used to encourage consumer spending.
- To list guidelines for shopping.
- To define shopping terms.
- To explain bar codes.
- To list and discuss methods of paying bills.
- To state the functions of advertising.
- To list advantages and disadvantages of advertising.
- To explain marketing and market research techniques.

Shopping

Each local area provides consumers with a variety of shops. Some areas have more variety than others.

Questions to ask when choosing items

1. Know your budget – can you pay for it?

2. Is the item good value for money?

3. Will it do the job for which it is intended?

4. Is it eco-friendly?

5. Is it well designed and durable?

6. Does it conform to safety standards?

7. Will it be easy to clean and maintain?

> **LINK**
> Consumer education (decision-making process) (p. 154)

Types of shops and outlets

Some large shops are found only in cities or large towns. Smaller shops may be located in suburban or rural areas. Chain shops may be found in larger towns and cities.

Types	Description	Examples
Supermarkets	• Self-service outlets stocking food and small household items. • Own-brand products are available.	Superquinn SuperValu

Types	Description	Examples
Department stores	• Large shopping areas divided into a number of smaller areas or units, each selling particular products or brands of similar products. • Products include clothing, cosmetics, furniture and fabrics. • Provide toilet and restaurant facilities.	Arnotts Clerys
Multi-chain stores	• Retail chains are located around the country, each providing the same range of goods arranged in the same way.	Dunnes Stores Marks & Spencer Penneys
Independent chain shops	• Shops belonging to this group are independently or individually owned. • They are small grocery shops and supermarkets.	Spar Centra
Hypermarkets	• Large warehouse buildings selling a vast range of goods. • They are generally situated in the suburbs.	Popular in other EU countries, e.g. Carrefour in France
Specialist shops	• These shops sell a specific category of goods, e.g. bread and cakes, crafts, jewellery, books, shoes.	Ethnic food stores Clothing boutiques
Discount shops	• Provide consumers with a range of goods that are reduced in price.	Euro shops

Specialist ethnic food stores

These stores supply authentic foods from different countries to cater for those who have come to live in Ireland from other countries and continents (e.g. African, Chinese, Polish, Russian).

Other shopping outlets

- Auction rooms • Door-to-door selling • Mail order • Markets
- Online shopping (internet) • Parties • Vending machines.

Self-service shops

Advantages	Disadvantages
• Convenient and fast.	• Impersonal compared to smaller shops.
• Quick turnover, foods fresher.	• Queues frequently occur.
• Goods well displayed and easy to see.	• Most foods are prepacked.
• Large range of goods.	• Danger of impulse buying.
• Own brands are cheap.	• Credit available only with credit cards.
• Lower prices due to bulk buying and lower overheads.	• You have to pack your own items.

Counter service shops

Advantages	Disadvantages
• Personal, friendly service by people known to the consumer.	• Smaller variety of goods.
• Credit facilities on offer in some small shops.	• Displays of goods limited.
• Advice is freely given.	• Higher overheads result in higher prices.
• Open late and on Sundays.	• Can be time-consuming to shop.

exam focus

Be able to compare self-service shops with counter service shops.

Techniques to encourage consumer spending

- Attractive background music.
- Interesting colours.
- Aroma of freshly cooked foods (breads, meats, etc.).
- Wide aisles for ease of movement around the shop.
- Essentials are at the back of the shop or on lower shelves.
- You pass luxury items to get to essentials.
- Luxury goods positioned at eye level or just above.
- Sweets, magazines and special offers at the checkouts.
- Food sampling on late-night opening.
- Large trolleys to hold a great range of items.

LINK
Marketing (pp. 182–83)

exam focus

Remember to learn six key techniques from this list for your exam.

General guidelines for shopping

1. Never shop for food when you are hungry.
2. Make a shopping list for the week and stick to the list.
3. Demand quality and a good after-sales service.
4. Shop around and be familiar with the goods available.
5. Compare prices, weights and date stamping.
6. Do not buy damaged foods or goods.

key point

Choose food shops that are hygienic and well organised, where foods are stored correctly and where staff follow personal and food hygiene laws.

Shopping terms

- **Bulk Buying:** Consumers buy goods in large amounts because they are cheaper. However, they are not good value for money if you do not need them.
- **Loss Leaders:** To encourage people to come into a particular shop, goods are sold at a loss in the hope that they will complete their shopping there.
- **Own Brands:** Some outlets sell products with their own name on them in simple packaging. They are generally cheaper than branded products.
- **Unit Pricing:** Fruits, vegetables, cheese and some other foods are sold according to cost per unit weight.

Other terms:

- Bar codes • Credit • Date stamping • Hire purchase
- Receipts • Stock control • Store cards • Store clubs.

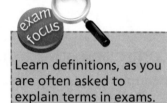

Learn definitions, as you are often asked to explain terms in exams.

Bar codes

A bar code is a series of bars and spaces printed on items that are read by electronic scanners. It helps the:

- Retailer with stock control.
- Buyer to see exactly what they bought.
- Checkout assistant to process items quickly.

LINK
Labelling (pp. 169–70)

Methods of paying bills

- Cash
- Credit card (Visa, MasterCard)
- Cheque and cheque card
- ATM card (Pass, Banklink)
- Debit card (Laser).

LINK
Budgeting and money
management (pp. 172–75)

Consumers and advertising

Advertising is used to sell goods and services. It carries a message for the consumer.

Functions of advertising

- To sell products or services.
- To promote new products and make them popular.
- To create a healthy, environmentally friendly image.
- To promote the company.
- To increase sales.

Advantages and disadvantages of advertising

Advantages	Disadvantages
• Provides information.	• Cost of advertising is included in the cost of the product.
• Creates interest in goods and services.	• Intrudes into people's lives, targets different age groups.
• Sells goods and services.	
• Encourages competition and may reduce prices of certain items.	• Can reinforce stereotyping.
• Provides employment.	• Creates a desire in people to buy products they cannot afford or do not need.
• Source of information for those buying, selling, renting or leasing.	
	• Encourages consumerism and dissatisfaction with life.

Controlling advertising standards

Control is exercised by a **voluntary organisation**, the Advertising Standards Authority for Ireland.

Legal control is exercised by:

- The Employment Equality Act 1977.
- The Consumer Information Act 1978.
- The EC Misleading Advertising Directive.

Popular advertising media/outlets

- Media (TV, radio, magazines, newspapers).
- Billboards and cinema ads.
- Sponsorship of public events and free products, e.g. key rings, pens.
- Bus shelters, buses, trains.
- Direct mail through the post.
- Internet sites, mobile devises.

> **LINK**
> Labelling (pp. 169–70)

Images used in advertising

> exam focus
>
> It is enough to learn six points.

- Music, bright colours and catchy phrases.
- Humour, comedy.
- The perfect family, healthy outdoor people.
- Romance, glamorous people.
- Luxurious lifestyle, idyllic locations.
- Environmental considerations.

Marketing

What is marketing?

Marketing uses the information gathered from market/consumer research to design advertisements to target the right group of consumers. Its main aim is to sell goods and services.

What Is market research?

To find out what people like, market research companies carry out surveys for advertisers. Sometimes questionnaires are used as part of a survey to gather information.

Market research gathers information on favourite:

- Clothes • Colours • Designers • Foods • Holiday destinations
- Leisure activities • Products • Restaurants • TV shows/films/music, etc.

Market research techniques

Selected samples of consumers are:

- Interviewed on the street or by phone.
- Surveyed individually by post.
- Surveyed personally (on the street, by phone).

Marketing techniques to encourage consumers to spend money

- Attractive packaging.
- Merchandising.
- Promotions, e.g. in-store, magazine.
- Special offers and free gifts.
- Unusual shop/window displays.

> **LINKS**
> Shopping (pp. 178–81)
> Packaging (p. 168)
> Labelling (pp. 169–171)

EXAM QUESTIONS AND SAMPLE ANSWERS

Sample exam question:
List **four** changes in how shops operate today.
1. Increase in customer loyalty schemes.
2. Shops open late and on Sundays, some are open 24 hours.
3. Shopping can be ordered online.
4. Delivery services available.
Higher Level 2008, Section A, Q.9 (4 marks)
Give **two** advantages of advertising.
(i)   Provides information on products, services and events.
(ii) Increases awareness and sales.
Ordinary Level 2008, Section A, Q.9 (5 marks)
Give **four** methods of advertising.
(i)   Media, e.g. TV, radio.
(ii) Billboards.
(iii) Internet.
(iv) Carrier bags with the shop's logo.

HL

Higher Level 2006, Section B, Q.3 (55 marks) (long question)

(a) Describe **each** of the following types of shopping outlets. (16 marks)

  (i) **Supermarkets**: *These are large self-service shops that sell food, newspapers and magazines, clothing, household goods and in some cases electrical goods.*
  Examples: Dunnes Stores, SuperValu, Tesco.

  (ii) **Department stores**: *These are large stores with a variety of individual departments (shoes, clothing, bags, household) in the same shop. Some stores sell electrical goods.*
  Examples: Arnotts, Clerys, Brown Thomas.

  (iii) **Specialist shops**: *These are shops that sell one product, e.g. shoes, electrical goods, breads.*

  (iv) Independent shops: *Family-owned shops, e.g. the local grocery, newsagent or chemist.*

(b) **List the guidelines** that should be followed when shopping for goods and services. (12 marks)

  1. Make a shopping list and stick to it.

  2. Shop around and compare prices.

  3. Keep receipts.

  4. Avoid over-packaging (be environmentally friendly).

(c) (i) Name **three** methods of payment that can be used when shopping.

    1. Cash.

    2. Credit card.

    3. Laser card.

  (ii) Give **one** advantage and **one** disadvantage of **each** method listed. (12 marks)

Method of payment	Advantage	Disadvantage
Credit card	Buy now, pay later.	High interest if bill is not paid on time.
Laser card	Money taken out of account directly.	Must have money in the account.
Cheque	Do not have to carry cash.	Need banker's card.

(d) Explain the benefit to the consumer of **each** of the following. (9 marks)

  (i) **Unit pricing**: *Consumers are able to compare prices of similar products, e.g. price per gram/kilogram.*

  (ii) **Keeping a receipt**: *Receipts are proof of purchase in case you need to return the goods for refund or exchange.*

  (iii) **Own-brand goods**: *Quality, cheaper foods made by larger supermarkets, e.g. Dunnes, SuperValu.*

PART THREE

Social and Health Studies

28 The Family

- To define the term 'family'.
- To list the types of families.
- To list the functions of a family.
- To identify factors influencing family life. **HL**
- To summarise the roles of family members.
- To describe relationships within the family.
- To explain what is meant by good communications skills.

What is a family?

A **family** is a social group of people related by blood, by marriage or by adoption. Families can be made up of adults, teenagers, elderly people, toddlers and babies.

Types of family

- A **nuclear family** consists of parents and children.
- An **extended family** consists of parents, children and other relatives, e.g. grandparent, aunts, uncles, cousins.
- **Single-parent or lone-parent families** have one parent and child/children.
- A **blended family** consists of two adults from other marriages/relationships and their children.

Functions of a family

The family satisfies the basic needs of the individuals in the family:

- Emotional needs (love, support and security).
- Physical needs (food, clothing, shelter, protection).
- Economic needs (money and belongings).

key point

The adults in the house may be biological parents, step-parents, guardians or other relatives, e.g. older siblings, grandparents.

key point

Parents may live on their own with children because they are divorced, separated or widowed.

Factors influencing family life

Cultural factors	Social factors	Economic factors
• Language • Media • Race • Religion • Rural/urban • Traditions	• Educational opportunities • Employment • Family background • Family size • Lifestyle	• Marriage breakdown • Cost of living • Income/salary • Unemployment

Roles within the family

Relationships exist between all family members, extended family members and friends.

key point

Provision must be made for children with special physical and emotional needs.

What is a role?

A **role** can be defined as the right way to behave within the family (acceptable and appropriate behaviour).

LINK

Adolescence (gender, gender role, gender equality) (pp. 187–88; 191)

Role of children

Childhood is generally a time free of responsibilities, allowing time for play. Children have few responsibilities.

Their main roles are:

- Helping with smaller tasks, e.g. setting the table, making their beds, putting dishes into the dishwasher.
- Behaving well, being polite and doing as they are told (go to bed, etc.).

Rights of children

Children have a right to:

- Love, care, security and understanding.
- A safe, secure and healthy environment.
- Protection from neglect, abuse and cruelty.
- Education.
- Freedom from discrimination.

Role of adolescents

As adolescents move from childhood dependence towards adulthood, there are many physical and emotional changes that take place. Adolescents may be confused about their role. Teenagers try to make parents aware of these changes as they try to become more independent. This sometimes causes conflict.

Adolescents' main roles may be:

- Taking on more responsibilities, e.g. household chores, babysitting younger siblings.
- Playing with younger siblings.
- Helping younger siblings with homework.

LINK
Adolescence (pp. 191–95)

Role of parents

Parents have a very responsible role in the family. Some of their roles are:

- Setting a good example for their children.
- Providing for the basic needs of their children.
- Creating a happy home environment.
- Teaching their children right from wrong.
- Listening to their children.
- Providing advice and guidance.
- Being supportive of each other.

Relationships in the family

The word 'relationship' describes how we get on with others. Relationships are influenced by the role adopted within a family.

Examples of types of relationships within a family

- Husband and wife.
- Parents and children.
- Siblings.
- Grandparents and grandchildren.
- Grandparents and their own children.

The key to good relationships is good communication (verbal and non-verbal), which includes effective listening skills.

Good communication skills

- Looking the person in the eye.
- Speaking calmly and explaining clearly.
- Listening and reacting to what is being said.
- Being respectful towards the other person.

exam focus

Keep to the point and do not waffle when answering a question. Give facts, not just opinions.

EXAM QUESTIONS AND SAMPLE ANSWERS

Higher Level 2009, Section A, Q.12 (4 marks)

State **two** factors that promote educational development in children.

(i) Encouragement and praise.

(ii) Consistency.

Higher Level 2004, Section A, Q.14 (4 marks)

Give **three** functions of the family.

(i) To provide love, support and security.

(ii) To provide food, clothing, shelter and protection.

(iii) To provide for the economic needs of family members.

Ordinary Level 2008, Section A, Q.12 (5 marks)

Having high self-esteem means:

Believing in yourself and having confidence.

Ordinary Level 2004, Section A, Q.10 (5 marks)

Tick (✔) the correct answer.

The nuclear family is made up of:

(i) Parents, children and grandparents

(ii) *Parents and children* ✔

(iii) Parents, children, aunts, uncles and cousins

Ordinary Level 2002, Section A, Q.11 (5 marks)

State whether **each** of the following are physical or emotional needs.

shelter, love, food, clothing, security

Physical needs	Emotional needs
Shelter	Love
Food	Security
Clothing	

Higher Level 2005, Section B, Q.4 (55 marks) (long question)

(a) Describe **two** different types of families. (2 x 4 marks)

　　1. *Nuclear family:*
- *Consists of parents and their children.*
- *Is small in size.*

　　2. *Extended family:*
- *Consists of parents, children, grandparents, aunts, uncles and cousins.*
- *Is large in size.*

(b) List **three** physical needs and three emotional needs provided by the family. (12 marks)

Physical needs:

(i) Food (ii) Clothing (iii) Protection.

Emotional needs:

(i) Love (ii) Support (iii) Security.

(c) Describe **three** different types of relationships that can exist within a family. (9 marks)

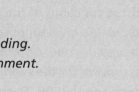
Give three points under each type of relationship.

   (i)   Parents and children.

   (ii) Siblings.

   (iii) Children and grandparents

(d) Outline the **rights** and **responsibilities** of children within the family. (18 marks)

Rights

Children have:

1. A right to love, care, security and understanding.

2. A right to a safe, secure and healthy environment.

3. A right to education.

Responsibilities

Children have a responsibility to:

1. Respect parents and siblings.

2. Help with tasks, e.g. set the table, make their beds.

3. Do their homework,

(e) Explain the term 'norms'. (4 marks)

Norms are the acceptable way of behaving in the society in which you live. Example: Going to school regularly and doing homework.

For full marks, you must:
- Define the term.
- Give an example.

Ordinary Level 2007, Section B, Q.4 (40 marks)

(a) Explain **each** of the following. (2 x 4 marks)

   (i)   Nuclear family: *This family consists of parents and children.*

   (ii) Extended family: *This family consists of parents, children, grandparents, aunts, uncles and cousins.*

(b) Give **two** functions of the family. (8 marks)

   (i)   *To provide for our emotional needs, e.g. love and security.*

   (ii) *To provide for our physical needs, e.g. food and clothing.*

(c) State whether **each** of the following are physical needs or emotional needs. (6 marks)

food, love, shelter, understanding, clothing, security

Physical needs	Emotional needs
Food	Love
Shelter	Understanding
Clothing	Security

(d) What are the main causes of conflict between teenagers and adults in the home? (9 marks)

   (i) Homework and study. (ii) Going out with friends. (iii) Style of dress.

(e) Suggest **three** ways to maintain good relationships between teenagers and adults. (9 marks)

   (i)   *Fairness and consistency.*

   (ii) *Giving them a sense of responsibility.*

   (iii) *Encouragement, support and praise.*

29 Adolescence

- To list the characteristics of adolescence.
- To summarise the physical, emotional, mental, social and moral development of growing up.
- To list the influences on adolescents.
- To explain the following terms: value, peer group, peer pressure, gender, gender role, gender equality and stereotyping.
- To define norms. (HL)
- To list the personal skills needed for communicating with others.
- To explain why conflict arises and how it should be handled. (HL)
- To identify leisure activities suitable for teenagers.

Characteristics of adolescence

Adolescence involves:

- Considerable change in moving from childhood to adulthood.
- Physical, emotional, social and moral development.
- Changing roles and relationships.
- Having greater independence from parents.
- Learning about one's self.

Adolescence may be a happy or an unhappy experience.

Changes in adolescence

Physical changes and development

Puberty begins at different times for different individuals. Hormones are responsible for the physical changes that take place during adolescence.

Some **physical changes** include:

- Very rapid growth – increase in height and weight.
- Growth of body hair – facial hair on boys, underarm and pubic hair on boys and girls.
- Girls develop breasts.
- Girls start menstruation.
- Boys may experience erections and ejaculations.

Emotional changes and development

During adolescence:

- Relationships develop and are taken very seriously.
- Confusion and pain result if relationships do not work out.
- Individuals learn how to manage feelings and emotions.

Signs of emotional development include:

- Increased self-esteem and confidence.
- Acceptance of self and acceptance by others.
- An ability to cope with emotions.

Personality development is influenced by:

- Heredity (what one inherits from parents).
- Environment (what one experiences at home).

Mental development

Mental development during adolescence involves the teenager:

- Thinking and questioning in a more adult way.
- Examining the world in which they live.
- Thinking about their future and planning for it.

Moral development

Moral development is an awareness of what is right and wrong. Parents help their children develop this awareness.

Social development

Social development means learning:

- How to behave towards others, e.g. being respectful.
- How to deal with others in a variety of situations.

> **key point**
>
> The moral and social values of teenagers are influenced by their relationship with parents and family and their peer group.

Other influences on adolescents

Adolescents are also influenced by:

- Community (neighbours, friends, employers).
- Media (TV, magazines, films).
- School (teachers and others).
- Experience of bullying.

During adolescence, young people:

- Examine attitudes, behaviour and ideas around them.
- Try to find a set of values that have meaning for them.

- Search for a personal identity.
- Develop greater self-esteem and self-confidence.
- Learn how to communicate and get on with others.

What is a value?

A **value** is the acceptable standard of an individual or a group.

What is the peer group?

The **peer group** is the group of people of one's own age and with similar interests.

What is peer pressure?

Peer pressure is when the peer group expects individuals to behave just like them or have the same interests, e.g. liking the same music, dressing the same way.

Gender

What is gender?

Gender is defined as the state of being male or female.

What is a gender role?

This defines separate roles for males and females. There is no exchange of roles. Gender roles are learned at a young age both in the home and outside the home. Examples of **traditional gender roles** include:

- Women minding children and doing housework.
- Men working outside the home.

Gender equality

This involves treating males and females equally at home, in school, at work and in the community.

Gender equality enables males and females to:

- Choose the same careers.
- Share household tasks.
- Develop skills free from stereotyping.
- Express their emotions.
- Develop self-esteem and self-confidence.
- Decide to stay at home to bring up their children.

Can you explain what gender equality means to you at home, at school, at work and in the community? Note that in this type of question there are **four** parts. You must explain **each** part separately.

What is stereotyping?

This means having a set or fixed image of how people should behave in any given situation.

Personal development

 ## What are norms?

A norm is the acceptable and appropriate behaviour for people living in society. Most people behave responsibly. Some people are irresponsible.

Examples of norms

- Respecting parents and others.
- Being polite (thanking people).
- Helping others.
- Being on time for school.
- Doing homework.

Examples of irresponsible behaviour

- Throwing litter on the street.
- Not going to school.
- Shouting on the street.
- Drinking to excess.
- Taking drugs.

exam focus

You only need to learn five points for each of these topics.

Personal skills for communicating with others

- Listening carefully.
- Speaking clearly and logically.
- Being co-operative and pleasant.
- Making eye contact and being interested.

Conflict

Why does conflict happen?

Conflict results from people having different views about the same situation.

Example: Parents and teenagers do not agree on how the teenager should dress, what colour their hair should be, what time they should come home, etc.

LINK
Peer pressure (p. 193)

Dealing with conflict

- Calm down (avoid being angry).
- Think before you speak.
- Consider the other person's view.
- Look at the other person.
- Listen attentively.
- Speak clearly and logically.
- Be co-operative and pleasant.
- Consider the options and negotiate an agreement together.

Leisure and adolescence

Adolescents should make use of their free time, away from their studies, to relax. Leisure provides adolescents with the opportunity to:

- Relax and refresh themselves.
- Reduce stress.
- Reduce boredom.
- Increase opportunities to make new friends.
- Learn something new.

Some leisure activities are expensive, while others cost nothing. Extracurricular activities at school ensure that young people can fit a sporting activity into the busy school day.

Examples of leisure activities

- Chess • Cinema • Cooking • Dance • Music • Reading • Sports
- Visiting friends • Voluntary work (helping someone else).

Guidelines for choosing a leisure activity

- It must be enjoyable.
- It must fit into your lifestyle.
- It must be affordable.

EXAM QUESTIONS AND SAMPLE ANSWERS

Higher Level 2007, Section A, Q.15 (4 marks)
Give **two** different examples of positive peer pressure among teenagers.
(i) Encouragement to do homework and study.
(ii) Encouragement to participate in team and individual sporting activities.

Higher Level 2006, Section A, Q.13 (4 marks)
Explain **each** of the following terms.
(i) Gender: Means being male or female.
(ii) Peer group: The people who share your background, age and interests.

Higher Level 2003, Section A, Q.12 (4 marks)
What factors contribute to the emotional well-being of teenagers?
(i)   A caring family.
(ii) Encouragement and praise.

Higher Level 2001, Section A, Q.13 (i) (2 marks) (Part question)
Explain **each** of the following terms.
(i)   Stereotype: *A fixed image of a person or a group.*
(ii) Peer group: *The people who share your background, age and interests.*

Ordinary Level 2008, Section A, Q.12 (4 marks)
Tick (✔) the correct answer.
High self-esteem means:
(i)   Treating males and females equally.
(ii) *Feeling confident and believing in yourself* ✔
(ii) Being able to tell right from wrong

Ordinary Level 2007, Section A, Q.12 (5 marks)
Tick (✔) the correct answer.
Physical development means:
(i)   Learning how to get on with others
(ii) Developing a sense of right and wrong
(iii) *Growing in height and weight* ✔

Ordinary Level 2005, Section A, Q.11 (5 marks)
State why it is important for teenagers to have hobbies.
(i)   Good for general health, e.g. swimming, team sports.
(ii) Reduces boredom, e.g. going to the cinema with friends.

Ordinary Level 2004, Section A, Q.13 (5 marks)
Give **one** example of positive peer pressure.
Friends are not involved in drinking.

Ordinary Level 2001, Section A, Q.1 (5 marks)
Name **one** physical change that occurs in boys and one physical change that occurs in girls during puberty.
Boys: *Growth of body and facial hair.*
Girls: *Menstruation.*

Higher Level 2002, Section B, Q.4 (55 marks) (long question)
'Adolescence is a time of change.'
(a) Outline **three** physical changes that occur in boys and **three** physical changes that occur in girls during puberty.

Physical changes in boys	Physical changes in girls
1. Increase in weigh/height.	1. Menstruation begins.
2. Voice breaks.	2. Breasts develop.
3. Erections, ejaculations.	3. Growth of underarm and pubic hair.

(b) List **four** guidelines that an adolescent should follow in order to maintain good personal hygiene. (12 marks)

1. *Shower or bathe every day.*

2. *Brush teeth twice a day.*

3. *Change shirt/blouse, underwear, socks/tights every day.*

4. *Use deodorant.*

(c) Describe **two** positive and **two** negative ways in which adolescents can be influenced by their peers. (16 marks)

Positive influences: (8 marks)

1. *Doing homework and studying.*

2. *Not drinking.*

Negative influences: (8 marks)

1. *Smoking.*

2. *Being late for school.*

(d) Name **one** organisation that offers support to teenagers and briefly outline how this support is provided. (9 marks)

Organisation: *Alateen*

How it supports teenagers:
- *Alateen is part of the Al-Anon group.*
- *It supports teenagers who are affected by alcohol by encouraging members to share ideas and experiences.*
- *It tries to help young people reach an understanding of alcoholism and learn how to reduce its impact on their lives.*

30 Good Health

aims
- To list the characteristics of a healthy lifestyle.
- To list the benefits of a good night's sleep.
- To explain the factors that contribute to health.
- To list the benefits of exercise.
- To explain stress and list ways to avoid it.

Good health is essential for people to enjoy a good quality of life. Health can be examined under the following categories of well-being:

- Emotional • Mental • Physical • Spiritual • Social.

Each of us is responsible for looking after our own health. The more vulnerable people in society will need others to look after them.

Characteristics of a healthy lifestyle

A healthy lifestyle depends on:

> **LINK**
> Adolescence (pp. 191–95)

- A healthy, balanced diet.
- Good personal hygiene.
- Good home hygiene.
- Rest.
- Exercise.
- A healthy attitude to life (positive).
- Avoiding health hazards.

Exercise: Improves stamina, muscle tone, suppleness, body systems.

Aerobic exercise: Makes your heart and lungs work harder. **Examples:** Brisk walking, swimming, running.

Rest and sleep: Increases energy and concentration, improves well-being.

Leisure: Improves fitness, brain activity, maintains interest in life.

Rest and sleep

The benefits of a good night's sleep are:

- Improved concentration.
- Improved study and work.
- Feeling better (better mood).
- Looking rested.

Mental health

Mental health influences:

- How we feel.
- How we behave towards ourselves and others.

Good mental health involves a positive state of mind and a positive attitude to life.

People with good mental health:

- Are able to like themselves.
- Can get on with others.
- Can cope with difficulties when they arise.

People with poor mental health find it difficult to cope on a day-to-day basis with:

- themselves • others • problems/conflict.

It is natural for all of us to feel at times that we cannot cope. When this happens, we depend on the love and support of family and friends.

Factors influencing good mental health

- Levels of confidence.
- Physical health.
- Experiences in life (positive or negative).
- Relationships with peer group.
- Family relationships.
- Attitude to life (being pessimistic or optimistic).
- Social environment (home and community).

Emotions

Our emotions influence our state of mental health. Emotions include anger, fear and love.

Stress

Stress is the feeling of tension we get when we feel we are not coping with the demands being made on us.

Stress-related problems

Problems associated with severe stress include:

- Anxiety • Breathing problems • Bowel problems • Heart problems • Ulcers.

Ways to avoid stress

- Develop a positive attitude to life.
- Develop strategies to cope with problems (ask for help and advice).
- Eat a healthy diet and relax while eating.
- Take some form of exercise daily, e.g. go for a walk.

- Relax after work.
- Get a good night's sleep.

Good physical health

To maintain good physical health, it is essential to:

- Eat a healthy, balanced diet.
- Get an average of eight hours of sleep each night.
- Have a good personal hygiene routine.
- Have regular health check-ups.
- Take regular exercise in the open air when possible.

Advantages of regular exercise

- Creates a feeling of wellness.
- Reduces risks of heart disease and stroke.
- Assists in weight loss.
- Reduces stress.
- Improves sleep.

key point

Some diseases can be prevented by regular health checks, vaccinations and a healthy lifestyle.

EXAM QUESTIONS AND SAMPLE ANSWERS

Higher Level 2003, Section A, Q.14 (4 marks)
Outline **two** benefits of regular exercise.
(i) Improves physical health, e.g. level of fitness.
(ii) Reduces stress.

Ordinary Level 2006, Section A, Q.13 (5 marks)
Give **two** effects of stress on teenagers.
(i) Poor concentration.
(ii) High levels of anxiety.

Ordinary Level 2005, Section A, Q.13 (5 marks)
What do you understand by the term 'mental health'?
Mental health means having a healthy mind and having a positive approach to life.

Ordinary Level 2002, Section A, Q.10 (5 marks)
Give **two** reasons why it is important to get enough sleep.
(i) Refreshes the body.
(ii) Improves concentration.

31 The Skin

aims
- To describe the structure of the skin.
- To outline the functions of the skin.
- To outline the guidelines for care of the skin.
- To outline the care of the hands, hair and feet.

Structure of the skin

Skin covers the whole body. The skin is made up of two layers: the epidermis and the dermis.

The epidermis

This is the outer layer of the skin.

Epidermis structure	Functions
Dead cells	These are constantly wearing away and being replaced.
Malpighian layer	Contains pigments that protect the skin from the damaging rays of the sun.

The dermis

This is the name of the inner layer of the skin. It has a complex structure.

Dermis structure	Functions
Blood vessels	Bring nutrients to the cells and remove waste.
Fat cells	Under the dermis, help insulate the body and act as an energy store.
Hair follicles	Hairs grow from the follicle and help keep the body warm.
Nerves	Make it possible for us to feel cold, heat and pain.
Oil glands	Oils keep hair lubricated and skin soft.
Sweat glands	Remove waste (water and salt) through the pores in sweat.

Functions of the skin

1. Protects the body (harmful rays of the sun, disease).
2. Enables us to feel sensations (hot, cold, pain).
3. Regulates body temperature and fluids.
4. Removes excess water and waste products (salt).

5. Acts as an insulator and energy reserve.

6. Manufacture of vitamin D when exposed to the sun.

key point

The body temperature is 37°C. The body releases about one litre of sweat per day.

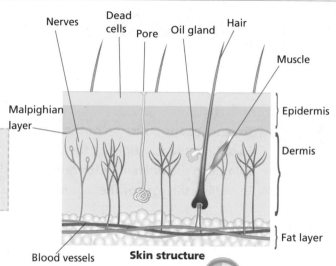

Nerves   Dead cells   Pore   Oil gland   Hair

Muscle

Malpighian layer

Epidermis

Dermis

Fat layer

Blood vessels   **Skin structure**

Skin care

Body odour (BO) is produced by bacteria on the skin. A good daily hygiene routine will prevent BO.

Daily hygiene routine

A good daily hygiene routine is essential for good health. Sweat and oil glands are very active during adolescence.

To feel fresh each day:

- Shower to remove sweat, bacteria and dead cells using warm water and soap.
- Shower after sporting activities and change into fresh clothes.
- Use deodorants or antiperspirants.
- Wear fresh clothes, especially underwear, every day.
- Wash hands frequently, especially after using the toilet.
- Wash hands before handling food.

exam focus

Make sure you are able to label the diagram of the skin.

Caring for the skin

- Eat a balanced diet.
- Drink plenty of water every day.
- Take plenty of fresh air and exercise.
- Get enough sleep.
- Avoid alcohol and cigarettes.
- Avoid overexposure to the sun (use high-protection sunscreens).

key point

To reduce the risk of skin cancer, do not lie out in the sun between 11.00 a.m. and 3.00 p.m. Select a high-factor sunscreen and reapply it often. Wear a hat and long-sleeved shirt/top when walking around to avoid sunburn.

Acne

Acne is a skin complaint resulting from overactive oil glands and blocked pores. It occurs during adolescence. Bacteria can become lodged in the pores and cause pimples or blackheads.

Acne can be controlled by:

- Establishing a skin care routine.
- Drinking lots of water.
- Washing the skin with a medicated soap.
- Eating fresh fruit and vegetables.
- Avoiding greasy foods.

LINK
Healthy eating (p. 33)

Caring for yourself

Hand care	• Wash hands frequently during the day. • Dry hands carefully after washing. • Use a hand cream to prevent chapping and dryness. • Manicure regularly. • Use gloves when doing dirty jobs.
Feet care	• Choose well-fitting shoes. • Change tights or socks each day. • Wash feet daily and dry well. • Pay attention to between the toes. Problems associated with feet: Corns, bunions, verrucae and athlete's foot.
Hair care	• Brush hair each day to remove tangles. • Wash hair at least once a week. • If hair is greasy, wash every three days. • Rinse well, condition, comb, towel dry. • Avoid using the hair dryer every time. • Avoid bleaching and colouring hair too often.

Brushes and combs

Keep brushes and combs clean. Wash them frequently. Do not lend your brushes or combs to other people, as dandruff and head lice can be passed on.

Examples of hygiene and care products

- Antiperspirant • Cleanser, toner and moisturiser • Deodorant • Hand cream
- Shampoo and conditioner • Soap • Toothpaste.

The skin and sun

Protect the skin by:

- Wearing a hat and long-sleeved top.
- Applying a high-protection sunscreen.
- Staying out of the sun between 11 a.m. and 3 p.m.
- Not falling asleep in the sun.

EXAM QUESTIONS AND SAMPLE ANSWERS

Ordinary Level 2008, Section A, Q.13 (5 marks)

List **three** personal hygiene guidelines that should be followed by adolescents.

Ordinary Level 2006, Section A, Q.11 and Q.12 (2 x 5 marks)

Q.11 Name **three** personal hygiene products.

(i)   Hand cream.

(ii) Toothpaste.

(iii) Soap.

Q.12 Suggest **two** ways of protecting the skin from the harmful rays of the sun.

(i)   Wear a hat and a long-sleeved top.

(ii) Apply a high-protection sunscreen.

Ordinary Level 2004, Section A, Q.11 (5 marks)

List **three** guidelines that should be followed in order to have good personal hygiene.

(i)   Shower every day.

(ii) Wear clean, fresh clothes every day.

(iii) Use deodorant or antiperspirant.

In preparation for exams, practise labelling diagrams.

Higher Level 2008, Section B, Q.4 (55 marks) (long question)

(a) Students were asked to label a diagram of the skin (hair, epidermis, oil gland, sweat gland, blood vessels).

(b) Outline **four** functions of the skin. (16 marks)

1. Excretory organ: Removes excess water and waste products.

2. Organ of touch: Enables us to feel sensations, e.g. pain.

3. Manufacture of vitamin D when exposed to the sun.

4. Regulates body temperature at 37°C.

(c) What guidelines should be followed to help promote healthy skin? (12 marks)

1. Shower every day.

2. Cleanse, tone and moisture daily.

3. Use mild soap and warm water.

4. Change into fresh clothes every day, e.g. underwear.

(d) What special guidelines should be followed by teenagers when caring for their feet and toenails? (12 marks)

Feet (2 x 3 marks)

1. Wash feet every day and dry carefully, especially between the toes.

2. Change socks/tights every day.

Toenails (2 x 3 marks)

1. Cut toenails straight across (never curved).

2. Keep clean and short.

32 The Teeth

aims
• To describe the structure and functions of the teeth.
• To explain plaque, periodontal disease and fluoride.

How many teeth do we have?

- Children have 20 teeth.
- Adults on average have 32 teeth.

Structure of the tooth

The tooth is made up of the crown, the neck and the root.

- The **crown** is the part of the tooth visible above the gum.
- The **neck** is the part between the crown and the root.
- The **root** is hidden in the gum.

What Is enamel?

Enamel is the outer covering of the tooth. It is the hardest substance in the body.

What Is dentine?

Dentine is just inside the enamel. It is not as hard as the enamel.

Types of teeth

Teeth	Functions
Incisors (8)	Biting, cutting and grinding food
Canines (4)	Tearing food
Pre-molars (8)	Crushing and grinding food
Molars (12)	Crushing and grinding food

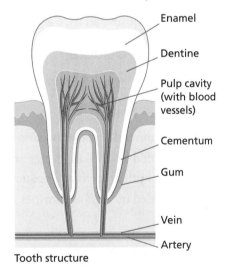

Tooth structure

Pulp cavity

The pulp cavity is the central part of the tooth. It contains nerves and blood vessels.

What is cementum?

Cementum covers the root of the tooth and holds the tooth in place.

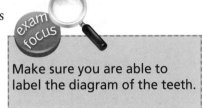

exam focus

Make sure you are able to label the diagram of the teeth.

Teeth problems

Bacteria, food and plaque are responsible for tooth decay or dental caries.

What is plaque?

Plaque is the substance that coats the teeth after a meal or a snack. Plaque sticks to the teeth. It contains bacteria. The bacteria work on the food, forming an acid. This acid then eats into the enamel, causing cavities to form. Gum disease may also result from a build-up of plaque and poor dental hygiene.

What is periodontal disease?

This is a dental disease that damages the area around the tooth. The parts affected include the bone, gum and tissues. Dental problems must be treated, as they can affect general health and well-being.

Rules for caring for teeth

1. Visit the dentist regularly (every six months).
2. Clean teeth twice a day with a fluoride toothpaste.
3. Eat a healthy diet rich in calcium and vitamin D.
4. Avoid sugary and acidic foods (they produce plaque).
5. Do not eat between meals.
6. Do not misuse teeth, e.g. cutting thread with your teeth.

> **LINK**
> Nutrients (calcium, vitamin D) (p. 23; 26)

Dental products

● Dental floss ● Disclosing tablets ● Mouthwash ● Toothbrush ● Toothpaste.

What is fluoride?

> **LINK**
> Water treatment (p. 261)

- A mineral that can occur naturally in water.
- Added to drinking water and to toothpaste to help strengthen teeth and reduce tooth decay.
- Added by local authorities to the water supply.

EXAM QUESTIONS AND SAMPLE ANSWERS

Higher Level 2006, Section B, Q.4 (55 marks) (long question)

(a) Name the four types of permanent teeth. (12 marks)

    1. Incisors.

    2. Canine.

    3. Pre-molars.

    4. Molars (wisdom).

(b) Outline the function of **each** of the following parts of the tooth. (12 marks)

   (i) Enamel: *The outer covering of the tooth that protects the tooth.*

   (ii) Pulp cavity: *The central part of the tooth that contains nerves and blood vessels. They keep the tooth alive.*

   (iii) Cementum: *Covers the root of the tooth and keeps it in place in the jaw.*

(c) List the guidelines that should be followed to maintain healthy teeth. (12)

Dental hygiene:

1. Visit the dentist twice a year.

2. Brush your teeth at least twice each day.

Diet:

1. Eat a diet rich in calcium and vitamin D.

2. Avoid sugary and acid-forming foods.

> **exam focus**
>
> Students must give four points, of which **one** point must relate to diet and **one** point must relate the dental hygiene.

(d) (i) What is plaque? (5 marks)

   Plaque is a mixture of saliva, food and bacteria that coats and sticks to the teeth.

   (ii) Explain how plaque affects teeth. (9 marks)

- *Plaque contains bacteria that work on food to form an acid. This acid eats into the enamel and causes tooth decay.*
- *Cavities can form. When the hole reaches the pulp cavity, pain is felt, as the nerves are exposed.*
- *Gum disease may also result.*

(e) Name the mineral that is added to the public water supply to strengthen teeth. (5 marks)

Fluoride.

Higher Level 2001, Section B, Q.4 (b) and (d) (Part of long question)

(b) Explain the importance of healthy teeth. (12 marks)

Healthy teeth are important for:

1. General good health: unhealthy teeth can cause medical problems.

2. Chewing food.

3. An attractive appearance.

(d) What are the benefits of using each of the following dental hygiene products? (15 marks)

- Antiseptic mouthwash:
  - *1. Prevents the growth of bacteria.*
  - *2. Keeps the mouth fresh.*
  - *3. Breath is fresher.*
- Fluoride toothpaste:
  - *1. Removes plaque.*
  - *2. Makes the enamel stronger.*
  - *3. Prevents tooth decay.*

- Dental floss:
    1. Helps to remove food from between the teeth.
    2. Helps to remove plaque from between the teeth.
    3. Helps to remove plaque from around the gums.

Ordinary Level 2004, Section B, Q.4 (b) and (c) (Part of long question)

(b) Choose the correct word from the following list to complete **each** of the sentences. (10 marks)

wisdom, incisors, canines, molars, temporary

(i) The *molars* help to chew and grind food.

(ii) The *incisors* cut and bite food.

(iii) The first set of teeth are called *temporary* teeth.

(iv) The *canines* help to tear food.

(v) The *wisdom teeth* grow at the very back of each row of teeth.

(c) Explain how diet affects the teeth. (6 marks)

1. Calcium and vitamin D strengthen teeth.

2. Sugary foods cause tooth decay.

3. Fluoride in water and toothpaste strengthen teeth.

Ordinary Level 2004, Section B, Q.4 (c) (Part of long question)

Choose the correct word from the following list to complete **each** of the sentences. (15 marks)

crown, root, cementum, enamel, pulp cavity

(i) Most of the tooth is protected by a hard substance called *enamel*.

(ii) The *cementum* holds the tooth in place in the jaw.

(iii) The space at the centre of the tooth is called the *pulp cavity.*

(iv) The visible part of the tooth is called the *crown.*

(v) The root of the tooth is embedded in the *gum.*

33 The Respiratory System

Structure

Position and shape of the lungs

Position

The two lungs lie above the diaphragm, in the chest cavity. The ribs, sternum (breast bone) and the back bone surround and protect the lungs. The heart lies between the lungs.

Shape

- The lungs are like two sponge bags when filled with air.
- The base (the wider end) rests just above the diaphragm. The pointed end is at the top.

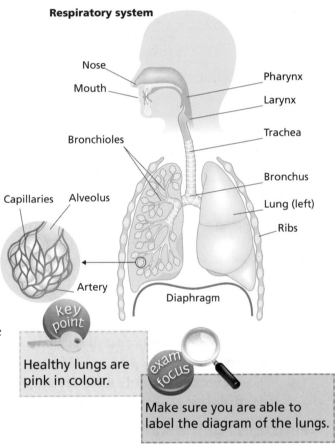

Respiratory system

key point

Healthy lungs are pink in colour.

exam focus

Make sure you are able to label the diagram of the lungs.

How the lungs work

The air passes via the nose and pharynx over the larynx, trachea and bronchus (plural is bronchi).

Respiratory tract	Functions
Nose and mouth	• Air is warmed and filtered as it is passed through the nose and mouth.
Pharynx and epiglottis	• The epiglottis is at the base of the pharynx. • This is a flap of skin that covers the windpipe or trachea and prevents food from going down the wrong way.
Larynx (voice box)	• The vocal cords are stretched across the larynx. • The larynx produces sound when air passes over the vocal cords. It is at the top of the trachea.
Trachea (windpipe)	• The trachea is a long tube made up of C-shaped rings of cartilage located just in front of the oesophagus. • It is lined with hairs that trap germs and dust and sends them away from the lungs as we breathe out. • The trachea divides into two bronchi, one entering each lung.
Bronchus	• From each bronchus, the air passes into the bronchioles.
Bronchiole	• From the bronchiole, the air is passed into the alveoli.
Alveoli (air cells)	• In the alveoli, the exchange of gases takes place between the capillaries and the lungs.

Exchange of gases

- Oxygen passes through the walls of the alveoli into the blood capillaries.
- Carbon dioxide and water pass through the walls of the blood capillaries into the alveoli.
- When we breathe out, carbon dioxide and water are expelled from the body in the stale exhaled air.

Functions of the lungs

- To take oxygen from the air.
- To remove carbon dioxide from the body.
- To release water vapour.

Diseases of the respiratory system

- Bronchitis • Cancer (throat, lungs) • Colds and flu
- Emphysema • Pneumonia • Tuberculosis.

LINKS
Health hazards (smoking) (pp. 219–20)
Kitchen ventilation (p. 240)

Guidelines for healthy lungs

1. Do not smoke or stay in a smoky atmosphere for a long time.

2. Learn to breathe correctly.

3. Look after colds and bronchitis before they develop into something more serious.

4. Ventilate the home properly.

5. Take aerobic exercise to strengthen the respiratory and circulatory systems.

6. If you suffer from asthma, follow the advice given by your doctor.

PAST EXAM QUESTIONS

- Higher Level 2007, Section A, Q.13 (4 marks): Label a diagram of the respiratory system.
- Higher Level 2007, Section A, Q.14 (4 marks): Functions of the lungs.
- Higher Level 2002, Section A, Q.12 (4 marks): Function of the larynx.

EXAM QUESTIONS AND SAMPLE ANSWERS

Ordinary Level 2002, Section B, Q.3 (40 marks) (long question)

(a) Give **two** functions of the lungs. (8 marks)

   (i) Remove carbon dioxide from the body.

   (ii) Provide the body with oxygen from the air to help release energy from food.

(b) Name **two** harmful effects of smoking on the lungs. (8 marks)

   (i) Cancer of the lungs.

   (ii) Affects the unborn child of smokers.

(c) Why do some young people smoke? (3 x 4 marks = 12)

   (i) Curiosity.

   (ii) Image – it looks 'cool'.

   (iii) Peer pressure – all their friends smoke.

(d) Suggest **two** ways that the government has tried to control cigarette smoking. (6 marks)

   (i) Health warnings on cigarette packages.

   (ii) Increasing taxes on cigarettes.

(e) What is meant by addiction? (6 marks)

- *Addiction means that the person in dependent on cigarettes, alcohol or other drugs.*
- *Addiction can be psychological or physical.*

34 The Circulatory System

Function of the circulatory system

The **circulatory system** brings blood with nutrients and oxygen around the body. It also carries impure blood with waste products away from the cells and brings it to the lungs to be purified.

The heart

Position and shape of heart

The heart is:

- Located in the chest cavity between the two lungs, above the diaphragm.
- A pear-shaped organ with the pointed end, or apex, turned downwards and the broad end at the top.

The heart pumps the blood around the body through blood vessels, arteries, veins and capillaries.

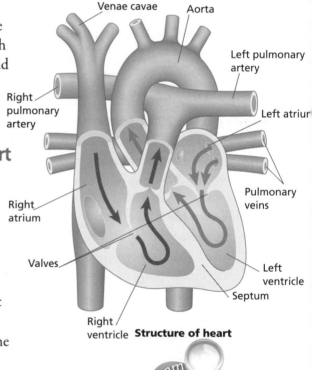

Venae cavae   Aorta

Left pulmonary artery

Right pulmonary artery

Left atrium

Right atrium

Pulmonary veins

Valves

Left ventricle

Septum

Right ventricle   **Structure of heart**

exam focus

Make sure you are able to label the diagram of the heart.

Structure

The heart is:

- Made up of **cardiac muscle**.
- Divided down the centre by a wall called the **septum**.
- Divided into **four chambers**, two on either side of the septum. The top chambers are called **atria**. The lower chambers are known as **ventricles**. The atria are separated from the ventricles by semi-lunar valves (tricuspid valve on the right, bicuspid valve on the left). The **valves** prevent blood from flowing back into the chambers.

Blood flow through the heart

1. Impure blood from the body is emptied by the superior and inferior venae cavae into the **right atrium**. The impure blood passes from the right atrium into the **right ventricle** through the tricuspid valves.

2. The right ventricle contracts and pushes the blood into the **pulmonary artery**, which brings the impure blood to the lungs.

3. The blood is purified in the **lungs**.

4. The purified blood leaves the lungs through the four pulmonary veins and returns to the **left atrium.** The blood is pumped from the left atrium into the **left ventricle**.

5. The **left ventricle** contracts and pushes the blood into the **aorta**. From the aorta, the purified blood is sent around the body.

Blood vessels

The body contains three types of blood vessels: arteries, veins and capillaries.

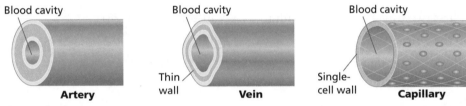

Blood cavity   Blood cavity   Blood cavity

Artery   Thin wall   **Vein**   Single-cell wall   **Capillary**

Arteries

All arteries except one (pulmonary artery) carry oxygenated blood. Artery walls are elastic and thick. Arteries divide into arterioles. Arterioles divide into capillaries.

Capillaries

Capillaries have thin single-cell walls that allow oxygen and nutrients to enter and carbon dioxide to leave body cells.

Veins

Vein walls are thinner than those of arteries. Veins carry blood towards the heart. The veins carry impure blood, except for the pulmonary veins, which are the exception. Veins have valves to prevent the backflow of blood. Veins divide into venules.

The blood

On average, the adult body has about five litres of blood. The blood is composed of plasma, red and white blood cells and platelets.

- **Plasma** is a yellow-coloured liquid in the blood in which red and white blood cells and platelets are found.

- **Red blood cells** are composed of haemoglobin, which picks up oxygen in the lungs and carries it around to the cells of the body.

- **White blood cells** fight infection by surrounding and killing the bacteria in the blood.
- **Platelets** help the blood to clot when we receive a cut.

Functions of the blood

1. To pick up and transport:
   - Oxygen to cells and tissues.
   - Nutrients around the body to cells and tissues.
   - Carbon dioxide from cells and to bring the impure blood to the lungs to be purified.
   - Hormones.
2. To fight disease.
3. To form clots over cuts.
4. To regulate body temperature.

Taking a person's pulse

1. Use the first two fingers (never the thumb).
2. Place on the wrist.
3. Count the beats per minute.

LINKS

Nutrients (pp. 18–28)
Special diets (p. 43)
Coronary heart disease (p. 49)

PAST EXAM QUESTIONS

 HL

- Higher Level 2007, Section A, Q.12: Coronary heart disease.
- Higher Level 2006, Section A, Q.11: Arteries, haemoglobin.
- Higher Level 2003, Section A, Q.12: The blood.
- Higher Level 2002, Section A, Q.15: Reducing the risk of heart disease.
- Higher Level 2001, Section A, Q.14: Haemoglobin.
- Ordinary Level 2001, Section A, Q.11: Risk of heart disease.

PAST EXAM QUESTIONS – SECTION B (LONG QUESTIONS)

HL

Higher Level 2004, Section B, Q.4 (55 marks)

(a) Label a diagram. (10 marks)
(b) Describe the position of the heart in the body. (6 marks)
(c) List the functions of the blood. (3 x 4 marks)
(d) Name three blood vessels and outline the differences between any two of the blood vessels you have named. (20 marks)
(e) Explain how a person's pulse is taken. (7 marks)

Marks Allocated
Names: 3 names x 4 marks = 12 marks.
Two differences: 2 points x 4 marks = 8 marks.

aims
- To describe the female reproductive system.
- To describe the male reproductive system.
- To define terms associated with reproduction.
- To explain menstruation.
- To explain fertilisation and pregnancy.

Female reproductive system

Structure of the female reproductive system

1. The ovaries are situated on either side of the lower abdomen. Two sex hormones (progesterone and oestrogen) are produced by the ovaries.

2. The ovaries contain a supply of unripened ova (eggs). Each month, one of the ovaries releases an ovum into the fallopian tube.

3. The fallopian tubes link the ovaries to the uterus.

4. The uterus (womb) is a muscular organ that carries the unborn baby during pregnancy. The neck of the uterus is called the cervix.

5. The muscular tube leading from the cervix out of the body is called the vagina.

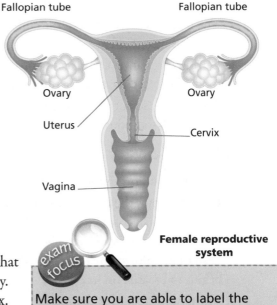

Female reproductive system

exam focus

Make sure you are able to label the diagram of the reproductive systems.

Menstruation

- Menstruation lasts from puberty to menopause.
- The menstrual cycle varies in length, but is 28 days on average. It can vary from month to month, depending on the individual.
- Each month, one of the ovaries releases an ovum (egg).
- The egg travels from the ovary through the fallopian tube to the uterus. The wall of the uterus has thickened in preparation for a baby.
- If conception does not occur, the egg and lining of the womb are expelled from the body during menstruation. This bleeding from the uterus is referred to as a 'period'.

Fertilisation, implantation and pregnancy

Fertilisation

- During sexual intercourse, the erect penis is placed into the female's vagina. Semen is released into the vagina.
- Sperm travel through the cervix, the uterus and into the fallopian tubes.
- If a fertile ovum is present, a sperm may fertilise it. If the ovum is fertilised, the female becomes pregnant.

Implantation and pregnancy

- The fertilised ovum begins to divide into more cells as it moves down the fallopian tubes.
- This group of cells becomes the embryo and attaches itself to the thick lining walls of the uterus. This area develops into the placenta.
- The placenta is attached to the embryo by the umbilical cord. The embryo develops into the foetus.
- During pregnancy, the placenta provides the developing baby with oxygen and food. The placenta acts as a filter between the mother and the developing baby.
- Amniotic fluid surrounds the baby and protects it during pregnancy. Pregnancy generally lasts about 40 weeks.

Birth and delivery

- After the waters (amniotic fluid) break, labour begins.
- During labour, the uterus contracts at intervals and the cervix dilates. The contractions become stronger and closer together as the mother is close to giving birth. The cervix widens to allow the baby to be born head first, followed by the rest of the body. The baby begins to breathe on its own.

> **LINK**
> Healthy eating during pregnancy (p. 40)

- The umbilical cord is clamped at the navel.
- Finally, the placenta and the remains of the umbilical cord are expelled (this is referred to as the afterbirth).

Male reproductive system

Structure and function of the male reproductive system

1. Two testes, which produce sperm from the time of puberty, lie outside the body in a sac called the scrotum.
2. The penis lies to the front of the scrotum.
3. The testes produce the hormone testosterone.
4. During sexual intercourse, mature sperm in semen travel from the testes via two sperm ducts to the penis.

5. They are released into the vagina and from there travel to the fallopian tubes, where fertilisation of an ovum might take place.

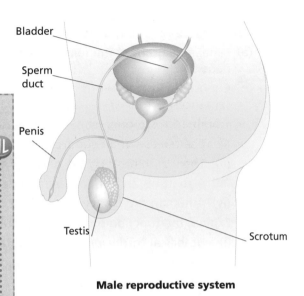

Male reproductive system

PAST EXAM QUESTIONS

- Higher Level 2009, Section A, Q.11 (4 marks): Label the male reproductive system.
- Higher Level 2006, Section A, Q.11 (4 marks): Label the female reproductive system.
- Higher Level 2005, Section A, Q.13 (4 marks): Define ovulation, menopause.
- Higher Level 2002, Section A, Q.13 (4 marks): Define menstruation, fertilisation.

EXAM QUESTIONS AND SAMPLE ANSWERS

Higher Level 2007, Section B, Q.4 (c) and (d) (Part of one long question)

(c) Outline the function of **each** of the following. (16 marks)

	Functions
(i) Testes	*Produce (a) the hormone testosterone and (b) sperm.*
(ii) Ovaries	*Produce (a) the female hormones, progesterone and oestrogen, and (b) eggs.*
(iii) Uterus	*Carries the developing baby until it is born.*
(iv) Sperm duct	*Carries sperm from the testes to the penis.*

(d) Briefly describe the menstrual cycle. (9 marks)

1. Each month, the ovary releases an egg. The egg travels from the ovary through the fallopian tube to the uterus.

2. The wall of the uterus has thickened in preparation for a baby.

3. If conception does not occur, the egg and lining of the womb are expelled from the body during menstruation. This bleeding from the uterus is referred to as a 'period'.

Ordinary Level 2003, Section B, Q.4 (40 marks) (long question)

(a) Label a diagram of the female reproductive system. (12 marks) See page 215.

(b) Choose the correct word from the following list to complete each of the sentences. (8 marks)

womb, testosterone, ovulation, pregnancy, foetus

(i) The release of an egg from an ovary is called *ovulation*.

(ii) The *womb* protects the developing baby.

(iii) A *foetus* is another name for a developing baby.

(iv) A human *pregnancy* usually lasts 40 weeks.

(c) Explain the function of <u>each</u> of the following. (2 x 7 marks)

(i) Umbilical cord: *Links the mother and the baby.*

(ii) Placenta: *Acts as a filter and removes harmful substances from the baby.*

(d) Give **three** guidelines that should be followed in order to promote good health during pregnancy. (6 marks)

(i) *Eat a healthy balanced diet.*

(ii) *Do not drink alcohol.*

(iii) *Never smoke.*

36 Health Hazards

What is health?

Health refers to our emotional, mental, physical, spiritual and social well-being. Factors that threaten our health are known as health hazards.

> **LINK**
> Good health (p. 198)

Smoking

Tobacco is used in cigars, cigarettes and pipes.

Harmful substances in cigarettes include nicotine and tar. These produce carbon monoxide and smoke particles when smoked. Cigarette smoke decreases the amount of oxygen being carried by the blood around the body.

Smoking affects the smokers themselves and people in their company. **Smokers** inhale the chemical contents of the cigarette smoke directly. Irritants in cigarettes cause smoker's cough. **Passive smokers** inhale some of these elements and this can affect them also. Smoking produces carcinogens, which may cause cancer.

Reasons young people smoke

- Peer pressure.
- Curiosity.
- To be part of the crowd and fit in.
- Advertising/business techniques.
- To appear cool.

> **key point**
>
> Pregnant women should not smoke because they run the risk of stillbirth, premature birth or miscarriage.

Effects of smoking

- Seriously damages health.
- Causes health problems, e.g. heart disease, lung cancer.
- Children born to smoking mothers generally weigh less at birth than those born to non-smokers.
- Damages the health of non-smokers.

What is passive smoking?

Passive smoking is when non-smokers inhale cigarette smoke from nearby smokers.

Government regulations

The government tries to control smoking in a number of ways:

- All cigarettes must carry a health warning.
- Cigarettes must be stored behind the shop counter in locked cabinets.
- It is illegal to sell cigarettes to under-18s.
- The display of 'No Smoking' signs is encouraged.
- Workplaces must be non-smoking areas.
- Smoking is not allowed in public places.
- Taxes are increased at Budget time.
- No cigarette advertising is allowed.

Remember to learn six points for your exam.

Alcohol

Alcohol is a legally available drug. Taken in moderation, alcohol is socially acceptable.

Reasons for drinking alcohol

- Peer pressure.
- The need for social acceptance.
- To relax and get rid of tension.
- To feel more confident and overcome shyness.

Effects of alcohol

The absorption of alcohol is determined by:

- Amount of food eaten before or with the drink.
- Gender of the drinker.
- Size of the drinker.
- Quantity of drink taken.
- Time taken to drink.

(a) Effects on the individual

Immediate effects (short term)	Long-term effects
Slower reactions and confusion.	Addiction to alcohol.
Loss of self-control.	Depression.
Loss of co-ordination.	Cancer of the mouth and throat.
Poor judgement.	Heart disease.
Mood changes.	Damage to liver and brain cells.
	Stomach ulcers.

(b) Effects on family

- Relationships break down.
- Financial difficulties.
- Violence.
- Illness.
- Unhappiness (children and adults).
- Absenteeism from school.

(c) Effects on society

- Road accidents, even death.
- Absenteeism at work and unemployment.
- Crime and social disorder.
- Increased cost to the state.

Sources of help

Organisation	What they do
Alcoholics Anonymous	Self-help adult group for alcoholics.
Alateen	Support teenagers affected by other people's alcoholism.
Al-Anon	Help families of alcoholics.

Drugs

What is a drug?

A drug is a chemical substance that induces particular effects, e.g. makes individual feel good. When people become dependent on the drug to produce this effect, they become drug abusers. Drug abuse causes illness and death.

Benefits of prescribed/controlled drugs

Some drugs can be beneficial when used for medical reasons under medical supervision. Drugs taken for medical reasons are referred to as controlled drugs.

Prescribed/controlled drugs can:

- Fight disease (antibiotics, etc.).
- Reduce pain.
- Improve the quality of life during certain illnesses.

Drug abuse

Why young people abuse drugs

- Out of curiosity.
- Peer pressure – to be part of the 'gang'.
- To escape from problems.

- To rebel against parents and society.
- To feed an addiction.

Solvent abuse

Inhaling substances, e.g. gases, vapours or fumes, from a variety of products gives hallucinogenic effects. Some people become addicted to these solvents. Death can be sudden.

Effects of solvent abuse:

- Hallucinations.
- Reduced ability to concentrate.
- Damage to the mouth, nose and internal organs.
- Difficulty breathing.
- Disruptive and aggressive behaviour.

Addiction

When a person becomes addicted to a drug, they crave the effect that the drug can produce and so become dependent on the drug. They may be unable to stop taking the drug without professional help. Addiction may be physical or psychological.

Effects of drug abuse

(a) Effects on the individual

- Addiction and dependence, mental illness.
- Accidental death (overdose), suicide.
- Danger of AIDS and hepatitis (sharing dirty needles).
- Addicts may become criminals to feed their drug habit.
- Unemployment and problems with family/friends.

(b) Effects on the family

- Violence, family rows.
- Financial problems, unemployment.
- Stealing money to fund drug habit.

(c) Effects on the community

- Crime and violence.
- Dirty used needles discarded in the locality.
- Drug pushers move into an area.
- Increased cost to the state.
- Absenteeism from school/work.

Sources of help

1. Drug treatment centres.
2. Narcotics Anonymous.
3. Health Boards.

PAST EXAM QUESTIONS

- Higher Level 2009, Section A, Q.14 (4 marks): Reducing alcohol consumption in Ireland.
- Higher Level 2008, Section A, Q.14 (4 marks): Substance abuse and young people.
- Higher Level 2007, Section A, Q.14 (4 marks): Define controlled drugs, passive smoking.
- Higher Level 2004, Section A, Q.15 (4 marks): Effects of alcohol abuse on society.
- Ordinary Level 2009, Section A, Q.12 (5 marks): Reasons for smoking.
- Ordinary Level 2005, Section A, Q.12 (5 marks): Effects of alcohol abuse on society.
- Ordinary Level 2005, Section A, Q.12 (5 marks): Smoking/government initiative.

EXAM QUESTIONS AND SAMPLE ANSWERS

Ordinary Level 2006, Section B, Q.3 (40 marks)

(a) Choose the correct word from the following list to complete each of the sentences.

inhale, bronchitis, exhale, nicotine, carbon dioxide

(i) To *inhale* means to breathe in oxygen.

(ii) A harmful substance found in cigarettes is *nicotine*.

(iii) Stale air contains more *carbon dioxide* than fresh air.

(iv) An example of respiratory disease is *bronchitis*.

(b) Suggest **three** reasons why teenagers smoke.

(i) Curiosity.

(ii) Peer pressure.

(iii) To be part of the crowd and fit in.

(c) Give **two** disadvantages of smoking.

(i) Causes serious health problems, e.g. lung cancer.

(ii) Damages the health of non-smokers.

(d) What is passive smoking?

Passive smoking is when non-smokers inhale cigarette smoke from nearby smokers.

(e) (i) What information does this symbol convey?

Smoking is forbidden.

(ii) Name **two** places where you would expect to find this symbol displayed.

(i) Restaurants.

(ii) Cinemas.

PART FOUR

Resource Management and Home Studies

37 Management Principles and Home Management

aims
- To define management terms.
- To list the characteristics/skills of a manager.
- To identify resources related to the home.
- To outline the steps in a management system.
- To list the effects of good management systems on a family.
- To apply management systems to the home.
- To list cleaning agents and give guidelines for their use.

Management terms

What is management?

Management involves setting goals, examining resources, making decisions, taking action and evaluating the results.

What is resource management?

Resource management involves researching, planning, budgeting, prioritising, controlling and using all the resources available to gain the most from them in order to avoid waste and to achieve goals.

What is home management?

Home management applies the same principles of management. It involves the use of the resources available to implement the goals (keeping the home running effectively and efficiently).

The main tasks in running a home include budgeting, shopping, cooking, caring for children, laundry, ironing, cleaning and maintaining the home and garden.

What is time management?

Time management is concerned with organising the time available to implement and complete goals in an efficient way so that there is free time left to do other things (leisure pursuits). Time is not wasted. It is sometimes referred to as ergonomics.

Managers and Management Skills

Managers	Management skills
Bank manager	Communicating
Factory manager	Decision-making
Farm manager	Evaluating
Home manager	Organising
Principal of a school	Planning
	Problem-solving
	Researching

Goals

What are goals?

Goals can be defined as the tasks or aims we set for ourselves or what we want to achieve. Goals will differ depending on the resources available to the person.

Types of goals

Goal	Example
Short term	Washing and ironing
Medium term	Saving for a new phone
Long term	Buying a house

Resources

Resources available

These include:

- Energy • Human resources • Knowledge and skills • Money • Time.

Community resources

- Agencies and organisations • Libraries • Schools • State services (postal service, etc.).

What are commodities?

Examples of commodities include:

- Electricity and gas • Food • Labour-saving equipment.

What are personal resources?

- Energy • Equipment in the home • Knowledge • Money available • Skills • Time.

Resources that could be limited in the home are energy, equipment, knowledge, money, skills and time.

Resources that money can buy include equipment, people's skills and knowledge, time and information.

Management systems

A **good management system** involves the following steps:

1. Identify and set the goal or aim.
2. Identify the resources available and other resources that might be needed (time, people, equipment, money).
3. Make a plan and include the time plan.
4. Implement the plan (take action).
5. Evaluate the plan.
6. Modify the plan.

Management plans will change according to the resources available and the resources that have to be found.

Effects of good management systems on the family

A **good management system** ensures that:

- Goals are set and plans are made.
- Resources are allocated effectively.
- Household tasks get done efficiently.
- Everyone in the family gets involved.
- The plan is evaluated and changed as needed.
- Resources are reallocated if necessary.

Family work plans

When organising work plans:

1. Involve the whole family.
2. Divide the tasks to be done into daily, weekly and seasonal categories.
3. Organise tasks to suit individual skills and time at work or school.
4. Use a rota for washing dishes, washing and ironing clothes and vacuuming.
5. Aim to get one or two of the weekly jobs done each day.
6. Use a system to get the tasks completed quickly.

Home management tasks chart

Daily	Weekly	Occasionally
Dusting	Ironing	Planning budgets
Tidying rooms	Shopping	Washing windows
Washing up	Vacuuming	
	Washing	

What is time and motion study (ergonomics)?

Time and motion study involves evaluating how much time and energy are required to achieve goals and complete tasks. Records are kept of everything that needs to be done to complete a task.

Work routines for household cleaning

Case Study A

Design a general work routine for **cleaning a room.**

General plan of action (adapt to any room):

1. Collect all the equipment needed to put the plan into action (cloths, cleaning agents, brush, duster, vacuum cleaner, etc.).
2. Open windows to let fresh air into the room.
3. Tidy room (collect newspapers, empty bin, hang up clothes, make beds, tidy cushions, books, etc.).
4. Clean out the fireplace if there is one in the room.
5. Sweep, dust and vacuum.
6. Wash windows, doors, skirtings and windowsills.
7. Polish furniture and other surfaces.

If asked for a cleaning plan for any room in the exam, use the above plan and make modifications specific to the room, e.g. for a bathroom, include cleaning the bath/shower/basin/toilet.

Case Study B

(i) Devise a list of guidelines for **general cleaning.**

(ii) List **four** cleaning agents used in the home.

Guidelines for general cleaning

1. Be organised.
2. Collect all the resources needed (equipment, cleaning agents, cloths, etc.).
3. In any room, clean from the higher surfaces to the lower surfaces.
4. Do not use harsh cleaning agents.
5. Follow the general plan of action, as above.

Keep the cleaning agents in one press away from children, food, equipment, dishes and saucepans. Mark all cleaning agents clearly. Never remove from the original containers.

Cleaning agents used in the home are:

- Bleach
- Detergents
- Lemon juice
- White vinegar.

Home hygiene

Basic rules for home hygiene

1. Ventilate the house every morning – open all windows.
2. Maintain even temperatures to prevent damp.
3. Clean the kitchen and bathroom daily.
4. Wash kitchen bins, cloths and tea towels daily.
5. Make beds and tidy the bedroom daily.
6. Clean out fireplaces, tidy and dust rooms.

7. Vacuum the whole house once or twice a week.

8. Keep drains clean and disinfect regularly.

9. Each week, wash, disinfect and dry outdoor bins.

Cleaning agents

- **Natural cleaning agents**: Lemon juice, vinegar.
- **Cleaning equipment:** Bucket, dustpan and small brush, sweeping brushes (indoor and outdoor), vacuum cleaner, mop, dusters, selection of cleaning cloths.

Cleaning agents and uses

Agents	Uses
Bleach	Removing stains.
Detergent	Washing clothes by hand or machine, washing-up liquid for dishes, dishwasher detergent for dishes and saucepans.
Disinfectant	Work surfaces, bins.
Non-abrasive cream cleaner	Sinks, work surfaces, ceramic hobs, cookers.
Oven cleaner	To remove stubborn oven stains and dirt.
Polish	Furniture, windows, floors.
Water	All purposes.

Guidelines for choosing cleaning agents

1. Is it value for money?

2. Is it an environmentally friendly product?

3. Can it be used for more than one purpose?

4. Could it harm surfaces?

5. Are there any warning symbols on the product?

6. Are the instructions for use clear?

Alternatives to commercial cleaning agents

Alternatives are now becoming popular as they are inexpensive, are easy to use, easily available in the home and do not contain chemicals. Examples include:

- Bicarbonate of soda ● Lemon juice ● White vinegar.

EXAM QUESTIONS AND SAMPLE ANSWERS

Higher Level 2001, Section B, Q.5 (55 marks) (long question)

(a) Give **four** guidelines necessary to ensure a high standard of hygiene in the home. (16 marks)

    (i)   Open the windows each day to ventilate the home.

    (ii) Disinfect sinks, toilets and drains regularly.

HL

(iii) Empty and wash out kitchen bins daily.

(iv) Tidy and dust rooms every day.

(b) Plan a simple daily routine that would help a teenager with asthma to maintain a high standard of hygiene in his/her bedroom. (9 marks)

(i) Open windows to ventilate the bedroom each day.

(ii) Turn back bed covers and air the bed daily. Change bed linen every week.

(iii) Wipe surfaces daily, vacuum twice a week.

(c) List **four** factors that should be considered when selecting and using household cleaning agents. (12 marks)

(i) Cost and value for money.

(ii) Versatility – multipurpose use or single use only.

(iii) Ease of use – easy to use and time efficient.

(iv) Environmentally friendly products.

Ordinary Level 2008, Section B, Q.5 (40 marks)

(a) List **four** guidelines that should be followed in order to keep a home clean and hygienic. (12 marks)

(i) Follow a regular cleaning routine.

(ii) Clean out fireplaces, dust and tidy rooms each day.

(iii) Empty and wash kitchen bins daily.

(iv) Open windows every day to air the house.

> **LINK**
>
> Quality and symbols (hazardous materials) (pp. 166–68)

(b) Suggest **three** points to be considered when choosing and buying cleaning agents. (9 marks)

(i) Are they environmentally friendly?

(ii) Do they give good value for money?

(iii) Can they be used for more than one cleaning task?

(c) Give a different use for **each** of the following cleaning agents. (10 marks)

(i) Detergent: *Dissolving grease on dishes.*

(ii) Bleach: *Removing stains.*

(iii) Cream cleaner: *Cleaning sinks, cookers, surfaces.*

(iv) Disinfectant: *Killing germs.*

(v) Wax polish: *Cleaning wooden furniture.*

(d) Why is it important to follow the manufacturer's instructions when using cleaning agents? (6 marks)

(i) To be aware of any dangers.

(ii) To use the product as intended.

(iii) To avoid using products that might damage surfaces.

(e) Explain clearly what this symbol means. (3 marks)

This symbol shows that the product:

(i) Should be stored out of children's reach.

(ii) Is toxic/poisonous.

(iii) Should not be eaten.

38 Home Studies

- To define shelter and a home.
- To list examples of homes.
- To identify the functions of shelter/home.
- To outline the guidelines for choosing a home.

What is shelter?

Shelter is a home that protects us from the elements (wind, rain, etc.) and provides us with a safe, secure and private environment in which to live.

What is a home?

A home is the friendly, familiar, warm, comfortable and safe place where we live.

Traditional homes	Modern homes
● Bamboo hut	● Apartment or flat
● Caravan	● Bungalow
● Cottage	● Detached house
● Houseboat	● Maisonette
● Igloo	● Residential housing
● Tent	● Semi-detached house
	● Sheltered housing
	● Terraced house

Homes can be:

- Temporary or permanent.
- Rented or owned.
- Privately owned or local authority owned.
- Rural or urban.

key point

Across the world, people live in different styles of homes/shelter.

Meeting basic human needs

The home meets basic human needs for shelter. These needs are:

- **Physical:** Protection from the elements.
- **Social:** A place for family, friends and people with special needs in society, such as the elderly, etc.
- **Emotional:** A place where we feel comfortable and safe; a private place in which to relax.

General guidelines for choosing a home

Some of the factors that influence people when choosing a home are:

- Money.
- Distance from facilities.
- Location (schools, shops, hospital, library).
- Type and size of home.
- Town or country location.
- Transport.
- Safety.

key point

Some people choose to buy rather than rent because they consider the house as a long-term investment that will increase in value over time.

exam Q

SAMPLE EXAM QUESTIONS, SECTION A

- Suggest **two** types of accommodation suitable for a student living away from home from Monday to Friday. (4 marks)
  - *(i) Apartment on the college campus.*
  - *(ii) Sharing a house with other students.*

- List **two** factors that should be considered when choosing a new family home. (4 marks)
  - *(i) Cost of the house.*
  - *(ii) Stage of family, e.g. retired with adult children.*

- List **four** amenities that you would like to have near your home. (4 marks)
  - *(i) Shops.*
  - *(ii) Park.*
  - *(iii) Library.*
  - *(iv) Health centre.*

exam focus

In these short questions, you apply your knowledge of individual and family needs.

39 Design Principles in the Home

- To define design, a designer and the design process.
- To explain design principles.
- To apply design principles to various areas of the home. HL
- To list and explain basic elements of design.
- To outline the rules for room planning.
- To outline the design process.
- To use the design process to design a kitchen.

What is design?

A design is a plan featuring a structure, with all the lines and shapes that make up the structure. Design shows the arrangement of objects.

What is a designer?

A designer is the person who creates the design and provides the plan to implement the design.

What is the design process?

The design process is the plan of action followed to create the design.

Design in home economics

Design is a part of many aspects of home economics and influences our lives in many ways.

Design across the home

Area	Example	End product
Equipment	Labour saving	Food processor
Food	Meal planning	Garnishes
Interior design	Room planning	Kitchen layout
Services	Electricity	Plugs
Textiles	Soft furnishings	Curtains

Factors involved in good design

The basic factors of good design are function, appearance, quality and durability.

Function

- Objects must fulfil their function, e.g. a chair must be comfortable, a table must be the right height.
- The main features of function are safety, comfort, ease of use, ease of maintenance and hardwearing (in the case of flooring in a kitchen).

Design principles

Good design follows certain basic rules. Designers make use of four design principles to achieve satisfactory results.

Proportion

Designs should be in proportion, e.g. small items of furniture in small rooms, mirrors in proportion to the fireplace, fireplace in proportion to the size of the room.

Emphasis

If a room or an object has a special feature that provides a focus in the design (e.g. fireplace, mirror, painting, small table), it is called emphasis of design.

Balance

Balance is achieved by arranging colours, patterns, textures, lines, shapes, proportion and emphasis in a way that is pleasing to the eye. A harmony is achieved in the design.

Rhythm

This refers to a repeated or a regular colour or pattern in the design that links the room/design together.

Basic elements of design

The basic elements are:

- Colour • Pattern • Texture • Shape • Line.

Colour

Colour is an important aspect of our environment. It is all around us. We also wear colour and we are affected psychologically by the colours we see:

- Colours can appear warm or cold.
- Pale colours make rooms appear bigger.
- Darker colours make rooms appear smaller.

Primary colours: Blue, red, yellow.

Secondary colours: Green, orange, purple.

Neutrals: Black, white, grey.

Shades: Black is added to any colour.

Tints: White is added to any colour.

Cool colours: Blue, green.

Warm colours: Orange, peach, pink, red, yellow.

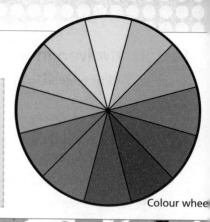

key point

Choose warm colours for north-facing rooms and cooler colours for south-facing rooms.

Colour wheel

Pattern

Functions of pattern

- Used to break up plain surfaces.
- Used to introduce interest.
- Provides contrast with plain surfaces.
- Used as a design feature by designers.

Types of pattern

- Floral • Geometric • Motifs
- Period style • Self-patterned • Trellis.

Floral pattern

General guidelines for using pattern

- Use small patterns in small rooms. Choose large patterns for larger rooms.
- The same pattern can sometimes be used on different surfaces (wall covering and curtains).
- Where two patterns are used, one should be larger than the other.
- Avoid patterns that create visual clutter.

Texture

- Texture describes the 'feel' of a surface.
- A variety of textures is pleasing to the eye.
- Some textures are suited to particular surfaces because of their characteristics (easy to clean, etc.).

Examples of textures

Soft	Hard	Rough	Smooth
Carpets	Brick	Brick	Glass
Curtains	Marble	Carpet	Marble
Towels	Wood	Towels	Stainless steel

General guidelines for using texture

- Choose smooth textures for kitchens and bathrooms, as they are easy to clean and do not encourage bacteria.
- Avoid having too many smooth textures in the living room, as they can look too clinical.
- Choose a mixture of rough, smooth and soft textures for balance.
- Rough textures look more comfortable than soft textures.

Shape

The basic shapes used in design are square, rectangular, triangular and circular. All items have a shape. Some combine shapes.

Line

Four types of line are used in design. Line influences the design.

- **Vertical:** These lines draw the eye up and down walls, rooms and objects. Rooms appear visually higher and objects appear taller.
- **Horizontal:** These lines draw the eye across the room. Horizontal lines make rooms look wider. There is less emphasis on height.
- **Curved lines:** Rooms or objects with curved lines look softer. They are easier on the eye.
- **Diagonal:** Lines crossing at the diagonal are used less frequently. They create a visual impact whether on a wall, fabric or in furniture design. Diagonal lines must be used with care.

Design and room planning

Design in the home aims to create a comfortable environment where people can relax and enjoy being at home. The functional aspects of a home are looked after in a well-designed home (room planning, furniture, lighting, heating, electricity).

General guidelines for room planning

Consider each of the following.

- Function of the room (kitchen, living- room, etc.).
- Space available (space for furniture and storage).
- Aspect of the room (this influences colour schemes).
- Storage space (for now and the future).
- Services (heating, lighting, electricity, ventilation).
- Type and size of furniture for the room.
- Space between furniture.
- Position of doors and traffic flow.
- Safety and hygiene.

> **key point**
>
> The type of room will determine the priorities when planning rooms, e.g. easy-to-clean surfaces for kitchens.

What is traffic flow?

Traffic flow is the movement of people within the room, between furniture and the door and around pieces of furniture.

What is a floor plan?

A floor plan is a scaled drawing of the room on graph paper that shows the position of windows, doors, light fittings, sockets and furniture.

The design process

The design process can be applied to room planning as well as many other areas.

Outline of the design process

1. Design brief (plan a new kitchen).
2. Analyse the task (what exactly are you asked to do?).
3. Research possible solutions and the resources needed.
4. Limit the ideas to a few and consider these carefully.
5. Choose one idea as the solution to the problem.
6. Draw a plan of action.
7. Implement the plan.
8. Evaluate the results.

> **exam focus**
>
> Use the design process to design any room in the house in an exam question.

> **LINK**
>
> See the design process in action with the exam questions at the end of the chapter (pp. 240–41)

Kitchen planning

The modern kitchen is planned so that all activities are carried out efficiently. The study of people and the efficiency of their surroundings is called **ergonomics**. Kitchens can be U-shaped, L-shaped or galley in design.

Examples of priorities in kitchen planning

1. Position and size of the work triangle.
2. Adequate storage space.
3. Traffic flow.
4. Hygienic surfaces.
5. Good ventilation systems.
6. Safe floor finishes (non-slip).

Sequence of activities in a kitchen

A natural sequence of activities takes place in the kitchen that determines the layout of the work units and the position of large appliances:

- Storage ● Food preparation ● Cooking ● Serving ● Washing up.

Arrangement of kitchen units and equipment

Function	Where
Food storage area	Cupboards, work surface, fridge
Food preparation area	Work surface, cupboards, sink, dishwasher
Cooking area	Work surfaces on both sides of the cooker
Serving area	Work surface

What is the work triangle?

The arrangement of the three large pieces of kitchen equipment (fridge, cooker and sink) in an imaginary triangle is called the **work triangle**.

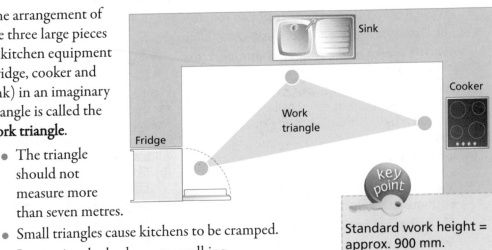

- The triangle should not measure more than seven metres.
- Small triangles cause kitchens to be cramped.
- Large triangles lead to extra walking.

key point

Standard work height = approx. 900 mm.

Characteristics of good kitchen design

- Well lit, well ventilated and comfortable with heat-resistant, easy-to-clean surfaces and equipment.
- Designed with the user in mind, e.g. a person using a wheelchair, a blind person (must be able to move around, work safely and comfortably).
- Unit heights may need to be altered to cater for someone with a physical disability.

Suitable surfaces for kitchens

- **Work units:** Modern, easy-to-clean melamine work surfaces with wood and man-made surfaces on doors. Hygienic surfaces are important in kitchens.
- **Flooring:** Vinyl is easy to clean, comfortable and reasonably hardwearing. Tiles are also easy to clean and hardwearing, but they are not comfortable for standing on for a long time.
- **Wall covering:** Washable paint, washable or vinyl wall coverings and tiles are suitable for the kitchen.

Kitchen ventilation

Efficient ventilation in a kitchen is important because it is needed to remove cooking smells and steam and to reduce the temperature in order to prevent condensation.

Types of ventilation include cooker hoods (ducted and ductless), extractor fans and open windows.

EXAM QUESTIONS AND SAMPLE ANSWERS

Ordinary Level 2002, Section B, Q.5 (40 marks) (long question)

(a) You have been asked to plan the layout of a teenager's study-bedroom. Give **four** guidelines that you would follow when planning the layout of the room. (12 marks)

   (i)   Function of room, e.g. sleeping, studying, relaxing.

   (ii) Size of room and space available for storage.

   (iii) Furniture required (bed, desk, chair, lamp).

   (iv) The aspect of the room will influence the colour schemes.

(b) Sketch and label the layout of the teenager's study-bedroom on the floor plan provided. Include a bed, wardrobe, study desk and chair, etc. (12 marks)

(c) Indicate **two** suitable positions for electrical sockets on the floor plan you have sketched and give two reasons why you think these positions are suitable. (10 marks)

   (i) Beside the bed for a light and radio.

   (ii) Beside the desk for a reading/study lamp.

Please note the marks allocated for each part. If you do not read the question very carefully it is easy to miss out on marks.

Allocation of Marks

(b) Sketch = 6 marks
    Label = 6 marks

(c) Two positions = 4 marks
    Two reasons = 6 marks

(d) Suggest **two** soft furnishings that you would consider suitable for the study-bedroom. (6 marks)

(i) *Curtains.*

(ii) *Cushions.*

Higher Level 2004, Section B, Q.5 (55 marks) (long question)

(a) List the factors that should be considered when decorating a family living room. (15 marks)

(i) *Cost involved and budget available.*

(ii) *Size, shape and aspect of the room.*

(iii) *Traffic flow through the room.*

(iv) *Function of the room (TV, music, studying, relaxing).*

(v) *Position of the doors, windows and services.*

(b) Draw a room plan and indicate on the plan the position of (i) window (ii) door(s) (iii) furniture and (iv) suitable lighting. (16 marks)

> **exam focus**
>
> When drawing your sketch, you must include a sofa, table, chairs, TV, central and side lamps, doors and windows.

(c) Suggest (i) a colour scheme (ii) a floor covering and (iii) a heating system suitable for a living room **and** give a reason for your suggestion in **each** case. (18 marks)

(i) **Colour scheme** (6 marks)

Cream and terracotta.

Reasons for choice: Bright, cheerful and warm.

(ii) **Floor covering** (6 marks)

Solid oak wood.

Reasons for choice: Easy to clean and hardwearing.

(iii) **Heating system** (6 marks)

Wood-burning stove.

Reasons for choice: Eco-friendly and safe to use.

(d) Explain the term 'upholstery'.

This term refers to the outer fabric covering sofas, chairs and beds.

40 Safety in the Home

aims
- To list the causes of accidents in the home.
- To suggest ways to prevent accidents in the home.
- To know how to apply safety rules in the home.
- To list organisations involved in community safety.

Causes of accidents in the home

- Badly designed homes.
- An elderly person's slow reactions.
- Incorrectly installed equipment.
- Mixing water and electricity.
- Faulty electrical equipment.
- Falls (down the stairs).
- A child's curiosity.
- Fires (e.g. open fire, deep-fat fryer).

key point

Some accidents that occur in the home can be prevented, and the risk of others can be reduced.

Prevention of accidents

Stairs and steps

- Ensure that stairs and steps have adequate lighting.
- Put safety gates on stairs where there are toddlers.
- Keep stairs and steps free of toys.

Fire

- Use a fire screen in front of open fires.
- Install smoke alarms (test regularly), fire extinguishers and fire blankets.
- Switch off and unplug all appliances at night.
- Close all internal doors at night.
- Never smoke in bed.

key point

Have a fire drill or plan that the family can implement in case of fire.

Electricity

- Never use faulty equipment.
- Never handle electrical items with wet hands.
- Never take an electrical appliance into the bathroom.
- Unplug the TV and all appliances at night.
- Do not overload sockets.

General safety measures

LINK
Design principles in the home (room planning) (p. 234)

- Use non-slip mats in baths and showers.
- Avoid putting rugs on highly polished floors.
- Install adequate lighting throughout the house.
- Store all chemicals in a locked cupboard.
- Keep all knives in a safe drawer away from children.
- Use childproof locks on kitchen units.
- Avoid trailing flexes in rooms.

Organisations involved in community safety

LINK
Statutory and non-statutory services (p. 265)

- Fire Brigade
- Garda Síochána
- Neighbourhood Watch

EXAM QUESTIONS AND SAMPLE ANSWERS

Higher Level 2005, Section B, Q.5 (55 marks) (long question)

(a) List the safety guidelines that should be followed in order to prevent a fire in the home. (15 marks)

   (i) *Use a fireguard around an open fire.*

   (ii) *Never air/dry clothes in front of an open fire.*

   (iii) *Never put hot ashes in paper or a plastic bin.*

   (iv) *Never smoke in bed.*

   (v) *Unplug TV and all electric appliances at night.*

(b) Name **three** pieces of fire safety equipment suitable for use in the home. (9 marks)

   (i) *Smoke alarm.*

   (ii) *Fire extinguisher.*

   (iii) *Fire blanket.*

(c) Outline the procedure to follow to ensure the safety of the occupants of the house in the event of a household fire. (12 marks)

   (i) *Remain calm and raise the alarm by warning the family.*

   (ii) *Ensure that everyone leaves the house and check that they are all outside.*

   (iii) *Close windows and doors only if possible on the way out.*

   (iv) *Call the Fire Brigade from outside the house using a mobile phone or a neighbour's phone.*

   (v) *Never re-enter the house.*

(d) Describe the first aid treatment for a major burn. (12 marks)

   (i) *If clothing is on fire, wrap in a coat or blanket to put out the flames.*

   (ii) *Do not remove clothing, as it could be stuck to the skin.*

(iii) Do not apply lotions or creams.

(iv) Cover the burned area with a clean, dry cloth to prevent infection.

LINK
First aid (p. 246)

(v) Treat the person for shock and loosen clothing.

(vi) Send for medical help.

(e) Explain why water should not be used to extinguish a fire caused by an electrical fault. (7 marks)

Water conducts electricity. Electricity can travel through water and cause an electric shock to the person trying to put out the fire with the water.

Ordinary Level 2003, Section B, Q.5 (Safety in the Home) (long question)

(a) Give examples of possible safety hazards in **each** of the following rooms in the home. (12 marks)

(i)   Kitchen: *Sharp knives, hot surfaces and equipment.*

(ii) Living room: *Open fire, trailing flexes, rugs.*

(iii) Bathroom: *Medicines and chemicals in unlocked cabinets, slippery floors, shower trays and baths.*

(b) List **four** examples of safety equipment that you would recommend for use in the home. (8 marks)

(i) Smoke alarm.

(ii) Fire extinguishers.

(iii) Locks on presses with chemicals and medicines.

(iv) Fireguard in front of open fires.

(c) Outline the procedure that you would follow if you discovered a fire in your home. (8 marks)

(i) Remain calm and raise the alarm.

(ii) Evacuate the house and check that everyone is present. Do not re-enter the burning house.

(iii) Close windows and doors only if possible.

(iv) Call the Fire Brigade from outside the house.

41   First Aid in the Home

aims
- To list the benefits of first aid.
- To know how to prevent accidents from happening to children.
- To list the contents of a first aid kit/box.
- To know the rules for dealing with accidents in the home.
- To list procedures for simple first aid.

Benefits of first aid

- To prevent the patient from getting worse.
- To help the patient recover.
- To preserve life (while waiting for emergency services).

Minor accidents can generally be attended to in the home.

If a more serious accident happens:

- Do not move the person.
- Cover the patient with a blanket and send for help.
- Remain calm until help arrives. Talk to the patient.
- Do not give them anything to eat or drink.

Avoid accidents to children by:

- Placing dangerous items out of reach.
- Strapping children into prams, buggies and baby chairs.
- Covering garden ponds.
- Using safety gates around the house.
- Locking up medicines, cleaning agents, poisons and plastic bags.

The first aid kit

A first aid kit should contain a selection of items that would help cope with minor accidents in the home. The best location for the first aid kit is the kitchen.

Contents of a first aid kit

- Adhesive plasters ● Antiseptic cream ● Bandages (selection) ● Burn spray
- Cotton buds ● Cotton gauze (sterile) ● Cotton wool ● Disinfectant
- First aid book ● Safety pins ● Scissors ● Thermometer ● Tweezers.

LINK
Safety in the home (p. 242)

Rules for simple first aid

Burns

The type and severity of the burn will determine the treatment that should be given.

(a) **Minor burns (dry heat) and scalds (moist heat):**

- Make the patient comfortable (treat for shock). Immerse in clean water.
- Spray with burn spray.
- Cover the area with a sterile dressing (burn gauze).
- Remove clothing and jewellery.
- Do not burst blisters or cover with ointment.
- Do not use adhesive plasters, creams or lotions.

(b) **Major burns and scalds (requires medical attention):**

- If a person catches fire, push them to the ground, wrap them in a blanket or coat and roll them over to put out the fire.
- Cover exposed burn areas with a clean, dry cloth to stop infection.
- Carefully remove watches, rings, belts and/or shoes.
- Do not remove clothing or apply dressings.
- Send for medical help _immediately_.

Sending for help:

- Send for an ambulance immediately.
- Wait with the patient until help arrives.
- Calmly explain the extent of the burns.

Choking

When the airways get blocked, a person begins to choke. If the obstruction is not removed very quickly, the person could die. Coughing might remove the object.

- **In the case of a child:** Place them face down over your knee, supporting the chest, and slap between the shoulder blades.
- **In the case of an adult:** Bend the person over and slap them on the back.
- **In a more serious case** of an adult choking, use the Heimlich manoeuvre. Repeat this if the object is not released. Do not exert too much pressure.

Cuts

Serious cuts

- Put a clean cloth over the cut and press firmly to stop bleeding.
- Do not remove the dressing until the bleeding stops.
- Take the person to the hospital or doctor.

Cuts from rusty metals and animal bites:

- These should be treated by a doctor..
- An anti-tetanus injection may be required.

Minor cuts and grazes:

- Lay the person down.
- Raise the bleeding limb above the level of the heart.
- Wash the wound gently.
- Dab dry and cover with a fresh sterile dressing.

Falls

Serious:

- Do not attempt to move the injured person.
- If they are unable to move, send for an ambulance.
- Cover the person with a blanket to keep them warm.
- Wait with the person until help arrives.

Less serious, e.g. sprain:

- Apply a cold compress.
- Raise the injured limb.
- Rest the injured limb.

Poisoning

- Go to the hospital immediately or call an ambulance.
- Bring the container of the poisonous substance and the patient's vomit to the hospital.
- If the patient is conscious, give sips of milk. This will help to neutralise a poison. Never make the patient sick. A corrosive poison will damage the throat.
- If the patient is unconscious, place them in the recovery position until help arrives.

key point

Follow instructions on containers with regard to hazardous substances and materials. Bring the container to the hospital.

LINK

Hazard symbols for materials/substances (pp. 167–68)

exam focus

Keep your answers concise and in point format. Avoid waffling and long-winded sentences.

exam Q   EXAM QUESTIONS AND SAMPLE ANSWERS

 HL

Higher Level 2009, Section A, Q.16

Describe a simple first aid treatment for a minor burn. (4 marks)

(i) *Pour cold water over the injured area. Spray with burn spray to exclude the air.*

(ii) *Remove clothing and jewellery.*

(iii) *Cover the area with a sterile dressing.*

(iv) *Do not use creams and adhesive plasters.*

Ordinary Level 2008, Section A, Q.14

Give **three** causes of accidents in the home. (5 marks)

(i) *Careless storage of medicines and chemicals.*

(ii) *Damaged electrical appliances.*

(iii) *Rugs on slippery floors.*

42 Technology and Kitchen Appliances

aims
- To define technology.
- To list the advantages and disadvantages of technology. **HL**
- To outline the application and benefits of technology in the home. **HL**
- To list the guidelines for choosing household appliances.

What is technology?

Technology is the application of science.

Examples of the use of technology in the home:

- Appliances (dishwashers).
- Central heating systems.
- Communication technologies (internet, interactive television).

HL Application of technology in the home

The use of technology in the home makes work easier, faster and efficient. Examples include the following:

Household tasks

- Washing and drying clothes, washing dishes.
- Built-in vacuum systems.
- Sewing machines with computerised functions.

Food preparation tasks

- Electric kettles (boiling water).
- Blenders (soups, sauces, milkshakes).
- Juicing fruits and vegetables.
- Food mixers and processors (mixing cakes).

Large appliances

- Microwave ovens (reheat, defrost and cook).
- Cookers with fan-assisted ovens, dual grills and rings and auto-timers.
- Fridges for keeping food fresh, chilling water and making ice.

A new range of materials has been developed for walls, floors, furniture, lighting, windows, utensils, paints and textiles due to technological developments.

Advantages and disadvantages of technology

Advantages	Disadvantages
• Work is easier.	• Initial cost can be high.
• Saves time.	• Machines can be expensive to run.
• In-built safety features.	• Energy consumed could be high.
• Energy-saving features.	• Machines cannot be left unattended.
• More time for leisure.	• Servicing is expensive.
	• Use of non-biodegradable materials.
	• Pollution.

Labour-saving food preparation machines

- Food mixer • Food processor • Liquidiser.

Energy-saving technology

Appliances in the home that make use of energy-saving technology include cookers, microwave ovens, fridges, dishwashers, washing machines, sewing machines and computers.

key point

All electrical appliances must carry an energy efficiency label. Appliances are rated A to G, with A being the most energy efficient.

General guidelines for choosing household appliances

Consider the following when choosing appliances.

1. Money available.

2. Energy efficiency.

3. Types/models available and special features.

3. Safety features.

4. Size of model and space available in the kitchen.

5. Delivery arrangements.

6. Guarantee.

7. After-sales service.

The fridge

- Is used to keep perishable foods fresh and to help foods last longer.
- Low temperatures (below 5°C) slow down the action of enzymes and micro-organisms that cause the food to decay.
- Reduces the number of visits to the shops during the week.
- Reduces food wastage (stores fresh and leftover foods).

How the fridge works

A special liquid (refrigerant) absorbs the heat from the food and air in the fridge and keeps the temperature low. The refrigerant evaporates and circulates through special coils. It recirculates continuously, keeping the inside of the fridge at the correct temperature. Temperatures should be between 2°C and 5°C.

Guidelines for buying a fridge

- Consider the size of family when choosing the size of the fridge.
- Method of defrosting.
- Star rating of frozen food compartment.

LINK

Guidelines for choosing household appliances (p. 249)

Modern features in fridges

- Cold drinks dispenser.
- Icemakers.
- Automatic defrosting.
- Star marking on freezer box.

Star markings

Star	Storage time	Temperature
*	1 week	−6°C
**	1 month	−12°C
***	3 months	−18°C
****	Up to 12 months	−18°C to −25°C

Guidelines for using a fridge

1. Do not open the door unnecessarily.
2. Cover and label food before putting it in the fridge.
3. Never place hot foods in the fridge.
4. Allow air to circulate around foods – do not overfill.
5. Store food on shelves/racks according to food type.
6. Defrost regularly (automatic, semi-automatic, manual).

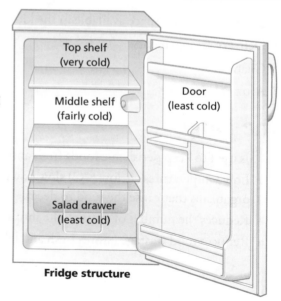

Top shelf (very cold)

Middle shelf (fairly cold)

Door (least cold)

Salad drawer (least cold)

Fridge structure

Routine for care and cleaning of the fridge

1. Do not place fridge near a cooker or radiators.
2. Unplug before defrosting and cleaning.
3. Remove all food and wrap to prevent it becoming warm.
4. Wash the inside of the fridge using a solution of bread soda and warm water. Rinse and dry with a clean cloth.
5. Wash and dry shelves and removable drawers.
6. Wash the outside of the fridge and the rubber door seal.

key point

When not in use, unplug the fridge and leave the door ajar to allow the air to circulate.

The cooker

Types of cooker

- Free-standing slot-in cooker that fits between units.
- Split-level cooker with hob in work unit and oven built in at eye level.
- Range style for larger kitchens.

Energy/fuel

The energy used to run cookers includes gas, electricity, solid fuel and oil.

Structure

Most **gas** cookers have:

- A grill at eye level or at waist level.
- Four to six burners of different sizes.
- Single or double oven with easy-to-clean oven linings.
- Glass panelled door to check the cooking process.
- Push-button ignition.
- Storage drawer at the bottom.

Most **electric** cookers have:

- A grill at eye level or in a small oven.
- Four to six hotplates or coiled rings of different sizes or a ceramic hob with halogen rings.
- Single or double oven with easy-to-clean or stay-clean oven linings.
- Fan oven to cook food more evenly and quickly.
- Glass panelled door to check the cooking process.
- Auto-timer to preset cooker to switch on and off.

Guidelines for care and cleaning of the cooker

1. Clean up spills as soon as they occur.
2. Wipe the hob, spill tray and oven surfaces after use.
3. Wash and rinse the grill pan each time it is used.
4. Clean ceramic hobs with the recommended cleaner.
5. Do not pull saucepans across ceramic hobs.
6. Wash and dry outside surface of the cooker and polish fittings with a soft cloth. Wash and dry all loose fillings, e.g. oven shelves.

hob

control panel

top oven with grill (with glass door)

main oven (with glass door)

Cooker structure

key point

Turn off the power supply to the cooker before cleaning.

exam focus

Learn the six points for care and cleaning.

Modern features and their advantages

Modern features	Advantages
Autotimers	Oven will automatically turn on and off.
Ceramic hob	Easy-to-clean surface.
Coloured surfaces	Can match kitchen.
Dual elements on grills/hotplates	Saves energy.
Fan ovens	Oven has even temperature, so food cooks more quickly.
Halogen hob	Food begins to cook as soon as the hob is switched on.
Hob lid	Hides the hob when not in use.
Keeps the hob clean.	Is an extra work surface. Self-cleaning ovens. Saves labour.
Simmerstat on hotplates	Prevents saucepans from overflowing.

The microwave oven

Microwave ovens are used to reheat, cook and defrost food. Microwaves ovens use energy to cook food. Food is cooked when:

- Microwaves produced are bounced off the oven walls, which are made of metal.
- These energy waves penetrate the food and are absorbed by water molecules.
- The water molecules in the food vibrate, causing friction.
- This friction produces heat and cooks the food.

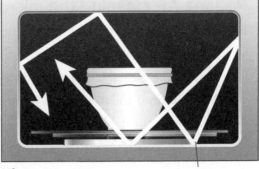

Microwave oven

rays bouncing off the oven walls

Advantages and disadvantages of microwaves

Advantages	Disadvantages
Ideal for busy households – cooks, reheats, defrosts foods.	Food does not brown unless using a browning dish or a combination microwave oven.
Begins to cook the food immediately.	
Cooks food quickly.	Some foods cannot be cooked in a microwave oven.
Less shrinkage and wastage in food.	
Food retains its colour and nutrients.	Special dishes must be used.
An economical method of cooking.	Standing time must be added to the cooking time.
Does not produce steam or cooking smells.	
Food can be cooked and served in the same dish.	
Less washing up (saves labour and time).	

Rules for buying a microwave oven

- Check the wattage of the oven.
- Does it have a turntable (more even cooking)?
- Examine the types of controls (dial or push-button).
- What are its special features?

LINK
Guidelines for choosing household appliances (p. 249)

Rules for using microwave ovens

1. Always follow the manufacturer's instructions.
2. Use special microwave covers on dishes or cover with microwave oven film. Prick the surface of the film before putting the dish in the oven. Prick any food with a skin before cooking, e.g. potatoes, egg yolk.
3. Arrange food in a circle to allow even cooking.
4. Stir liquids during cooking and turn food, e.g. potatoes.
5. Allow standing time when food is removed.
6. Clean up spills immediately.
7. Do not use if the door is faulty.

key point

Danger!
- Never operate a microwave oven when empty.
- Never use metal in a microwave oven.

Routine for cleaning the microwave oven

Note: Check the manufacturer's instructions.

1. Turn off the power supply.
2. Remove the turntable and wash, rinse and dry.
3. Wash the door and inside with warm soapy water; rinse and dry.
4. Replace the turntable.
5. Wipe and polish the outside of the microwave oven.

Small appliances

Advantages of small appliances

- Labour saving.
- Save time.
- Inexpensive to buy.
- Do not require a lot of storage space.
- Help speed up food preparation techniques (shredding, blending, chopping, grating).

Types of small appliances

Some small appliances use a small motor to do the work. Others use thermostats to control heat.

Appliances with a motor	Appliances with a thermostat
Blender or liquidiser	Deep-fat fryer
Electric can opener	Kettle
Electric carving knife	Sandwich maker
Food mixer (large/small)	Slow cooker
Food processor	Toaster

Choosing and buying small appliances

- How much money is available?
- Will the appliance be used frequently?
- Is the appliance the right size or capacity?
- How many tasks can the appliance perform?
- How efficiently does it perform these tasks?
- Is it easy and safe to use and easy to clean?

LINKS

Guidelines for choosing household appliances (p. 249)

Home management systems (p. 227)

Guidelines for using small appliances

1. Read and follow the manufacturer's instructions.
2. Use with care, especially appliances with sharp blades.
3. Do not overfill blenders, liquidisers and food processors with hot liquids (e.g. soups).

4. Choose soft margarine for food processors.

5. Use the correct attachments for the task in hand.

6. Select the recommended speed on all appliances.

Routine for cleaning small appliances

1. Follow the manufacturer's instructions.

2. Take appliances apart carefully (blades, bowls, etc.).

3. Never put parts containing motors or thermostats into water – wipe with a cloth rinsed out in warm soapy water.

4. Wash, rinse and dry blades, bowls and other attachments as indicated in the instruction booklet.

5. Do not put lids into place (allow the air to circulate so that the appliances do not develop stale smells/odours).

key point

Thermostats contain bimetal strips, which are made up of two metals, brass and invar. When heated, brass expands more than invar and bends away from the source of the electricity.

exam Q

EXAM QUESTIONS AND SAMPLE ANSWERS

HL

Higher Level 2004, Section A, Q.17 (4 marks)
Explain the purpose of each of the following in relation to microwave cooking.
(i) **Standing time:** *When food is removed from the microwave oven, it continues to produce heat and to cook. Each food/dish has a recommended standing time allocated as part of the cooking process.*
(ii) **Turntable:** *This is the part of the microwave oven on which food is placed. It rotates during cooking and the food is cooked more evenly as a result.*

Higher Level 2003, Section A, Q.17 (4 marks)
Name a **different** electrical appliance under **each** of the following headings.
Appliance with a motor   **Appliance with a heating element**
Electric hand mixer   *Electric kettle*

Ordinary Level 2007, Section A, Q.15 (5 marks)
Tick (✔) which of the following electrical appliances has a heating element or a motor.

Electric Appliances	Heating element	Motor
Toaster	✔	
Food mixer		✔
Kettle	✔	
Carving knife		✔
Deep-fat fryer	✔	

Ordinary Level 2004, Section A, Q.15 (5 marks)
(i) Give **one** advantage of using cordless appliances in the home.
   Cordless appliances are safe, easy to use and move around.
(ii) Name **one** cordless appliance used in the kitchen.
   Electric kettle.

HL

Higher Level 2003, Section B, Q.5 (55 marks)

(a) List **four** features of modern cookers and suggest one advantage of each feature. (24 marks)

Feature	Advantage
1. Autotimer	Can be preset to cook and turn off when you are not at home.
2. Self-cleaning oven	Food is burned off and oven is clean.
3. Fan oven	Food can be cooked on all shelves at the same temperature.
4. Dual grill/rings	Half the grill/rings can be heated, making it economical to use.

(b) Give **three** guidelines that should be followed when positioning a cooker in a kitchen. (9 marks)

(i) Do not place a cooker beside a fridge.

(ii) Never place a cooker at the end of a run of units. Make sure that there is a work surface on either side of the cooker.

(iii) Do not place a gas cooker in a draught.

(c) List the methods of heat transfer. (9 marks)

(i) Conduction.

(ii) Convection.

(iii) Radiation.

(d) Suggest **three** ways to save energy when using a cooker. (9 marks)

(i) Cook a complete meal in the oven rather than just one dish.

(ii) Turn off the oven 10 minutes before the end of the cooking time. The dish will continue cooking in the residual heat.

(iii) Use dual rings for small saucepans.

(e) Explain the function of a thermostat. (4 marks)

A thermostat is an energy-saving mechanism that maintains an even temperature in appliances and prevents overheating.

Ordinary Level 2005, Section B, Q.5 (40 marks) (Part question)

(a) List **four** points that should be considered when choosing a household refrigerator. (16 marks)

(i) Cost of item – is it affordable?

(ii) Capacity of fridge – is it adequate for the size of the family?

(iii) Method of defrosting.

(iv) Star rating of frozen food compartment.

(b) Give **three** advantages of using a refrigerator. (9 marks)

(i) Perishable foods stay fresh and last longer, e.g. milk.

(ii) Due to low temperatures, fridges reduce the risk of food poisoning.

(iii) Reduces food wastage (stores fresh and leftover foods).

43 Services in the Home

- To list the services supplied to the home.
- To explain how electricity, gas and water are supplied.
- To give guidelines on how to wire a plug.
- To explain the function of fuses.
- To outline the importance of good lighting.
- To list the lighting arrangements for different rooms.
- To state the guidelines for good lighting.
- To list the safety guidelines for using gas.
- To outline procedures to follow if there is a gas leak.
- To describe procedures for blocked sinks, frozen pipes and burst pipes.
- To explain methods of heat transfer.
- To list methods of heating the home.

Important services supplied to the home

- Electricity • Gas • Paper collection • Sewage and refuse collection
- Telephone • Television • Water.

Electricity in the home

- A service cable attached to the fuse box in the home brings electricity from the generating station to the home.
- Electricity is carried around the house to the various points by wires.

Energy used to generate electricity

- Fossil fuels (turf, oil, gas, coal) • Hydroelectric power • Wind power.

How is electrical consumption measured?

Electrical consumption is measured in units called kilowatt-hours.

How is electrical consumption recorded?

Consumption is recorded by a meter in the home. A second meter may be used to record the use of off-peak 'Nightsaver' electricity.

Electric wires

The three wires found in an electrical appliance are:

- **Earth:** The earth wire acts as a safety device should a fault occur.
- **Live:** The live wire brings electricity to the appliance.
- **Neutral:** The neutral wire carries the current back to the generator.

Wiring colour code for plugs

Earth   Green/yellow

Live   Brown

Neutral Blue

Rules for wiring a plug

1. Unplug the appliance.

2. Loosen all screws and put the wires into position.

3. Make sure the plug has a cord grip.

4. Tighten the screws into place.

Safety symbol: Doubly insulated, with two square boxes, one inside the other.

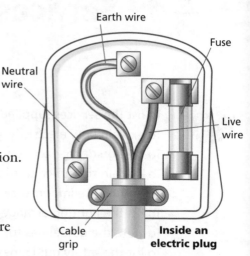

Earth wire

Neutral wire

Fuse

Live wire

Cable grip

Inside an electric plug

Fuses

What is a fuse?

- A fuse is a weak link that melts when a fault occurs.
- This breaks the circuit and stops the electrical current.
- Fuses are found in appliances and in the fuse box.
- Circuit breakers are used in modern systems.

LINK

Consumer education (p. 152)

Causes of blown fuses

- Overloaded circuits.
- Faulty thermostats in appliances.
- Live wires touching neutral wires.

What is a residual current device (RCD)?

This is a safety device found in immersion heaters and electric showers.

Lighting in the home

Good lighting is important for safety and comfort in the home. Sources of light are natural sunlight and artificial light.

- **Natural light:** The main source of natural sunlight is through windows and glass doors. The aspect of the room and the position of the windows will influence the quality of the natural light.
- **Aspect:** This refers to the direction the room faces (north, south, east or west).
- **Artificial light:** Filament bulbs, fluorescent bulbs and strips and compact fluorescent lights (CFLs) are sources of artificial lighting. The function of the room will influence the type and strength of the artificial lighting chosen.

- **CFLs:** Compact fluorescent lights (CFL) are energy-efficient artificial lighting systems. CFL bulbs are expensive compared to ordinary filament bulbs. CFLs use 80 per cent less electricity and will last eight times longer than filament bulbs. The shape of CFLs is rather unattractive.

Importance of good lighting

- Prevents eye strain when reading, studying or sewing.
- Allows us to see everything we do (washing, cooking, etc.).
- Prevents accidents (on stairs, when using kitchen knives, etc.).
- Does not produce glare, shadows or flickering.

Lighting arrangements in the home

Kitchen	Spot lights or CFLs. Fluorescent lights under wall units.
Living room	Table lamps, wall lights, central light.
Bedroom/study	Table lamp, desk lamp, central light.
Hall/landings	Central light fittings that light up both areas and the steps of the stairs.
Bathroom	Central light, fluorescent light over washbasin.

Guidelines for good lighting

1. Choose energy-efficient bulbs and systems.
2. Choose good-quality fittings with suitable shades.
3. Buy fittings and lampshades that are safe.
4. Always use shades over bulbs and fluorescent tubes.
5. Light up stairs and steps.
6. For detailed work, use strong, direct light.

Replacing a bulb

- Turn off the switch.
- Allow bulbs that have blown to cool down.
- Remove the blown bulb and dispose of it safely.
- Insert a new bulb and check that it is secure.
- Turn on the switch to check that it is working.

Gas in the home

Piped gas is available in cities and some large towns. It is a quick and efficient form of energy. Bottled gas is used where piped gas is unavailable. As gas is a non-renewable energy source, use it economically.

Types of gas available

Natural gas	• A service pipe brings the gas into the house.
	• A meter records the amount used.
	• A valve is located at the point of entry.
	• The gas can be turned off if there is a leak or during servicing of the system.
Bottled gas	• Is used for heating and cooking in houses, caravans, mobile homes and when camping.
	• Local shops stock bottled gas.
	• Liquid petroleum gas (LPG) is delivered to large home storage tanks.

How is gas consumption measured?

It is measured in cubic metres.

Safety guidelines for using gas

- Buy gas appliances that carry a recognised safety label.
- Qualified people should install gas appliances and systems.
- Service systems and appliances regularly.
- Use gas appliances in well-ventilated rooms, as gas uses oxygen when it is burning. A balanced flue removes gas fumes.
- Never block wall vents in the house.
- If you smell gas in your home, take action immediately.

What to do when there is a gas leak:

1. Act immediately and evacuate everyone in the house.
2. Check that everyone is present. Do not re-enter the house.
3. Turn off the gas supply at the point of entry.
4. Do not light a match or a cigarette or turn on a light switch, as there is a danger of an explosion.
5. Open all windows and doors to allow the gas to escape.
6. Send for the gas company – phone from someone else's house.

key point

Be careful when lighting pilot lights on gas appliances.

Water in the home

A clean, pure water supply is an essential service to homes.

Uses of water in the home

• Cleaning • Cooking • Drinking • Preparing food • Washing.

How does water get into homes?

1. Local authorities are responsible for supplying water to homes in their area from a reservoir.
2. From the reservoir, water is sent through the mains pipe and a service pipe into homes. This supplies the cold tap in the kitchen.
3. A separate pipe brings water to an attic storage tank. This sends water to sinks, toilets, baths, boiler and hot water cylinder.
4. Wells supply water to some homes in country areas.
5. Some homes in rural areas are attached to rural water schemes.

What is hard water?

Water that contains dissolved minerals which make it difficult to form a lather is called hard water. Hard water forms limescale, which builds up in kettles and pipes.

Water treatment plants

- Water is filtered through layers of sand and gravel **to remove harmful solid substances**.
- Chlorine is added **to destroy harmful bacteria**.
- Fluoride is added **to prevent tooth decay and strengthen teeth**.

Blocked sinks – what to do

The plunger method

- Remove any food from the sink.
- Half-fill the sink with water.
- Put the plunger over the plug hole.
- Push down and release until the blockage is cleared.

The washing soda method

- Put washing soda crystals down the plug hole and pour over boiling water to dissolve the washing soda into the waste pipe.

U-bends

- If the above methods fail, put a basin under the U-bend.
- Unscrew the pipe at the U-bend under the sink.
- Remove the blockage manually.
- Rinse out the U-bend pipe with hot water and put back into position.

Frozen pipes – what to do

- Turn off the water coming into the house.
- Wrap the pipes with towels dipped in hot water.

- Use a hairdryer on a low setting to thaw out the pipes. Work from the taps back along the pipes.

Burst pipes – what to do

- Turn off water coming into the house at the mains.
- Turn on all cold water taps to empty the water system.
- If a solid fuel cooker or a stove with a back boiler is linked into the central heating system, allow it to go out. Do not refuel.
- Send for the plumber immediately.

key point

Condensation results from warm air coming in contact with cold air or surfaces. Problems associated with condensation include dampness, rotting of wood, growth of mould (mould spores are dangerous) and metals rusting.

Heating in the home

An efficient heating system is essential to make the home energy efficient and to save money.

Fuels used to run central heating systems include oil, gas and solid fuel (open fires, solid fuel cookers, enclosed stoves).

Gas is supplied via the mains **or** from a supply tank in the garden.

Factors that influence the choice of heating system

- Effectiveness, energy efficiency and safety of the system.
- Money available.
- Lifestyle.
- Size of house.
- Location of house.

Heat transfer

Heat is transferred in the home in three ways:

1. **Convection**, e.g. a poker in a fire.
2. **Conduction**, e.g. fan heaters, convector heaters.
3. **Radiation**, e.g. open fire, coal, gas and electric fires.

LINK

Revise Heat Transfer in Cooking Methods (p. 75)

Methods of heating the home

- **Full central heating** provides heat for the whole house from a central source and circulates it around the house through pipes and radiators.
- **Partial central heating** gives background heating and may only heat some areas of a house.
- **Spot heating** is provided by electric or gas heating appliances and open fires.

EXAM QUESTIONS AND SAMPLE ANSWERS

Higher Level 2006, Section B, Q.5 (55 marks) (long question)

(HL)

(a) Explain **two** methods of heat transfer. (10 marks)

1. *Conduction*
   - *Heat passes from one molecule to the next molecule along a solid metal object.*
   - *Metals are good conductors of heat.*
   - *Example: A poker used in an open fire.*

2. **Radiation**
   - *Heat travels in straight rays from the source of the heat to the first solid object they hit.*
   - *The heat does not heat the air in between the heat source and the object.*
   - *Example: Radiant heater.*

(b) (i) Name **three** fuels used for home heating. (6 marks)

   1. Oil.

   2. Gas.

   3. Solid fuel.

(ii) Give **two** advantages and **two** disadvantages of one of the fuels named. (12 marks)

Advantages of oil	Disadvantages of oil
1. Clean and efficient.	1. Storage is needed.
2. Easy to use.	2. Can be expensive.

(c) Outline the benefits of using a central heating system in the house. (8 marks)

1. Can be operated on a timer to come on and off at specific times.

2. Heats the water for sink, baths and showers.

3. Rooms can be heated to different temperatures.

4. A comfortable atmosphere is created by heating the house.

(d) List **four** ways of saving energy when using a central heating system. (12 marks)

To save energy:

1. Turn off the heat in unused rooms.

2. Turn down the main thermostat and individual thermostats on radiators.

3. Use a timer on the heating system.

4. Get boilers serviced each year.

(e) What is the function of a thermostat? (7 marks)

A thermostat is a device that regulates the temperature of central heating systems and kitchen appliances.

Ordinary Level 2007, Section B, Q.5 (40 marks) (long question)

(a) List **three** different uses of water in the home. (6 marks)

    (i) Heating.

    (ii) Washing dishes.

    (iii) Preparing and cooking food.

(b) Suggest **three** ways of reducing the amount of water used in the home. (12 marks)

    (i) Use economy buttons on washing machines.

    (ii) Use the dishwasher only when full.

    (iii) Take showers instead of baths.

(c) Give **two** common causes of water pollution. (8 marks)

    (i) Farm waste, e.g. slurry escaping into rivers.

    (ii) Overuse of detergents in the home.

(d) Give **two** effects of water pollution. (8 marks)

    (i) Food poisoning outbreaks in local areas.

    (ii) Fish and vegetation in rivers die.

(e) Apart from water, give **two** other examples of basic household services. (6 marks)

    (i) Electricity.

    (ii) Refuse collection (green and brown bins).

SHORT QUESTIONS, SECTION A

Higher Level 2008, Q.18 (4 marks)

Outline **four** methods of conserving water in the home.

(i) Take showers instead of baths.

(ii) Use the dishwasher only when full.

(iii) Use economy buttons on washing machines.

(iv) Avoid running the taps when not in use.

Higher Level 2007, Q.16 (4 marks)

What actions should be taken in the event of a gas leak in the home? (4 marks)

(i) Open doors and windows and evacuate the house.

(ii) Turn off gas at the mains.

(iii) Call the gas supplier from a neighbour's house.

(iv) Never light a match or turn on an electric switch in the vicinity of a gas leak – there is a danger of explosion.

44 Community Resources and Amenities

- To define community, community resources and amenity.
- To list community services and amenities.
- To examine what services and amenities are in your own area.

What is a community?

A group of people who live in the same area are collectively called a community.

What are community resources?

These are services available, such as schools, library, community centre, hospital and post office. The people who live in the area are also a community resource, because they bring with them knowledge and skills.

What is an amenity?

An amenity can be described as an attractive feature in a local area that can be enjoyed by those who live there.

LINK

Home Studies (choosing a place to live) (pp. 232–3)

Community services and amenities

Statutory	Voluntary	Amenities
Gardaí	Heritage groups	Banks
Health Board	Meals on Wheels	Bus service
Libraries	Residents' groups	Gardens
Post office	Sports clubs	Parks
Public housing	The Samaritans	Playgrounds
Schools	Youth clubs	River walks
Social welfare		Shops
		Sports centres

exam focus

List the amenities and services in your own area and use them as examples when answering exam questions.

exam Q

EXAM QUESTION AND SAMPLE ANSWER

Higher Level 2009, Section A, Q.15 (4 marks)

HL

(a) What do you understand by local amenities?

An amenity can be described as a feature in a local area that can be enjoyed and used by those who live there.

(b) Give **two** examples of amenities found in your community.

(i) Local park.

(ii) Shopping area.

45 Energy-friendly Homes

- To list ways of saving energy.
- To make suggestions for insulating the home.

Energy-friendly homes

Saving energy in the home is very important if we are to use the resources available efficiently. Using less energy saves money and protects the environment. A poor energy rating could mean that a house will have a lower resale value.

key point

New regulations state that all houses need a Building Energy Rating Certificate if they are to be sold or rented.

Ways of saving energy: general guidelines

Area	Suggestions
Electricity	• Make full use of the oven (cook several dishes together). • Keep appliances serviced and in good working order. • Buy appliances that have energy-saving features. • Take showers instead of baths. • Use a pressure cooker to cook complete meals.
Lighting	• Switch off lights when not needed. • Use CFL bulbs for internal/external lighting.
Central heating	• Turn down thermostats. • Turn off radiators in rooms when not in use. • Close curtains to prevent heat escaping.
Water heating	• Lag the cylinder. • Put timer on immersion heater. • Use 'Nightsaver' electricity.

exam focus

Learn eight guidelines for saving energy in the home. Ensure that you have two suggestions from the four areas identified in the table.

Insulating the home

Area	Suggestions
Attic	Fibreglass blanket Loose-fill insulating material
Floors	Underlay fitted correctly Fitted carpets
Hot water cylinder	Lagging jacket or preinsulated cylinder
Walls	Cavity walls Foam or polystyrene insulation
Windows/doors	Double glazing Heavy lined curtains Draught excluders (metal, plastic, foam)

EXAM QUESTIONS AND SAMPLE ANSWERS

Higher Level 2007, Section A, Q.17 (4 marks)
Give **two** reasons why houses should be insulated.
(i) Reduces energy, e.g. heating bills.
(ii) To prevent heat loss.

Higher Level 2001, Section A, Q.15 (4 marks)
Name a different type of insulation suitable for **each** of the following areas in the home.

	Area	Type of insulation
(i)	*Attic*	*Fibreglass*
(ii)	*Hot water cylinder*	*Lagging jacket*
(iii)	*Walls*	*Inject foam*
(iv)	*Windows*	*Double/triple glazing*

Ordinary Level 2008, Section A, Q.16 (5 marks)
Match the most suitable form of insulation with each of the following.
walls, windows, floors, attic, hot water cylinder

Form of insulation	Area
Curtains	*Windows*
Lagging jacket	*Hot water cylinder*
Fibreglass	*Attic*
Carpet	*Floors*
Polystyrene sheets	*Walls*

Ordinary Level 2000, Section A, Q.14 (5 marks)
Name **two** areas in the home that should be insulated to prevent heat loss.
(i) Attic.
(ii) Windows.

46 Environmental Issues

aims
- To list the causes and effects of pollution.
- To define/explain environmental terms.
- To explain the ozone layer. **HL**
- To identify types of waste.
- To list methods of waste disposal.
- To list examples of recycling in the home.
- To outline the main recycling rules for consumers.
- To name the organisations associated with environmental issues.
- To name the recycling symbols.

The quality of our lives is influenced by the products we use and how they affect the environment around us. Air and water are frequently damaged by pollution.

Causes of pollution

Where	Causes
Air	Toxic chemical fumes from factories and industry
	Lead in petrol
	Fumes and lead from cars, buses, lorries
	Aerosols and fridges releasing CFCs (chlorofluorocarbons)
Water	Organic waste (slurry, sewage)
	Dead animals
	Rubbish
	Toxic chemical waste from industry
	Excess fertiliser seeping from land
	Phosphates
Noise	Constant traffic
	Loud music/radios/television
Others	Plastic bags and containers
	Rubbish and litter (paper, fast food containers)
	Old equipment (fridges, washing machines)
	Old cars and scrap metal
	Graffiti
	Illegal dumping

key point

Biodegradable means that the product is not harmful to the environment and breaks down easily.

What is the ozone layer?

The ozone layer is a layer of the upper atmosphere that protects us against ultraviolet rays from the sun. CFCs (chlorofluorocarbons) disrupt and damage the ozone layer by causing it to become thinner, thereby allowing the ultraviolet rays through the atmosphere. This results in an increased risk of:

- Skin cancer.
- Eye disorders.
- Damage to plant and marine life.

Environmental guidelines – saving the planet

- Avoid aerosols that contain CFCs – replace with ozone-friendly alternatives.
- Choose products in biodegradable packaging.
- Choose energy-efficient kitchen equipment.
- Use CFL bulbs.
- Avoid detergents with phosphates.
- Dispose of old fridges properly.

key point

CFLs = compact fluorescent lights.

Waste disposal

Waste must be disposed of safely and hygienically to avoid health hazards. Local authorities collect waste in cities and some towns. In some country towns and rural areas, private companies collect waste from households for a fee.

Types of waste

Dry:

- Cans • Cardboard • Glass • Metal • Newspapers • Plastic.

Liquid:

- Sewage • Waste from sinks and baths.

Waste can also be classified as **inorganic** or **organic**.

What is organic waste?

Waste that can be broken down, e.g. biodegradable food waste, natural materials (paper, wood), human waste, sewage.

What is inorganic waste?

Waste that does not break down easily, e.g. non-biodegradable materials, metal, glass, plastic.

Disposal of organic household waste

- Waste is removed from the house through pipes that are linked to a sewage treatment plant or a septic tank.
- The waste is broken down by bacteria into harmless substances.

- These substances are released into the sea, lake or river.
- By law, raw, untreated sewage cannot be pumped into the sea, lakes or rivers.
- Septic tanks are emptied and their contents removed for treatment.

Bins

Bins are used to hold waste in kitchens (pedal bins) and outside the house (dustbins, green and brown bins). Keep bins covered at all times. Empty, wash and disinfect regularly. Weekly bin collections are a feature of many cities, towns and country areas.

Recycling

- Recycling systems dispose of waste products in an environmentally friendly way if they are planned correctly.
- Have a recycling plan for the home.
- There are many ways the home can be organised to dispose of waste in a manner that would not damage the environment.

Recycling in the home

Items	Methods of recycling
Glass, paper, metal and oils	• Return to collection banks. • Collection banks can be found in car parks and community spaces.
Clothes	• Put in a clothes bank. • Donate to a charity shop. • Recycle at home by making new clothes.
Natural materials (vegetable peelings, grass and wood cuttings, paper)	• Add to the compost heap.

LINK
Consumer studies (recycling symbol) (p. 271)

The **main rules for consumers** are:

1. *Reduce* the amount of items you buy.
   Alternative: Repair items instead of replacing them.
2. *Refuse* overpackaged items and plastic bags.
   Alternative: Buy items loose and bring your own bag.
3. *Reuse* plastic bags and household items.
   Alternative: Use refillable containers.
4. *Recycle* all resources.
   Alternative: Donate cloths and books to charity. Bring glass to the recycling bins. Use a compost heap.

key point

Develop a recycling plan for the home.

Environmental organisations

- An Taisce • Environmental Protection Agency • Green Schools Programme
- Greenpeace.

Name of symbol	Symbol	What it means
Glass recycling		Glass can be put into a glass recycling bank.
The Green Dot		European trademark to advise consumers that they have contributed to the recycling of the product's packaging.
Mobius Loop		Product's packaging can be recycled.
Tidyman		Do not litter.
Plastic recycling	PET	Symbols can be used to identify the different types of plastic.
Wood recycling	© FSC	The product contains wood from a sustainably managed forest.

EXAM QUESTIONS AND SAMPLE ANSWERS

Higher Level 2008, Section A, Q.17 (4 marks)

In waste management, suggest a different method of disposing of **each** of the following items.

Items	Method of disposal
(i) Vegetable peelings	Compost heap
(ii) Clothes	Donate to a charity shop
(iii) Coloured glass	Bottle bank, e.g. green, brown
(iv) Paper	Recycling bin or centre

Higher Level 2006, Section A, Q.16 (4 marks)

Suggest **two** ways in which the ozone layer can be protected.

(i) Dispose of fridges at the designated centre.

(ii) Choose ozone-friendly products.

HL

Higher Level 2005, Section A, Q.18 (4 marks)
(a) Explain the term inorganic waste.

This is waste that will not break down over time, i.e. non-biodegradable.

(b) Give one example of inorganic waste.

Glass.

Higher Level 2001, Section A, Q.18 (4 marks)
Give **two** advantages of using compact fluorescent lights (CFLs) in the home.

(i) Cheaper running costs, uses less electricity.

(ii) Lasts longer than filament bulbs.

Ordinary Level 2004, Section A, Q.14 (5 marks)
Suggest **one** way in which the environment can be protected.

Use energy-efficient kitchen appliances.

Ordinary Level 2003, Section A, Q.15 (5 marks)
List **five** household items that can be recycled.

(i) Paper

(ii) Glass

(iii) Clothes

(iv) Tins

(v) Plastic bags

PART FIVE

Textile Studies

47 Textiles

aims

- To list the functions and uses of textiles and clothing.
- To explain terms associated with textiles. **HL**
- To list the factors that influence fashion trends. **HL**
- To outline the factors influencing the choice of clothes.
- To list desirable and undesirable properties of textiles.

What are textiles?

Textiles can be described as cloths, fabrics and materials that are used to make a variety of items.

Functions of textiles/clothing

Textiles fulfil the basic needs of:

- Modesty.
- Protection against fire or injury.
- Protection against dirt and grime.
- Protection against the weather.
- Identification.

How textiles identify people:

- Self-expression (e.g. by wearing colourful, creative or unusual outfits).
- In sport (clothes worn by athletes, divers, mountaineers).
- At work (uniforms or clothes worn by bus drivers, doctors, mechanics).

What is fashion?

Fashion describes the style of clothing that is popular.

Factors that influence fashion trends

- Aesthetic.
- Fashion/interior design industry.
- Celebrities.
- The media.
- Historic events.
- Culture and tradition.

Factors that influence the choice of fabrics

- Fashion trends and personal style.
- Quality of fabric.
- Money available and value for money.
- Fabric care (easy to care for).

LINKS
Consumer Studies (p. 154)
Advertising (fashion) (p. 181)

Uses of textiles

Textiles are used in the home, in public buildings, shops, hotels, workplaces and leisure.

Personal items	Household items	Others
Clothing	Bathroom items	Flags
Footwear	Bed linen	Parachutes
Sportswear	Carpets and rugs	Sails on boats
	Soft furnishings	Upholstery
	Table linen	
	Upholstery	

Properties of textiles

How a fabric drapes, feels, looks and reacts to wear and tear can be described as the characteristics or properties of the fabric.

key point

Properties may be desirable or undesirable.

Desirable properties	Undesirable properties
Absorbent	Burns readily
Closely woven texture	Creases easily
Comfortable	Delicate
Cool, crisp, warm, soft	Irritates the skin
Crease resistant	Loosely woven
Drapes well	Shrinks easily
Durability and strength	Stains easily
Flammability (flame resistant)	Surface pills
Insulates	
Resilient	
Shrink resistant	
Stain resistant	
Suitable weight	
Washable	
Waterproof	

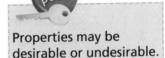

exam focus

Watch out for questions on this chapter in Section A (short questions) or in Section B, where the theory is integrated into the longer question on textiles.

EXAM QUESTIONS AND SAMPLE ANSWERS

Higher Level 2009, Section A, Q.19 (4 marks)

What influences fashion trends?

(*i*)   *Historic events.*

(*ii*) *Culture and tradition.*

(*iii*) *Celebrities.*

(*iv*) *Fashion design industry.*

Higher Level 2008, Section A, Q.19 (4 marks)

List **four** functions of clothing.

(*i*)   *Modesty.*

(*ii*) *Protection against fire.*

(*iii*) *Protection against dirt and grime.*

(*iv*) *Identification.*

Higher Level 2005, Section A, Q.23 (4 marks)

Give **two** desirable properties of **each** of the following: (i) winter jacket and (ii) bed sheets.

(i) **Winter jacket**

   1. Insulates the body against cold.

   2. Waterproof.

(ii) **Bed sheets**

   1. Cool and crisp.

   2. Washable.

48 Textiles in the Home

aims
- To list the uses of textiles in the home.
- To identify the functions of soft furnishings.
- To give the desirable properties of textiles. **HL**
- To list the factors for choosing soft furnishings.
- To list the functions of soft furnishings.
- To outline the desirable properties of soft furnishings.
- To identify suitable fabrics for household furnishings and upholstery.

Uses of textiles in the home

Textiles are used in every room for many different items. Examples include:

- Accessories • Bath towels • Bed linen
- Carpets and rugs • Soft furnishings • Table linen.

LINKS
Resource management (p. 226)
Design principles in the home (p. 234)

Soft furnishings

Soft furnishings refer to furnishings made from textiles, e.g. blinds, curtains, cushions. Some soft furnishings are also considered to be accessories, e.g. cushion covers.

Functions of soft furnishings

- Aesthetic (add style) • Comfort and warmth • Insulation • Privacy
- Protection against fire • Self-expression.

Desirable properties of household furnishings

Household item	Desirable properties
Bed linen	Absorbent, cool, durable
Carpets/rugs	Resilient, soft, stain resistant
Duvet	Comfortable, insulates
Shower curtain	Water resistant, mildew resistant
Tea cosy	Insulates, aesthetically pleasing
Towels	Absorbent, soft, durable, colourfast
Upholstery	Hardwearing, stain resistant

Choosing soft furnishings

The factors to consider are:

- Suitability for purpose (function).
- Care and cleaning (washing, dry cleaning).
- Durability (hardwearing).
- Cost (suits your budget).
- Range of fabric (colour, pattern, texture).

key point

The function of the household item will determine the properties required in the fabric.

Curtains

Types of curtain include full length, short (to windowsill or to the top of the radiator), lined and net.

Functions of curtains

- Exclude or reduce draughts.
- Insulate (keep heat in).
- Keep the light out when pulled.
- Provide privacy.
- Reduce noise.

HL Desirable properties of curtain fabric

- Hangs and drapes well.
- Colourfast, resistant to fading.
- Easy to clean (washable).
- Flame resistant.
- Pre-shrunk.
- Closely woven, durable.

Fabrics suitable for curtains include cotton, linen, wool, velvet and man-made fabrics.

Blinds

Blinds are used on their own or with curtains. Their functions are the same as for curtains.

Types of blinds

- Austrian • Roller • Venetian • Vertical.

Upholstery

Upholstery fabrics are heavier and stronger than those used for curtains and blinds.

Desirable properties of upholstery fabrics

- Tough and durable, closely woven to prevent sagging.
- Colourfast, resists fading.
- Easy to clean (washable or spongeable).
- Stain resistant.
- Conforms to fire safety regulations.

Fabrics suitable for upholstery include heavy cotton, linen, linen union, velvet, leather and man-made fabrics.

Note: Fabrics and fillings for new upholstered furniture must comply with 1988 Safety Regulations (look for the safety labels and symbols on upholstery).

Fire-resistant care label

Carpets and rugs

Types of carpets and rugs

Carpets and rugs may be looped, tufted or woven. The pile may be embossed, long, short or twisted.

LINK
Labels (p. 169)

Desirable properties in carpets and rugs

- Comfortable underfoot, resilient.
- Closely woven or tufted.
- Durable and hardwearing.
- Warm underfoot.
- Moth proofed.
- Fire resistant.

key point

Rugs should be non-slip.

Carpet grading system

The grading system is based on the wear and tear carpets will get in the different locations within the home. Luxury domestic is the best quality for halls, stairs and living rooms. Carpets in bedrooms will get less wear and tear.

Grades	Uses and suitability
General domestic	Living room, TV room
Heavy domestic	Halls and stairs, living room
Light domestic	Bedroom
Luxury domestic	Halls and stairs, living room
Medium domestic	Dining room

Fibres in carpets

- Main fibres are acrylics, nylon, silk and wool.
- Wool and nylon are blended together in an 80 per cent to 20 per cent ratio, respectively. The properties of both make the carpet hardwearing.
- In luxurious, expensive carpets, wool and silk are blended together.

LINK
Safety labelling (pp. 167–8)

Questions related to this section frequently focus on household items. You should be able to:

- Design, sketch and describe the item.
- Draw a care label to go with it.
- Name and list the properties of the fabric.
- Say why you chose the fabric.
- Suggest and sketch a decorative feature for the item.
- Define textile terms.

PAST EXAM QUESTIONS

- Higher Level 2009, Section B, Q.6: Household textiles.
- Higher Level 1999, Section B, Q.6: Household item.
- Ordinary Level 2005, Section B, Q.6: Textiles in the home.
- Ordinary Level 2001, Section B, Q.6: Textiles in the home.

EXAM QUESTIONS AND SAMPLE ANSWERS

Higher Level 2003, Section B, Q.6 (55 marks)

(a) Discuss the factors that should be considered when choosing soft furnishings for the home. (12 marks)

When answering this question:
- List four factors.
- Give an explanation for each factor.

Factors	Explanation
(i) Function	*Will it suit the purpose of the room, e.g. keep out light in the case of curtains?*
(ii) Care and cleaning	*Are they easy to clean, e.g. washing, dry cleaning?*
(iii) Cost	*Can you afford the items? Are they within your budget?*
(iv) Interior design	*Will the colour, pattern and textures suit the style and design of the room?*

(b) Give **four** functions of curtains. (12 marks)
(i) *Insulate the room by excluding or reducing draughts.*
(ii) *Provide privacy.*
(iii) *Add to the decoration of the room.*
(iv) *Reduce sounds from outside.*

(c) List **three** desirable properties of textiles suitable for curtains. (12 marks)

The fabric should:

(i)   *Hang and drape well.*

(ii) *Be flame resistant.*

(iii) *Be easy to clean, e.g. washable.*

(d) Name **two** soft furnishings, other than curtains, that you consider suitable for a living room. (6 marks)

(i) Cushions (ii) Lampshades.

(e) (i) Explain what is meant by a fabric finish. (7 marks)

A fabric finish is a chemical process applied to fabrics to give the fabric a specific characteristic. Example: Crease-resistant fabric.

(ii) Suggest **two** fabric finishes that could be applied to textiles for use in soft furnishings. (6 marks)

(i)   *Flame retardant.*

(ii) *Stain repellent.*

Ordinary Level 2007, Section B, Q.6

A diagram of a care label found on a pair of curtains starts the question.

(a) Using the information on the care label, answer the following questions. (12 marks)

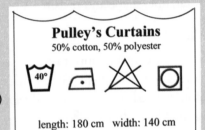

(i)   How would you wash these curtains?

Machine wash at 40 degrees Celsius.

(ii) How should these curtains be dried?

Tumble dry.

(iii) What is the recommended heat setting for the iron?

Cool iron.

(iv) Can these curtains be bleached?

No, as there is a 'do not use bleach' symbol on the care label.

(b) Name **two** fabrics suitable for curtains. (6 marks)

(i) Cotton. (ii) Velvet.

(c) Suggest **three** reasons why curtains are used in the home. (12 marks)

(i) Privacy. (ii) Keeps the light out. (iii) Insulates the room.

(d) Curtains are soft furnishings. Give two other examples of soft furnishings used in the home. (4 marks)

(i) Chair covers. (ii) Rugs.

(e) State **one** advantage and one disadvantage of making soft furnishings. (6 marks)

Advantage: You can make items to suit your own style and taste.

Disadvantage: You need a sewing machine.

49 Design and the World of Fashion

- To list the principles of fashion design.
- To outline the design process.
- To explain terms associated with the fashion industry.
- To outline the factors that influence fashion trends. **HL**
- To explain fashion style.
- To list guidelines for buying clothes.

Basic principles of fashion design

The basic principles of textile design are similar to the general design principles of colour, line, shape and texture. A basic knowledge of each is required for fashion design.

Colour

Colours are divided into primary, secondary, hues, shades and tints. There are few rules in the use of colour for fashion, but seasonal trends influence what is available. Colours can appear warm or cold.

> **LINK**
> Design principles in the home (colour wheel) (p. 236)

- **Primary colours:** Blue, red, yellow.
- **Secondary colours:** Green, orange, purple.
- **Neutrals:** Black, white.
- **Shades:** Black is added to a colour.
- **Tints:** White is added to a colour.
- **Cool colours:** Blue, green.
- **Warm colours:** Orange, peach, pink, red, yellow.

Line

Curved, diagonal, horizontal and curved lines can be used to visually alter the proportions (slimmer) and height (taller) of an individual.

Shape

The outline of the garment, which is determined by the latest trends, is referred to as its shape.

Texture

Texture is the softness, crispness or hardness of a fabric. The fibre and the type of weave determine the texture of a fabric. Loosely woven fabrics tend to be soft, while tightly woven fabrics are firmer.

Visual principles of fashion design

Balance, emphasis and proportion are important visual design principles associated with fashion design.

LINK
Design in the home
(p. 234)

Practical principles of fashion design

As well as the basic and visual principles, fashion design must consider practical factors such as comfort, care, safety and suitability for the purpose.

The design process

The designer must apply the principles of good design when following the design process. The design process is a problem-solving approach used in textile design and other areas of design (e.g. interior design, meal planning).

Summary of the design process

The steps involved are as follows:

1. A design brief is received.
2. Analyse the design brief.
3. Research possible solutions.
4. Consider the resources available.
5. Select one solution and create a proposal.
6. Make a plan.
7. Implement the plan (make the item).
8. Evaluate the results.
9. Modify the solution and plan for the next time.

Designing an outfit

Use the design process when designing an outfit. The **factors to consider when designing an outfit are:**

- Budget available (cost of materials, etc.).
- Fashion trends.
- Personal style.
- Event.
- Colour and texture of fabric.
- Size.

The fashion industry

What is fashion?

Fashion can be described as the prevailing popular style in clothing, footwear, soft furnishings and various other items.

What are fashion fads?

This is the latest trend or craze, which is generally popular for a short period of time (e.g. platform shoes and boots).

What are fashion trends?

Fashion trends are the latest changes in fashion styles for the next season or collection (swimwear, winter collections, etc.).

What is a couturier?

Professional dress designers are called couturiers. Their collections are shown twice a year at the major fashion centres.

What is haute couture?

Couturiers design and make original designs that are available for wealthy individuals to order during their haute couture shows. Some individuals employ couturiers to create once-off original designs. Haute couture is not available in the shops as off-the-peg collections.

What is prêt-à-porter'?

Prêt-à-porter refers to ready-to-wear garments, based on haute couture design, that are available in the shops. Cheaper fabrics and mass production ensure more economical prices for these collections.

(HL) Fashion trends

Changes in fashion trends may occur because of:

- Designer influence.
- Manufacturing techniques.
- Fabrics available and new fabrics.
- Time of year.
- Historical events.

The basic design features change from season to season and from collection to collection. For example, hems are raised or lowered, neckline shapes change, jackets become looser or more tightly fitted or shirt collars change shape.

Fashion styles

A style is the look created by accessories, garments, hairstyles and make-up. There are a variety of styles that can be created from the latest clothes in the shops and older clothes in the wardrobe. Each style has a particular mix of clothes, colours, footwear and accessories.

Examples of styles

- Casual • Classic • Country (tweeds) • Executive or work wear
- Outdoor (hiking, mountaineering) • Special occasion (weddings, parties)
- Sporty • Teenage or trendy.

Fashion and the consumer

Factors influencing the choice of clothes

When choosing clothes, we may be influenced by:

- Advertising • Age • Appearance • Care label • Comfort • Cost • Designers
- Fashion industry • Fashion trends • Fit • Image • Lifestyle • Suitability.

Guidelines for shopping for clothes and footwear

Before shopping:

- Examine the clothes and footwear already in your wardrobe.
- Make a list of what is really needed.
- Consider how much money is available.
- Know the latest fashion trends.

When shopping:

- Buy the best quality that you can afford.
- Consider the cost (keep within your budget).
- Consider the construction (must be well made).
- Consider the fit, colour, shape and size.
- Read the care label (clothes should be washable).
- Consider value for money.
- Avoid buying cheap clothes and shoes.
- Keep the occasion in mind (work, party).

When shopping for footwear:

- Do not try on shoes with bare feet.

> **LINK**
> Consumer education
> (receipts) (p. 160)

Developing a personal style

- Know what suits your colour, shape and size.
- Be familiar with the latest fashion trends.

Accessories for a total 'look'

Accessories include bags, beads, belts, gloves, hats, jewellery, scarves, shoes, socks, ties and tights. It is important to:

- Invest in good-quality accessories that will last.
- Choose inexpensive, fun accessories in the latest colours for short-term use.

PAST EXAM QUESTIONS

The following are examples from past exam questions, Section B.

Designing outfits.

Higher Level	Ordinary Level
● Garment made from silk	● Garment you made as part of your textile studies
● Leisure wear	● Outfit for teenagers
● Outfit for a wedding	

PE sports top

For this type of question, you should be able to:

- Design, sketch and describe the garment.
- Draw a care label to go with it.
- Name and list the desirable and undesirable properties of the fabric chosen. **HL**
- Answer questions related to the fabric being used, e.g. stages involved **HL** in the production.
- Say why you chose the fabric.
- Suggest and sketch a decorative feature that would personalise the garment.
- Define fashion terms.

SAMPLE EXAM QUESTIONS, SECTION A

Higher Level:

- Suggest two ways to accessorise an outfit.
- Explain each of the following terms: (i) accessories and (ii) prêt-à-porter.
- Explain each of the following fashion terms: (i) haute couture and (ii) prêt-à-porter.

Ordinary Level:

- Explain the term **fashion accessory**. Give **one** example of a fashion accessory.
- List **three** factors that would influence you when buying clothes.
- Name one popular accessory for teenage boys **and** teenage girls.

EXAM QUESTIONS AND SAMPLE ANSWERS

Higher Level 2007, Section B, Q.6 (55 marks) (long question)

You have been asked to make a sports top suitable for your PE class.

(a) Name the fabric you would choose for the sports top **and** give **three** reasons for your choice. (12 marks)

Fabric: 100% cotton (3 marks)

Reasons for choice: (3 x 3 marks)

   (i)   Comfortable.

   (ii) Absorbent.

   (iii) Washable.

(b) List the guidelines to be considered when buying the fabric. (6 marks)

   (i)   Budget available.

   (ii) Range of fabric available.

   (iii) Pattern and other requirements.

(c) Sketch **and** describe the sports top that you would make. (15 marks)

Sketch:

The new PE sports top is deep pink in colour and made from cotton, which is cool to wear and is soft in texture.

Sketch

For the description of a garment, describe its style, level of comfort, colour and texture.

When sketching a household item or garment, the diagram must be labelled fully.

(d) Suggest **two** methods of personalising the sports top. (2 x 3 marks)

   (i) Machine embroidery.

   (ii) Appliqué.

(e) **Sketch and describe** a suitable care label for the sports top you have made.

LINK

Fabric care symbols (p. 300)

- In the **sketch**, you are expected to draw **four** care symbols.
- Symbols must suit the **named fabric** in part (a) of the question.
- In the **description**, you are expected to give **four** points of information.

50 Fabric Composition

Fibres and fabrics

Fibres are the smallest strands of a fabric. Individual fibres are twisted together to form a yarn that can then be made into fabric.

Type	Source	Examples
Natural	Animal	Silk, wool
	Vegetable	Cotton, linen
Regenerated	Cellulose	Acetate, triacetate, viscose
Synthetic	Chemicals	Acrylic, nylon, polyester

Natural fibres

Examples of natural fabrics

- **Silk:** Chiffon, crêpe de chine, raw silk, shantung.
- **Wool:** Cashmere, flannel, tweed, gabardine.
- **Cotton:** Canvas, denim, gingham, muslin, organdie.
- **Linen:** Cambric, damask.

Uses of natural fabrics

- **Silk:** Blouses, dresses, lingerie, shirts, soft furnishings.
- **Wool:** Clothing, carpets, furnishing fabrics, upholstery.
- **Cotton:** Clothing, furnishing and household fabrics.
- **Linen:** Clothing, bed linen, soft furnishings, table linen.

The symbols for fibres must be known for Higher and Ordinary level papers.

Silk

- **Origin:** Silk originates from the cocoon of the *Bombyx mori* silkworm.
- **Producers:** China, Japan, India.

Pure silk symbol

Production of silk

1. Female silkworms lay eggs on mulberry leaves. The eggs are incubated and hatch out into silkworms.

2. Small silkworms eat mulberry leaves continuously until they get very large (about 6.5–8 mm).

3. After about 35 days, the silkworms spin a cocoon of silk around themselves. The silk is held in place by a gum called sericin.

4. The cocoons are sorted out. Some moths are allowed to hatch to produce the next batch of eggs and the remaining cocoons are dipped in hot water to soften the sericin and kill the silkworms.

5. The silk threads are then unwound from the cocoon. The raw silk is wound onto reels. This process ('throwing') makes silk stronger by twisting and doubling the silk fibres.

6. The gum is removed from the silk. It is then ready for dyeing, weaving and printing.

Desirable properties of silk	Undesirable properties of silk
• Absorbent	• Tends to be expensive
• Beautiful, lustrous surface	• Easily damaged by chemicals, careless washing and moths
• Comfortable	
• Crease resistant	• Expensive
• Drapes well	• Prone to rotting in sunlight and from perspiration
• Resilient	

Wool

- **Origin:** Wool is the fleece of a variety of sheep.
- **Producers:** Australia, Argentina, New Zealand, UK, Ireland.

WOOLMARK

Production of wool

1. Sheep are sheared to remove the fleece.

2. The wool is baled, graded and sent for cleaning and spinning.

3. Scouring removes dirt, grease, sweat and twigs from the fleece.

4. The wool is carded to separate the fibres.

5. Long fibres are spun into worsted yarn for weaving.

6. Short fibres are spun into woollen yarn for knitting.

7. The wool is ready for dyeing, weaving or knitting and finishing.

Desirable properties of wool	Undesirable properties of wool
• Absorbent. • Comfortable, soft and warm to wear. • Mixes well with other fibres. • Resilient and holds its shape. • Resists flames, smoulders slowly. • Resists static electricity.	• Easily damaged by bleach, hot water and moths. • Expensive. • Hairy surface can irritate delicate skin. • Liable to pill. • Scorches easily. • Weak when wet.

Cotton

- **Origin:** Cotton comes from the cotton plant.
- **Producers:** Egypt, India, USA.

Production of cotton

1. Cotton bolls (seed heads) are gathered or harvested from cotton plants.
2. Cotton fibres (2–3 cm long) are separated from the seed using a cotton ginning machine.
3. The fibres are compressed and baled.
4. At the mill, cotton is graded according to its quality (length of fibre) and remaining seeds are removed.
5. Carding and combing separate the fibres.
6. Fibres are put through several processes before they are spun.
7. Finally, the cotton is woven, knitted, dyed, printed and finished.

Desirable properties of cotton	Undesirable properties of cotton
• Absorbent. • Comfortable and cool to wear. • Dyes readily. • Strong when wet and dry. • Washes, dries and irons well.	• Burns and scorches easily. • Cheap cottons become limp. • Creases easily unless treated. • Damaged easily by mildew. • Shrinks readily.

Linen

- **Origin:** Linen is made from the inner fibres of the flax plant.
- **Producers:** Belgium, France, Ireland.

Production of linen

1. The flax stalks are pulled and dried and the seeds are removed.
2. The flax stalks are soaked to ferment or rot the woody core. This can be done in the traditional way or using chemicals.
3. The flax fibres are dried and are separated from the rest of the stalk during a process called scutching.

4. The long fibres are separated by combing the fibres.

5. Carding, drawing, spinning and bleaching prepare the fibres for weaving.

Desirable properties of linen	Undesirable properties of linen
• Absorbent and dries quickly.	• Creases quickly.
• Comfortable.	• Damaged by mildew.
• Cool to wear in summer.	• Expensive.
• Durable (wears and washes well).	• Shrinks easily.
• Resists dirt and grime.	• Wears along the creases.

Man-made fibres

There are **two** groups of man-made fibres:

- Regenerated.
- Synthetic.

Man-made fibres were created to replace or blend with natural fibres.

Origin of man-made fibres

- **Regenerated fibres** are made of cellulose from plants. e.g. acetate, triacetate and viscose.
- **Synthetics fibres** are developed from chemicals, e.g. acrylic, nylon and polyester.
- **Other man-made fabrics** are fibreglass, Lycra, rayon, PVC and metallic fibres.

Production of man-made fibres

1. Man-made fibre is made by copying the production of silk.

2. A liquid is forced through a spinneret and thin silk-like filaments emerge and harden.

3. The filaments are stretched, drawn and twisted.

4. Filaments can be cut into staple fibres or spun using a continuous filament.

Properties of man-made fibres

Different fibres have different properties.

Advantages of individual fibres

Fibres	Advantages
Acetate	Absorbent, attractive, drapes well and is mothproof.
Acrylic	Launders well, is durable, light and soft and is resistant to creasing, mildew and moths.
Nylon	Durable and strong, launders well, is crease resistant and resilient.
Polyester	Resistant to creasing, mildew, moths and sunlight and is warm.
Triacetate	Can be permanently pleated, is shrink resistant, warm to touch and washes well.
Viscose	Absorbent, comfortable, drapes well and is mothproof.

HL Disadvantages of individual fibres

All man-made fibres	Flammable except modacrylic, which is flame resistant.
Acetate	Damaged by acids, alkalis and sunlight and is weak when wet.
Acrylic	Attracts dirt, has poor absorbency and loses its shape when wet.
Nylon	Pills, uncomfortable in warm atmospheres and is damaged by strong sunlight, bleach and hot water.
Polyester	Non-absorbent, attracts dirt easily and develops static electricity.
Triacetate	Attracts dirt easily, develops static electricity and is not suitable for children's clothes.
Viscose	Creases easily, must not be wrung out during laundering, weak when wet.

Uses of man-made fabrics

Some of the uses of man-made fabrics are clothes, evening wear, lingerie, soft furnishings, ties, tights, rainwear, ribbons, shower curtains, ski wear, swimwear, umbrellas and underwear.

exam focus

Be prepared to identify the symbols associated with each of the fibres.

The burning test – identifying a fibre

1. Take a small sample of fibre.
2. Using a pair of tongs, burn the sample slowly over a metal plate.
3. Take note of the burning process, colour of the flame, smell and residue.
4. Write down the results.

Results for natural fibres

Fibre	Burning result
Animal fibres	Wool and silk burn slowly and smell like burning feathers or hair. A black or grey ash remains.
Vegetable fibres	Cotton and linen burn quickly and smell like burning paper. A grey ash remains.

Results for man-made fibres

Fibre	Burning result
Acetate	Burns with a smell of vinegar and leaves behind a brittle black bead.
Acrylic	Burns quickly with a dark, smoky flame and has an unpleasant sooty smell. An uneven hard bead remains.
Nylon	Melts and shrinks. Smells like celery. Nylon leaves a hard grey bead behind.
Polyester	Melts and shrinks quickly, producing a black sooty flame. A smooth hard bead is left behind.
Viscose	Burns with a smell of burning paper. There is a white afterglow and grey ash remains.

PAST EXAM QUESTIONS

- Higher Level 2009, Section A, Q.22 (4 marks): Identify symbol – pure new wool.
- Higher Level 2007, Section A, Q.21 (4 marks): Desirable and undesirable properties of linen.
- Higher Level 2006, Section A, Q.20 (4 marks): Two examples of synthetic fibres and suggest a different use for each one.
- Higher Level 2004, Section A, Q.21 (4 marks): Two desirable and two undesirable properties of wool.
- Higher Level 2003, Section A, Q.21 (4 marks): Uses for (a) Lycra and (b) polyester.
- Higher Level 2002, Section A, Q.22 (4 marks): Two examples and uses of natural fibres.
- Higher Level 2001, Section A, Q.20 (4 marks): Two examples of synthetic and regenerated fibres.
- Higher Level 2000, Section A, Q.22 (4 marks): Properties of denim.
- Ordinary Level 2007, Section A, Q.17 (5 marks): Symbol: Pure new wool.
- Ordinary Level 2006, Section A, Q.17 (5 marks): Indicate with a tick (✔) whether each of the following fabrics is natural or man-made – wool, linen, nylon, polyester, silk.

 EXAM QUESTIONS AND SAMPLE ANSWERS

Higher Level 2002, Section B, Q.6 (55 marks) (long question)

'Cotton is a very versatile and popular fabric.'

(a) Outline the stages involved in the production of cotton. (20 marks)

  (i) *Bolls (cotton balls) are removed from the plant and cleaned.*

  (ii) *Fibres are separated from the seed using a ginning machine. Fibres are compressed and baled.*

  (iii) *Cotton is classed and graded according to its quality and remaining seeds are removed.*

  (iv) *Carding and combing separate the fibres. Fibres are put through several processes before they are spun.*

  (v) *Finally, the cotton is woven, knitted, dyed, printed and finished.*

> **exam focus**
>
> Be prepared for the following:
> - Recognising symbols.
> - Analysing labels.
> - Designing a household item (sketch and describe).
> - Designing a care label to go with the item.
> - Choice of fabric for item and reasons for choice.

(b) List **three** examples of cotton fabric. (9 marks)

  (i) *Denim.* (ii) *Gingham.* (iii) *Towelling.*

(c) Suggest **three** fabric finishes that can be applied to cotton. (12 marks)

  (i) *Brushing (brushed cotton).* (ii) *Crease resistant.* (iii) *Shrink resistant.*

(d) State **two** desirable properties of cotton as a household textile. (8 marks)

(i) *Absorbent.* (ii) *Strong.*

Higher Level 2008, Section B, Q.6 (55 marks)

(a) Silk is a natural fabric. List **three** other natural fabrics.

(i) *Cotton.* (ii) *Linen.* (iii) *Wool.*

(b) Choose a natural fabric and outline the stages involved in its production.

Fabric: *Linen.*

Production:

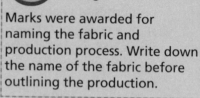

Marks were awarded for naming the fabric and production process. Write down the name of the fabric before outlining the production.

(i) *Flax stalks are pulled and dried and seeds are removed.*

(ii) *Flax stalks are soaked to ferment or rot the woody core. This can be done in the traditional way or using chemicals.*

(iii) *The flax fibres are dried and then separated from the rest of the stalk during a process called scutching.*

(iv) *The long fibres are separated by combing the fibres.*

(v) *Carding, drawing, spinning and bleaching prepare the fibres for weaving.*

(c) State **four** desirable properties of the fabric you have chosen.

(i) *Absorbent, dries quickly.*

(ii) *Cool to wear in summer.*

(iii) *Durable, wears and washes well.*

(iv) *Comfortable.*

(d) Name, sketch and describe a household item or garment that could be made from this fabric.

Household item: *Linen cushion with embroidered musical notes.*

Description of cushion:

(i) *The cushion is made from two squares of cream linen and has a zip closure at the side.*

(ii) *A row of black musical notes is embroidered on the front using satin stitch.*

(iii) *The zip is inserted into one of the side seams and then the other three sides are stitched together.*

(iv) *All seams are neatened using zigzag machine stitching.*

(e) Design a care label that could be attached to the household item you have named.

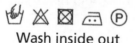

100% linen

Wash inside out

The care symbols must suit the fabric chosen above. You must include wash, dry, iron and one other symbol.

51 Fibres into Fabrics (Construction)

aims
- To describe how fibres are made into fabrics.
- To describe how fabric is woven.
- To outline the uses, advantages and disadvantages of woven fabrics.
- To outline the uses, advantages and disadvantages of bonding **HL** or felting and knitted fabrics.

Basically:

- Fibres are spun into yarn.
- Yarns are bonded or felted, knitted or woven into fabrics.

Woven fabrics

Uses of woven fabric: Household items, clothing.

Types of yarn:

- Filament yarn (made from filament fibres).
- Staple yarn (made from short, small staple fibres).
- Monofilament yarn (made from one continuous filament).

Construction of woven fabric

Woven fabric is made using a loom. The process is called weaving.

1. Threads are arranged lengthways down the loom. These threads are called selvage or warp threads.
2. Weft threads are woven under and over the warp threads to fill in the weave.
3. The way the threads are woven under and over will determine the type of weave.

Types of weave

Examples of different weaves are:

- Simple (plain weave).
- Complex (basket, herringbone, towelling, twill, velvet).

key point

Straight grain is the direction of the warp threads in a fabric.

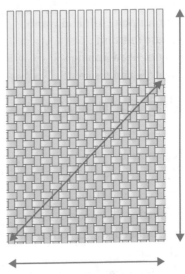

Plain weave (showing construction of warp and weft)

Advantages of woven fabrics	Disadvantages of woven fabrics
● Hangs and drapes well. ● Easy to sew. ● Looks well.	● No give or stretch in fabric. ● More fabric is needed for items and garments.

Non-woven fabrics

Bonding or felting

Fibres can be bonded or felted together to produce a non-woven fabric that does not fray. The bonding process involves the use of glue, heat, moisture, pressure and suitable fibres.

> **key point**
>
> The bias is the diagonal line of the fabric. When the fabric is pulled on this line, it becomes stretchy.

Uses of bonded fabrics

● Blankets ● Carpet underlay ● Hats ● Interfacing.

Advantages of bonded or felted fabrics	Disadvantages of bonded or felted fabrics
● Do not fray. ● Easy to use. ● Economical. ● Inexpensive.	● Felt is damaged by water. ● Not as warm as wool.

Knitted fabrics

Yarns can be linked together using a looping process called knitting. This can be done by hand or machine. Knitting can be thin or thick. All knitted fabric has a stretchy quality, is crease resistant and only needs pressing.

Uses of knitted fabrics

● Cardigans ● Dresses ● Jackets ● Jumper ● Lingerie ● Socks;
● Sportswear ● Thermal underwear and tights

Advantages of knitted fabrics	Disadvantages of knitted fabrics
● Comfortable, soft and warm. ● Crease resistant. ● Do not need ironing. ● Stretchy and resilient.	● Lose their shape easily. ● Fray or run easily.

Making textured yarns

● **Looping:** A loopy effect, e.g. bouclé.
● **Crimping:** Makes fabric stretchy and thick.
● **Knotting:** Knots are introduced at intervals in the yarn.
● **Mixing yarns** (one smooth, one hairy).

EXAM QUESTIONS AND SAMPLE ANSWERS

Higher Level 2008, Section A, Q.22 (4 marks)
Suggest a different use for **each** of the following types of fabrics.
(i) Woven fabric: *Jeans.* (ii) Bonded fabric: *Blankets.*

Higher Level 2004, Section A, Q.22 (4 marks)
State **two** ways in which yarn can be made into fabric.
(i) *Knitting.* (ii) *Weaving.*

52 Fabric Finishes

aims
- To name and list the uses of fabric finishes.
- To explain how pattern is applied to fabric.

Fibres are blended together to create fabrics with new properties.

Fabrics are treated in a variety of ways to improve their desirable properties.

Fabric finishes generally involve a chemical process. Finishes improve fabrics, making them perform better and look better.

Labelling

Labels on fabrics provide valuable care and cleaning information. Follow the manufacturer's instructions exactly. Fabrics with special finishes require care when cleaning them.

> **LINKS**
> Consumer education (p. 152)
> Care labels (p. 300)

Fabric finishes

Types of finishes	Uses
Anti-static	Carpets, clothing
Brushing or napping	Brushed nylon
Crease resistant	Clothing, furnishings
Drip-drying	Clothing, household fabrics
Flame resistant	Children's nightwear, furnishing fabrics
Mothproof	Carpets, clothing
Non-shrink	Clothing, furnishing fabric
Permanent press	Skirts, trousers
Polishing	Glazed cotton, curtains
Stain repellent	Carpets, clothes, upholstery
Water repellent	Raincoats, outdoor jackets
Waterproof	Raincoats, outdoor wear

key point

> **SAFETY**
> Remember the importance of flame-resistant fabric for children's nightwear and furnishing fabrics.

exam focus

Learn the names and uses of six fabric finishes.

Applying pattern to fabric

Dyeing and printing

Dyeing and printing are finishes that are applied to fibres and fabrics.

Dyeing:

- May take place during a variety of stages of fabric production, e.g. fibre, yarn or fabric stage.
- Gives fabric its colour.
- May be natural or synthetic.
- Can be used to apply pattern, e.g. batik, tie-dying.

Printing:

- Applies colour and a pattern to one surface.
- Uses a dye to fill in or outline the design, e.g. screen printing, block printing.

Colour and pattern can be applied using:

- Fabric paints.
- Fabric pens.
- Transfer crayons.
- Arrangement of yarns (in woven and knitted fabrics, yarns and fibres are placed in different ways to produce patterns).

Technology and textiles

Technology has influenced textiles as a result of automation in factories. It has resulted in:

- New fibres.
- New fabric finishes.
- The development of computer-aided design (CAD).

EXAM QUESTIONS AND SAMPLE ANSWERS

Higher Level 2007, Section A, Q.22 (4 marks)
Name **two** suitable finishes that can be applied to a fabric for a school jacket.
(i) Water repellent. (ii) Brushing.

Ordinary Level 2005, Section A, Q.18 (5 marks)
Name **one** fabric finish and give its purpose.
Water repellent: Prevents water from soaking into the fabric.

Ordinary Level 1999, Section A, Q.17 (5 marks)
Suggest a different garment that might benefit from **each** of the following finishes.
(i) Crease resistance: *Shirt.*
(ii) Waterproofing: *Raincoat.*
(iii) Flame proofing: *Children's nightwear.*

53 Caring for Textiles

- To list the guidelines for taking care of clothes.
- To outline the points to follow when storing clothes.
- To describe the care labelling system.
- To list the guidelines for washing clothes.
- To explain stain removal methods. **HL**
- To outline the use of commercial products. **HL**
- To list the effects of detergents on the environment. **HL**

General guidelines

1. Fasten buttons, belts and zips before storing clothes.
2. Fold jumpers and store flat in drawers or on shelves.
3. Hang up clothes when not in use.
4. Mend clothes if torn and sew in buttons before washing.
5. If clothes are to be dry cleaned, do not wash them at home.
6. Stained clothes should be washed immediately.

key point

Separate the whites and coloureds before washing.

Storing clothes

Before folding and storing winter or summer clothes for the following year, wash, clean, dry and air them.

Care labels

An international care labelling system shows how to care for clothes and textiles. There are five basic symbols that act as guides to caring for clothes. They are:

1. **Washing** (bar symbols: a tub with temperatures).
2. **Drying** (box symbol: with lines and circles).
3. **Ironing** (iron: with or without dots).
4. **Dry cleaning** (circles: with or without letters).
5. **Bleaching** (triangles: with or without letters).

Main guidelines for care labels

- Read all care labels on garments carefully.
- Follow the instructions given by the manufacturer.
- Delicate fabrics are best washed by hand using a gentle detergent.

Symbols

Washing (the bar symbols)

For Sections A and B, be able to explain what each of the following fabric care symbols indicate.

Symbol	Washing machine	Fabrics
95	Maximum wash in cotton cycle	White cotton and linen without special finishes
60	Maximum wash in cotton cycle	• Cotton, linen or viscose • No special finishes • Colourfast at 60°
50	Medium wash in synthetic cycle	Suits mixtures, such as: • Polyester/cotton • Cotton/viscose • Cotton/acrylic
40	Maximum wash in cotton cycle, normal washing action and spin	Cotton, linen, viscose with colours fast at 40° but not at 60°
40	Medium wash in synthetic cycle, short spin	Acrylics, acetate and triacetate, mixtures with wool, polyester/wool blends
40	Minimum wash in wool cycle, normal spin	Wool, wool mixed with other fibres, silk
	Hand wash only	Fabrics that must not be machine washed
	Do not wash	Check label for dry cleaning instructions

Ironing

Do not iron	Cool iron (110°C)	Warm iron (150°C)	Hot iron (200°C)

Dry cleaning

Do not dry clean	Dry clean A	Dry clean P	Dry clean F
	(A)	(P)	(F)

Bleaching

Chlorine bleach can be used	Do not use bleach

Drying

Dry flat (wool)	Drip dry	Do not tumble dry	Tumble dry	Line dry

Organising the washing

Guidelines for organising the washing

1. Close buttons and zips.
2. Empty all pockets.
3. Remove stains before washing if possible.
4. Repair tears and sew on buttons before washing.
5. Separate coloured clothes from whites and wash separately.
6. Sort into care label categories.
7. Choose a suitable detergent.
8. Select the appropriate wash cycle for the clothes.

key point

Sort clothes by colour, whites, lights, brights and darks, and by garments care label.

Delicate fabrics

1. Follow the care label, e.g. silk.
2. Wash by hand.
3. Use a low temperatures and mild detergents.
4. Handle lightly – do not rub and only squeeze gently.
5. Rinse a few times until the water runs clear.

Removing stains

- Before using a stain removal product, try rinsing the garment in cold water as soon as the stain occurs.
- If this is unsuccessful, soak the garment in warm water with a little detergent.
- Remove the stain before washing.

key point

Always test commercial stain removal agents first on a hidden part of the garment before treating the stain.

- Rinse, wash and dry according to the care label instructions.
- If all this fails, use a commercial stain removal agent.

Storing stain removal agents

All stain removal agents should be labelled correctly and stored with care. Keep well away from children.

LINK
First aid (accidents in the home – poisoning) (p. 247)

Steps to follow when removing stains

1. Protect your clothing and surrounding surfaces.
2. Read and follow the instructions on the label.
3. Use in a well-ventilated and airy room.
4. Do not use near a flame.
5. Test on a small piece of the fabric.
6. Use the weakest solution at first, then increase strength if necessary.
7. Wash, rinse and dry in the recommended way.
8. After use, wash your hands.

Higher Level students: Do you know how to remove the following stains at home? Protein, gravy, tea, chocolate, coffee, grease/fat, felt pen, biro, ink, grass, chewing gum, nail polish, mildew, paint, perspiration, tea.

Detergents

Detergents are products that remove dirt, dust, grime and grease from clothes.

Composition of detergents

Detergents or washing powders contain bleaches, brighteners, cleaning chemicals, enzymes, perfume and water softeners.

Types of detergent

- Biological detergent.
- Concentrated detergent.
- Liquid or powder detergent for washing by hand.
- Low-foaming detergent.
- Special detergent for delicate fabrics.

Biological detergents contain enzymes that break down protein stains, e.g. gravy, blood.

Functions of detergents

- To wet the fabric.
- To dissolve grease.
- To loosen dirt, dust and grime.
- To remove dirt from the fabric.

Biological detergents harm flame-resistant and waterproof finishes on household textiles and garments.

Environmental effects of detergents

Phosphates encourage the increased growth of algae in rivers and lakes. Algae use more oxygen, which reduces the oxygen levels available to plants and fish.

Buy phosphate-free detergents (environmentally friendly detergents or 'green' detergents).

LINK
Consumers and the environment (p. 268)

Fabric conditioners

Fabric conditioners are used in the final rinsing water.

Functions of fabric conditioners

Fabric conditioners are used to:

- Aid ironing.
- Reduce static electricity.
- Soften the fibres and fabrics.

key point

Liquid conditioners are used in washing machines and conditioning sheets are used in tumble dryers.

Washing machines

- When **buying** a washing machine, choose one that is energy efficient. Some washing machines also function as dryers.
- When **using** a washing machine, choose suitable phosphate-free and low-foaming detergents.
- Use **energy-efficient** programmes and wash cycles suitable for the clothes. Check all care labels.

Using washing machines

1. Check pockets and remove coins, receipts, etc.
2. Sort clothes according to colours and care labels.
3. Remove stains.
4. Load the washing machine.
5. Add detergent and fabric conditioner.
6. Select the washing programme.
7. Use eco-friendly programmes, e.g. half load.

LINK
Guidelines for removing stains (p. 301)

Methods of drying clothes

The following methods can be used:

- Line dry clothes in the fresh air.
- Dry clothes in a tumble dryer.
- Use a clotheshorse for indoor drying.

key point

Check the care labels for recommendations on drying.

- Avoid putting clothes on radiators to dry, as this may damage the paint or wallpaper and cause condensation.
- Never place a clotheshorse near an open fire or a gas or electric heater, as the clothes could catch on fire.

> **key point**
>
> Some clothes cannot be put in a dryer because they would shrink.

Ironing and pressing

Most clothes benefit from ironing or pressing, unless the care label indicates that this is not recommended. Useful ironing and pressing equipment includes:

- Clothes hangers.
- Sleeve board.
- Iron and ironing board (for cuffs, necklines and sleeves).
- Pressing cloths.
- Pressing pad (useful for embroidery).
- Seam roll (for pressing seams).

Rules for ironing and pressing

1. Examine the care label instructions. Set the temperature dial to suit the fabric.
2. Clothes should be slightly damp.
3. Avoid creasing the garments as you iron or press.
4. Hang up clothes when ironed or fold them carefully.
5. Air freshly ironed clothes fully before storing in drawers and wardrobes.

 EXAM QUESTIONS AND SAMPLE ANSWERS

Check out the fabric care symbol questions in Section A of the following exam papers:

- **Higher Level 2008 (Q.21), 2006 (Q.23) and 2005 (Q.22).**
- **Ordinary Level 2009 (Q.17), 2006 (Q.20) and 2002 (Q.19).**

Higher Level 2007, Section A, Q.23 (4 marks)

Name **four** guidelines to be followed when washing a delicate item of clothing.

(i) Use a mild detergent in warm water.

(ii) Do not rub, just squeeze the fabric very gently.

(iii) Gently press out water and rinse a few times.

(iv) Roll in a towel to remove excess moisture, dry flat and press with a cool iron.

Higher Level 2003, Section A, Q.20 (4 marks)

List **four** items of information that you would expect to find on a care label attached to a pair of jeans.

(i) The fabric that the jeans are made from.

(ii) Temperature at which to wash the jeans.

(iii) How to dry the jeans.

(iv) Whether or not the jeans can be tumble dried.

54 Needlework Skills and Techniques

aims
- To list the contents of a sewing box.
- To outline the guidelines for choosing fabric.
- To name, describe and state the uses of basic hand stitches.
- To name, describe and state the uses of embroidery stitches.
- To describe the methods of neatening/finishing flat seams.

Contents of a sewing box

A basic home sewing box should contain a selection of essential sewing equipment, such as:

- Needles ● Pin cushion ● Pins ● Plastic ruler ● Scissors ● Stitch ripper
- Tailor's chalk ● Tape measure ● Thimble ● Thread.

Choosing fabric for sewing

1. Estimate the amount of fabric needed for the item/garment (check the pattern in the case of a garment).
2. Choose a fabric that is easy to handle and sew.
3. Avoid fabrics that have one-way designs, are shiny, stretchy or fray easily.
4. Choose a fabric that suits the item/garment, e.g. colour and weight.
5. Choose fabrics that are easy to care for, e.g. washable.

key point

Examples of nap fabrics are velvet and corduroy. If you brush these fabrics one way they have a smooth surface, but if you brush them in the other direction they are rough.

Basic hand stitches

Tacking

Tacking is a temporary stitch that is removed when the permanent stitching has been completed. Use a different colour thread when working tacking stitches.

Uses:

- Holding two pieces of fabric together for machining or hand stitching.
- As a guide for machining.
- To hold fabrics together for the first fitting.
- To hold interfacing in position for machining.

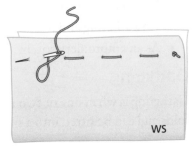

WS

Tacking stitch

Hemming

Hemming is a permanent slanted stitch done by hand. It should not be used on hems of dresses, skirts, shirts and trousers, as the slanted stitch will show on the right side.

Uses:

- To finish off hem edges on cuffs, collars, waistbands, etc.
- To sew tapes into position.

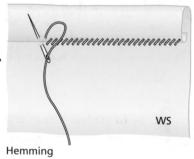

Hemming

Tailor tacking

Tailor tacking is used to transfer pattern symbols or markings from the paper pattern pieces to doubled fabric, e.g. balance marks, construction marks for darts, position of buttons and buttonholes.

Tailor tacking

Slip hemming

Slip hemming barely shows on the right side of garments. Its V shape can be seen on the wrong side only.

Uses:

- For hems of dresses, skirts, shirts and trousers.
- For attaching a lining to any garment.

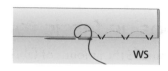

Slip hemming

Running

Running is a permanent small straight stitch similar to tacking.

Uses:

- For holding two pieces of fabric together (seams).
- For gathering and making tucks.
- As an embroidery stitch.

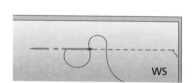

Running

Gathering

Gathering is when one or two rows of small running stitches are pulled so that the fabric folds and can be fitted into a smaller piece of fabric.

Uses:

- To reduce the size of one piece of fabric so that it fits into a smaller piece (gathered sleeves, cuffs, aprons, skirts, etc.).
- As a fashion feature on garments.

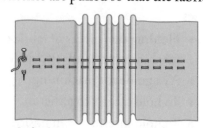

Gathering

Top-sewing

Top-sewing is a small slanted stitch worked along the folded edge of two pieces of fabric. It is worked from the right side of the fabric.

Uses:

- To join two folded edges of fabric together.
- For attaching lace.
- For securing ribbons and tapes.

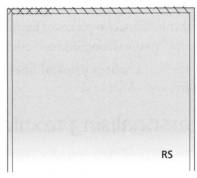

Top-sewing

Embroidery stitches

Stem

Uses: Outlines, motifs and stems.

Stem stitch

Satin

Uses: Leaves, motifs and petals.

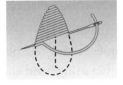

Satin stitch

Chain

Uses: To fill in or outline designs.

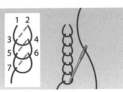

Chain stitch

Long and Short Stitch

Long and short stitch

French knots

Uses: Centre of flowers as a fill-in stitch, single knots or for shaded clusters of knots.

Basic seams

Plain seam

A plain seam is simply two pieces of fabric joined together with the raw edges neatly finished.

Uses: With medium- and heavyweight fabrics used for dresses, jackets, skirts and trousers.

Seam finishes for plain flat seams:

- Blanket stitch.
- Edge machining.
- Overcasting.
- Pinking.
- Zigzag.

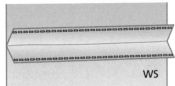

Edge machining

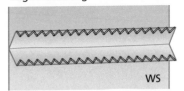

Zig-zagging

French seam

For this seam, two pieces of fabric are joined with wrong sides facing. The raw edges are turned to the wrong side and enclosed in a narrow seam on the inside of the garment.

Uses: With lightweight and fine fabrics used for blouses, children's clothes, lingerie, shirts and underwear.

Personalising textiles and garments

Decorative finishes can be created using:

- Appliqué ● Batik ● Block printing ● Creative embroidery ● Crochet
- Fabric collages ● Fabric painting ● Hand and machine embroidery
- Patchwork ● Plain hand sewing ● Quilting ● Soft sculpture
- Stencilling ● Tie-dyeing

Appliqué: Sewing one piece of fabric on top of another using hand embroidery or a machine stitch for decorative purposes.

Bias: This is the line (which is very stretchy) that runs diagonally to the straight grain of fabric.

For Higher and Ordinary level, it is important that you are able to identify diagrams of all stitches, label them and state their uses.

55 The Sewing Machine

aims
- To label a sewing machine.
- To outline the guidelines for buying a sewing machine.
- To explain how a sewing machine stitches.
- To list the guidelines for using a sewing machine.
- To explain how to use a sewing machine.
- To list the guidelines to be followed when caring for a sewing machine.
- To name the machine stitches and their uses.
- To list and explain machine faults.

The sewing machine

exam focus

Students should be able to label a sewing machine in the exam.

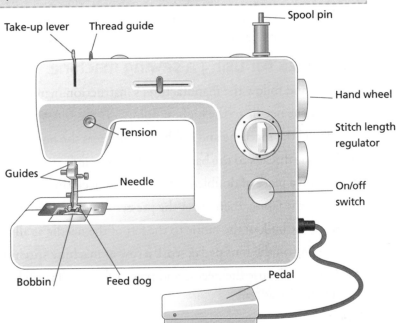

Questions to ask when buying a sewing machine

- How much can I spend?
- Do I need a basic machine or one that does embroidery?
- What attachments are included in the price?
- Can attachments be bought separately?
- Will I need lessons in its use?
- Is there a guarantee with the sewing machine?
- What is the after-sales service?
- Does the shop have a demonstration model for sale if I cannot afford the new machine? (Check the guarantee and after-sales service arrangements in this case.)

How a sewing machine works

- Two separate threads are linked together, one from the bobbin with one from the spool and needle to form a stitch.
- The tension is adjusted so that each thread is evenly linked into the other. If the tension is too loose, loops will form. The tension disc may be loosened or tightened to adjust the tension.

Using a sewing machine

Before using the sewing machine

- Learn the name of each part.
- Know the function of each part.
- Know how the machine works.
- Get a demonstration.

Guidelines for using a sewing machine

1. Read and follow the manufacturer's instruction manual.
2. Raise the needle to the highest point.
3. Thread the machine and bobbin, then insert the bobbin.
4. Pull the threads to the back. Keep the presser foot and needle up.
5. Test on a piece of doubled scrap fabric. Check the tension, stitch and stitch length.
6. Insert the fabric, then lower the presser foot and needle.
7. Keep the bulk of the fabric to the left of the needle at all times.
8. Pressing on the foot pedal, work a row of machine stitching.
9. At the end, raise the needle and presser foot, pull the fabric towards the back and cut the threads.

Never:

- Use a faulty machine (get advice and help).
- Use the machine in poor light.

Caring for a sewing machine

1. Follow the manufacturers' instructions.
2. Never use the machine without fabric.
3. Never push or pull fabric under the presser foot.
4. Cover when not being used.
5. Get the machine serviced every year.

Machine stitches

Types	Stitches	Uses
Basic stitches	Straight stitch	Sewing seams together, sewing non-stretch fabrics.
	Zigzag	Neatening seam edges, decorating fabric, appliqué.
	Blind hem	Sewing up hems, decorating edges.
	Overlocking	Neatening seams.
	Buttonhole stitch	Finishing buttonhole edges.
Embroidery stitches	Shell, satin, chain	Decorating household items and garments.

Machine and stitch faults

Fault	Reasons for fault
Looped stitches	• Wrong size of needle • Machine not threaded correctly • Upper thread tension too loose
Needle breaks	• Poor quality thread • Needle inserted incorrectly • Needle too low when removing fabric • Upper tension too tight
Skipped stitches	• Different quality threads • Fabric forced through • Needle damaged or blunt • Needle inserted incorrectly
Top thread breaks	• Damaged or blunt needle • Machine threaded incorrectly • Needle inserted incorrectly • Poor quality thread • Upper thread tension too tight
Uneven-sized stitches	• Fabric forced through • Feed dog faulty, loose or worn • Incorrect stitch length for fabric • Presser foot not lowered correctly

EXAM QUESTIONS AND SAMPLE ANSWERS

Higher Level 2009, Section A, Q.24 (4 marks)

List **four** guidelines that should be followed when caring for a sewing machine.

(i) Always follow the manufacturers' instructions.

(ii) Never use the machine without fabric.

(iii) Cover when not being used.

(iv) Have the sewing machine serviced every year.

Higher Level 2005, Section A, Q.20 (4 marks)

Give **two** reasons why the thread may break when using a sewing machine.

(i) The upper thread tension is too tight.

(ii) Poor-quality thread.

ORDINARY LEVEL, SECTION A

Rules/Guidelines for Using a Sewing Machine
Question: 2009 (Q.20), 2007 (Q.18), 2005 (Q.17) and 2003 (Q. 20).

> **LINK**
> Refer to the diagram of a sewing machine at the beginning of this chapter (p. 309)

Higher Level 2006, Section B, Q.6 (55 marks) (long question)

(a) Diagram of a sewing machine.
 Students are asked to label it. (12 marks)

(b) List the guidelines that should be followed when:

 (i) **Choosing a sewing machine.** (8 marks)

 ● *Consider the cost of the machine. How much can I afford? Do I need a basic machine or do I need one with more functions, e.g. computerised embroidery stitches?*

 ● *What special features are available on the machine, e.g. automatic buttonhole, embroidery stitches, thread cutter?*

 (ii) **Using a sewing machine.** (8 marks)

 ● *Read the instruction manual.*

 ● *Thread the machine carefully, following the instructions given in the manual.*

 (iii) **Caring for a sewing machine.** (8 marks)

 ● *Cover when not in use with a plastic or fabric cover.*

 ● *Service regularly (at least once a year).*

 ~~ive~~ **one** reason for each of the following faults. (9 marks)

 ~~breaking:~~ *Top tension is too tight.*

 ~~es:~~ *Tension is too loose.*

 ~~king:~~ *Machine is not threaded correctly.*

 ~~rent~~ machine stitch suitable for **each** of the following.

 ~~:~~ *Zigzag stitch.*

 ~~up~~ a hem: *Blind machine hemming stitch.*